Cash, Crisis, and Corporate Governance

Cash, Crisis, and Corporate Governance

The Role of National Financial Systems in Industrial Restructuring

Victoria Marklew

Ann Arbor
THE UNIVERSITY OF MICHIGAN PRESS

Copyright © by the University of Michigan 1995
All rights reserved
Published in the United States of America by
The University of Michigan Press
Manufactured in the United States of America
© Printed on acid-free paper

1998   1997   1996   1995   4   3   2   1

A CIP catalog record for this book is available from the British Library.

Library of Congress Cataloging-in-Publication Data

Marklew, Victoria, 1961–
    Cash, crisis, and corporate governance : the role of national financial systems
in industrial restructuring / Victoria Marklew.
      p.   cm.
    Includes bibliographical references (p. –) and index.
    ISBN 0-472-10504-3
    1. Steel industry and trade—Great Britain—Finance. 2. British Steel
Corporation. 3. Steel industry and trade—France—Finance. 4. Automobile
industry and trade—Great Britain—Finance. 5. Automobile industry and
trade—France—Finance. 6. Industrial policy—Great Britain. 7. Industrial
policy—France. I. Title.
HD9521.6.M37   1995
338.4'3669142'0941—dc20
                                    95-8273
                                      CIP

For my Mother,
who taught me to read;

for Michael,
who encouraged me to write;

and
in loving memory of

my Mother-in-Law
Myrna Wagner
(1931–89)

and of
my Grandma,
Violet Moss
(1904–94)

Acknowledgments

This work was made possible by the support and advice of many people. Any errors are, of course, my own. The initial research was conducted while I was a doctoral candidate at the University of Pennsylvania. My thanks to the university, and to Jack Nagel of the Political Science Department in particular, for financial support. Michaela Richter gave of her time and help, far beyond her role as dissertation supervisor. Her detailed criticisms and consistent moral support were integral to this work and to my sanity. Fred Block's enthusiasm for the subject and his extensive analyses were essential in clarifying the arguments advanced here. He subsequently invited me to take part in a three-day conference in May 1992 on "Efficiency and Ownership: The Future of the Corporation," under the auspices of the Program for Economy, Justice, and Society at the University of California, Davis. My thanks to the conference participants for invaluable feedback on my paper, "State Ownership and Finance," and in particular to Michael Useem, Colin Mayer, and Steven Kaplan. James Womack graciously answered questions about national financial systems and the industrial performance of Peugeot SA.

From his first insistence that I should consider a Ph.D. in the United States, Andy Markovits has been an invaluable friend. He has advised, cajoled, and supported to great effect over the years. I hope he thinks it was worth it.

The transition from doctoral dissertation to publishable manuscript was made possible by the advice and insight of Colin Day of the University of Michigan Press and by reader Stephen Wilks. The latter's focus on the need for a consistent theoretical approach, and the former's patience and wit, made the whole process both interesting and worthwhile.

My thanks also to The Northern Trust of Chicago, and in particular to the denizens of the Economic Research Department, for granting me the time and the encouragement needed to complete this work. My especial thanks to Chief Economist Robert Dederick (who taught me, among many other things, the idiosyncrasies of American grammar and punctuation) and to International Economist Elizabeth Hart (mentor and friend, teacher of macroeconomics, and winner of the World's Best Boss Award).

I also owe a great debt of thanks to Stephen and Katarina Thomson, who made my research in London not only possible, but also fun. Jim Steiker and Wendy Epstein kept us sane through some difficult times, with unfailing generosity and great blintzes. Jackie Pearce, Lisa Rudy, and Rhonda Lovell each helped more than they can know.

Finally, and most important of all, I must thank Michael Golden— advisor, husband, and best friend. His support and cooking made it possible to finish the Ph.D. and then to write the book. His encouragement and affection made it all worthwhile.

Contents

Introduction   1

Chapter

   1. Industrial Crisis and Finance in the 1980s   5

   2. The British Steel Corporation   55

   3. The French Steel Industry   85

   4. Peugeot SA   113

   5. British Leyland: From BL to Jaguar
     and the Rover Group   141

   6. Extending the Argument: Government, Industry,
     and Finance in the 1990s   175

Appendixes

   1. The Steel and Auto Industries   227

   2. Abbreviations Used in Text   231

Notes   233

Bibliography   247

Index   257

Introduction

The problems of industrial restructuring dominate economic policy debate in the industrialized democracies. Manufacturing firms have to grapple with the rise of new competitors, rapid technological developments, and shifting markets at home and abroad. They need vast sums of cash to adapt to a changing world, and even just to survive.

During the 1980s, competitive, technological, and economic changes came together in a distinctive way to produce a veritable upheaval among manufacturing industries in Europe and the United States. As some firms were bailed out by their governments and others teetered on the verge of bankruptcy, popular and academic attention focused on the question of state versus private ownership as the key to the survival and restructuring of industrial firms. The pronationalization Mitterrand government in France, and the pro-privatization Thatcher government in Britain, exemplified the two apparently very different approaches. By the 1990s, it seemed that the proprivatization arguments had prevailed in the debate. Even the *dirigiste* French government planned a program of equity sales to shift the ownership of a number of industrial concerns from the state to the private sector. In Eastern Europe, emerging capitalist economies began grappling with even more ambitious plans to "get the state out of industry."

However, in the industrialized economies, government's impact on the fortunes of major manufacturers does not begin with nationalization and end with privatization. The role of the state in ensuring the survival and adaptation of such firms is more subtle, yet more profound. The key issue in industrial restructuring is not whether the state attempts a rescue, but how each national financial system channels financing to industry. Governments have a profound impact on industry through their role in maintaining, regulating, and, occasionally, altering, the national financial system.

The best way to uncover the workings of different national financial systems is to start at the level of the firm, rather than at the level of national institutions and the organization of the state. This "bottom-up" approach reveals a more accurate picture of the ways in which national financial systems actually work, and it throws up some surprising conclusions.

The following pages examine events surrounding four large manufacturing firms in Britain and France, starting in the late 1970s and continuing through 1993. As direct and indirect employers of many thousands of people, the fate of individual firms in the auto and steel industries had a high political profile and a profound economic impact. These firms were especially hard hit by the upheavals of the 1980s. Four firms in particular exemplified the very different ideological approaches to industrial restructuring of the Thatcher and Mitterrand governments. During this period, the British Steel Corporation metamorphosed from state-owned "national champion" to private sector company, while the French steel industry evolved from myriad private firms into Usinor Sacilor, a nationalized giant. In the auto industry, Peugeot SA established itself as a leading European carmaker and a dominant firm in the French private sector, while the state-owned British Leyland was split into component parts, with first Jaguar, and then the rump car-making division, Rover, returned to private ownership.

The first startling discovery revealed by this analysis is that these two apparently very different governments in fact behaved in some remarkably similar ways, and not only during times of crisis, when the short-term survival of a firm was at stake. There were, indeed, fundamental differences in what happened to these companies, but not because of the governments' competing ideologies or because one state was in some way stronger than the other. Rather, what happened to each firm was the result of the forms of financing to which it had access, regardless of whether it was state or private-sector owned. The second discovery is that nationalization and privatization are wholly inadequate labels for defining the boundaries of government-industry relations. In fact, large manufacturing firms straddle the public-private divide in many ways, and the divide itself is decidedly unclear.

The most important lesson of the period of industrial restructuring that swept Europe from 1978 to 1993 is that capital is not neutral. The forms of financing to which a firm has access—particularly a capital-intensive firm subject to intense international competitive and cyclical pressures—are crucial to that firm's ability to survive a crisis and to adapt, irrespective of whether ownership is formally public or private. The availability and costs of financing, and, most important, the attitudes of its providers—whether they are concerned with short-term profit maximization or with long-term relationship building; whether they see themselves as dominant stakeholders in a firm's future or as only one voice among many—reflect the national system of finance and corporate governance. The fundamental role of national financial systems in industrial restructuring only becomes clear when we start the analysis of government-industry relations at the level of individual firms and their financing.

Finally, as financial markets become increasingly globalized, and as some of the national differences in corporate governance begin to erode, so do the financial options open to major manufacturers change. This is especially the case in the nations of the European Community (EC), where the move toward a single market has led to rapid changes in national financial systems, and to a marked decrease in the more overt forms of state financial aid to industry. Given the importance of industrial financing, and given the impact of different systems of finance and governance on industrial survival and adaptation, the developments now unfolding across the EC's financial markets (and in the emerging capitalist economies of Eastern Europe) will have a profound impact on individual firms, and on the national economies of which they are an integral part.

Note: The case studies end in December 1993, and hence do not take into account developments in 1994, such as the sale of the Rover Group to BMW of Germany. Although the European Community, or EC, has now been renamed the European Union, or EU, the former "EC" is used throughout.

For the sake of brevity, the word "tonnes" is used throughout the text, to designate metric tonnes.

obscures our view of how government, industry, and financial markets really interact. The view of a national financial system is very different from the ground-up level of the firm than from the top-down level of national structural constraints. By approaching the problem of industrial change from the opposite direction—from the level of the firm, rather than the level of the state—we get a more accurate picture of what the key differences between national financial markets really are. We also see that the government is the ultimate mediator and regulator of the national financial system, and that governments can and do act quite outside the "constraints" of those systems.

Starting the analysis of the relationship between government, industry, and finance at the level of the firm sheds new light on some of the standard stereotypes of how these countries' political economies work. First, it reveals that government-industry relations in Mitterrand's France and Thatcher's Britain actually had far more in common than is generally supposed. Each government became intimately involved in providing the firms with access to financing, despite their apparently very different ideologies and "structural constraints." Second, the analysis reveals that where the financing of major manufacturers was concerned, the distinction between public and private spheres of action and decision making was nowhere near as sharp as is generally supposed. These two points, taken together, suggest that some of the differences in government-industry relations across countries may be breaking down. On the other hand, crucial differences do still remain. As the case studies will show, the outcomes in these two nations were very different, and the financing of major manufacturers continues to be a point of distinction between them. Once we discount the notion that structural constraints are the key factors that lead some governments to be more involved in industrial restructuring than others, it becomes apparent where the key point of difference between them does lie—namely, in the workings of national financial systems, and what these imply for the costs and availability of financing and the attitudes of providers.

Indeed, a clear understanding of the implications of financial issues for such firms is a necessary component of the analysis of any nation's financial system. Whether we are discussing Europe, North America, or Asia, the national financial market is a crucial component of industrial policy and government-industry relations. Governments regulate, and sometimes change, national financial markets; and ultimately governments decide how national financial systems will respond to international economic pressures. The financing of industry is the place at which government, industry, financial institutions, and international economic change meet. The implications of such variations in national financial markets are enormous. Could national variations in systems of industrial financing and corporate governance help to explain why one nation's manufacturers seem better able to ride out the peaks and troughs of a cyclical industry? If government-industry relations in Thatcher's Britain and Mitterrand's France had more in common than is generally supposed, does this imply that national differences in government-industry relations are breaking down across Europe, perhaps across the industrialized world? Is there really a distinct division between the public and private spheres in modern capitalist economies?

Financial resources, of different kinds, are integral to any firm's short-term survival and long-term investment for adaptation. In the cases presented here—large, capital-intensive manufacturers in two different industries in two different countries—the key to survival and adaptation and, ultimately, to the differences between cases, was the individual firms' financial structures and forms of corporate governance, as determined by the national financial systems. To reveal these differences, the analysis of each case starts first at the level of the individual firm, rather than at the level of the institutions of the state or the constraints on the state's actions, and asks a different set of questions designed to unravel how the way manufacturers in crisis are financed affects their survival. Did the firm get enough capital to survive, even to adapt? If so, where did it come from? How did the government concerned, irrespective of its stated policies or of apparent institutional constraints, actually get involved in providing the firm access to financing? Are there similarities in the financial options open to "successful" adapters, or to firms that are struggling to survive? What exactly is the most important aspect of financing for a firm caught in the throes of intense competition and restructuring—is it the relative cost of various forms of capital; the availability of, say, debt versus equity to firms in this sector, in this country; the conditions attached by the provider(s) of investment capital; or some other factor? Most important of all, what do the answers to these questions tell us about the national financial system and the role of the government in maintaining or altering national financial markets?

Yet the 1978 rescue of the French steel industry was not just an historical blip, the product of a particularly severe shakeout in European manufacturing combined with the last gasp of Gallic state intervention in industry. The 1990s are likely to bring more of the same. By 1993, the worldwide steel and auto industries were once again in a state of crisis, facing problems of serious overcapacity at a time of expensive technological developments. Talk of costly "restructuring" is once again in the air. The problems are particularly acute in Europe. With every major European steel producer losing money, the EC has approved new rescue plans for the industry, while production from the new Japanese-owned auto manufacturing plants based in the UK is making the already highly competitive European market even more cutthroat. With stricter EC rules governing state aid to industry, and after a decade of financial market liberalization and the advent of a common market, European governments and manufacturers are operating in a very different world in 1993 than in 1978. But access to financing will still be a crucial—perhaps *the* crucial—aspect of manufacturers' ability to adapt and to survive the latest upheavals. The workings of national financial systems will still play a key role in determining how firms such as British Steel and Peugeot SA are financed, and national governments will still be concerned not only with making sure that "their" firms are the ones that survive, but also with ordering and reordering national financial markets. The events of the 1980s will serve as lessons for the 1990s, not only for firms in the EC, but across the industrialized world, including those in the emerging capitalist economies of Eastern Europe.

Going beyond National Differences, Institutions, and Structural Constraints

The French and British governments have adopted very different policies with regard to their auto industries over the years. These differences have been especially striking since the mid-1970s, with France maintaining high protectionist barriers against foreign producers, which helped its two indigenous car firms to survive, while Britain actively welcomed Japanese manufacturers, even as the domestic market share of the one remaining British-owned mass-market carmaker declined. It is such differences in policy toward industries in adaptation that has attracted the attention of much comparative political science literature in recent years. A great deal of this literature has focused on the differing political capacities of governments to resist demands for protection or subsidy, and on governments' different technical capacities to promote industrial advantage—differences in national institutional structures and in industry organization; in the ability of one firm to affect government policy outcomes in ways that another could not; in degrees of state capacity, variously defined; and so on.

There is a strong assumption in contemporary comparative political economy that "structure constrains strategy." In studies of government-industry relations and industrial policy, when national outcomes and policies differ, the initial reaction is to look for the national-level institutions and structures that explain those differences.[1] Given this assumption, Britain and France are popular comparative cases: the "weak" British state apparently lacks the institutional means to affect industrial outcomes, while the "strong" French state supposedly possesses greater structural capacities for intervention in the national economy. The organization of a nation's financial and banking sectors, for example, and the institutions through which their interests are mediated, may affect the extent to which government is able to manipulate financing for industrial investment strategies. The organization of industrial relations, the structure of trade unions, and the degree and form of business interest organization, may also be deemed relevant in the workings of government-industry relations (Hall 1986; Elbaum and Lazonick 1986).

Zysman's (1983) ground-breaking analysis of the financial systems of Britain and France treats the national financial system as the opportunity and constraint structure through which the state must work to try to direct economic and industrial adjustment. He finds that the structure of the national financial system has major implications for a government's capacity to intervene in the market, and for the types of political conflicts that emerge when it does act. He characterizes France as having a state-led model of industrial change because it has a credit-based, price-administered financial system. Britain, on the other hand, has failed to make any particular choice about an approach to adjustment. Zysman concludes that the particulars of the national financial system limit the marketplace options of firms and the administrative choices of governments, and that this is one element defining the ways in which business and state can interact.[2]

To a large extent, Zysman's approach is very insightful. The structure of national financial systems does indeed have great implications for government-industry relations. While Peugeot was struggling to maintain its markets and to re-equip its factories in the mid-1980s, it had financial options that were not available to the British auto firms in the early 1970s. The British Treasury may historically have eschewed most forms of public-private capital mixes for industrial financing largely because it did not have the control over both monetary and industrial policies once found at the French Ministry of Finance. The postwar organization of the French state, with public savings institutions and Funds designed to channel investment capital to industry through the private banking sector, probably encouraged the development of financing options deemed impossible in Britain.

However, by starting the analysis at the level of national institutions, Zysman's definition of a market, of what counts in terms of finance and industry, is limited to savings flows at the national level. He focuses on the institutions that aggregate savings, and on how these are structured. What Zysman and other political scientists concerned with industrial policy do not consider are financial issues at the level of the firm itself, and the extent to which these give a far more accurate picture of how government, industry, and financial markets actually interact. The "top-down" approach makes it hard to see the extent to which a major manufacturer's short-term survival and long-term adaptation are dependent upon the precise characteristics of the national financial system. In particular, this approach tends to obscure the differences that exist between firms in the same country; the extent to which the dividing line between public and private financing of industrial adjustment strategies is blurred; and the striking similarities that also exist across sectors and countries in terms of the involvement of the state in financing industrial restructuring.

In addition, the example of the Phoenix schemes (chap. 2) shows that state and industry can "negotiate" ways around these apparent constraints (Samuels 1990), and even just ignore them altogether. Financial institutions are not immutable. In France, the government itself has radically altered the financial system. Zysman was overly pessimistic about the extent to which governments can change markets (albeit often in unintended ways). In the past ten to fifteen years, financial sector liberalization and the loosening of regulations and capital controls have sped up the pace of change to an extent that no doubt seemed highly unlikely in 1982. To some extent, the developments in the markets pressured governments to act, but to a very great extent, the governments themselves initiated radical changes. France is the most striking example of this, liberalization being very much a part of the post-1981 governments' strategy of maintaining French industry's international competitiveness.

The broad sweeps of comparative theory do not capture the subtleties and complexities of contemporary government-industry relations (Wilks and Wright 1987), or of contemporary industrial adaptation, because such theories begin their analysis at the level of the institutions of the state. If we credit the French state with a close, *dirigiste* relationship with industry, why did all of its major steel firms face bankruptcy in the late 1970s, and why was one manufacturer actually "allowed to fail"? If the British state has an arm's-length and uninvolved relationship with industry, how did it manage to become closely involved in the management and resuscitation of the British Steel Corporation (BSC), even as it pointedly failed to do so in the case of British Leyland (BL)?[3] The answers to these questions lie primarily in the financial structures and forms of corporate governance of each firm. Just as Zysman pointed out that all capitalist market systems do not function in the same way at the national level, so it is also true that not all capital is alike, as far as the individual firm is concerned. Financing is not a neutral issue for any firm, least of all for a major manufacturer in a highly competitive and capital-intensive industry. In the cases analyzed here, the kinds of capital on each firm's balance sheet, and the form of its governance beyond a simple public-private ownership distinction, had a profound impact both on its day-to-day survival and on its longer-term process of crisis management and strategic adaptation.

The most obvious difference between kinds of capital is that of debt versus equity financing, a question that has generated a slew of analysis and research from microeconomists and business theorists.[4] The question of ownership is closely tied to a firm's financing. Holders of various forms of debt and equity take on different levels of risk and have different interests in a firm's financial health and future prosperity. These differences show up especially clearly when a firm is on the brink of failure—hence corporate bankruptcy laws (which vary markedly in different national legal systems) try to strike a balance between creditors and shareholders.[5] These issues have, to date, made few inroads into the broader field of government-industry relations theory. Political science needs to incorporate the issues of corporate financing and the role of governments in national financial markets in order to explain adequately the myriad responses to, and outcomes of, the industrial restructuring of the 1980s. Differences in the financial and governance structures of the firms involved go a long way toward explaining why, for example, the British state was able to play such a dominant role with regard to BSC, whereas the widely held debts of the French steel firms delayed the state's ability to come to grips with broader adaptation strategies.

It must be emphasized that this is not an argument that national institutional constraints are irrelevant—far from it. The differences in national financial markets and financial policies described in part 2 below are very relevant in explaining why the French steel firms were so debt-laden by 1978. Rather, starting the analysis at the national level limits our view of how finance, government, and industry interact, and leads to an overemphasis on, for example, the aggregation of national savings, rather than on their distribution. What these firms' stories illustrate is the extent to which firm-level financial structures have a profound effect on industrial survival strategies. Once we focus on government-industry relations at the level of the firm, it becomes clear that contemporary national governments are, directly and indirectly, intimately concerned with the financing of industry. This was as true for a laissez-faire proprivatization Thatcher government as for an interventionist, pronationalization one under President Mitterrand.

The remainder of this chapter lays out these arguments in more detail. Section 1 discusses the role that each government played in providing these manufacturers with access to financing, and the increasingly blurry lines between nationalized firms and those operating in the private sector. The conclusion is that nationalization and privatization are wholly inadequate labels for defining the boundaries of government-industry relations. In any case, the major manufacturers studied here straddled the public-private divide in numerous ways. Section 2 outlines each nation's financial system and the varieties of financing to which firms may have access. These are the kinds of national differences that comparative political economists usually dwell upon at length. The description given here forms a background and reference for the subsequent case-study chapters, and begins to show that the financing of industry is neither politically neutral nor merely technical, but rather a key aspect of industrial restructuring and of government-industry relations.

Section 3 considers the argument that Britain and France are historically fundamentally different in terms of the relationship between government and industry, and especially so under the Thatcher and Mitterrand governments of the 1980s. Nationally specific variations in the structure and operation of financial markets are still profound, but we find that in Thatcher's Britain and in Mitterrand's France, the solutions to the question of how to help large industrial firms to cope with crisis and adaptation were often strikingly similar. These similarities are illustrative and important. They show both the extent to which these kinds of crises require the same kinds of responses, no matter what labels are used to describe those responses, and what the more fundamental sources of differences in outcomes were. As we shall see in the case studies, and as explored more fully in chapter 6, these more fundamental differences had to do with the forms of financing to which the firms had access. Finally, part 4 of this chapter describes the European steel and auto industries in the 1980s, and the kinds of international competitive change and domestic political pressures to which they were subject. As Keohane (1984) points out, comparative government-industry relations analysis without some conception of the common international economic pressures facing national economies will be misleading. (The appendix gives further details on each industry.)

1. Government-Industry Relations

How did firms manage to survive, even adapt to, the pressures and problems of the 1980s? One of the answers explored in the following chapters is that, in the cases of the British Steel Corporation, Usinor Sacilor, Peugeot SA, and British Leyland, each national government was involved in providing the firms with access to both short-term funds and stable sources of long-term finance for adjustment. It is this involvement that leads to two of the conclusions put forward here. First, that the supposed distinction between the activist French and hands-off British is not nearly so sharp as is usually assumed. Each government could, and often did, act in ways apparently quite contrary to its "structural constraints." Second, that in each country the public-private divide is increasingly blurry. Most important, however, is that the key to understanding the outcome of restructuring for these firms in the 1980s is not the capacity of the state or institutional constraints, but rather the financial structures involved at the level of the firm itself. These are a function of the national financial system, as regulated, and sometimes even reordered, by the national government.

At first glance, the above points about finance and ownership might seem irrelevant to the cases studied here, given that three of the four following chapters deal with firms that were nationalized (i.e., owned by the state) for most or all of the 1980s. If the state is the owner, doesn't that end all discussion of a firm's corporate governance? How can the workings of the national financial market in any but the crudest sense possibly be of relevance? The answer to this has to do with the blurring of the public/private-sector divide. Nationalization does not whisk a firm away into a black hole of state ownership, any more than privatization suddenly returns it to the bright lights of the private market. The French and British governments were involved in providing all of these firms with access to capital and, more to the point, they did so in ways that confound any neat separation between public- and private-sector adjustment strategies, between market-driven and state-led change. Zysman argued that in a credit-based government-pricing system, which is how he characterized France, the borderline between public and private disappears. But when we look closely at events in the apparently capital-market-based system of Britain, the borderline disappears there, too. Each government repeatedly intervened to deal with the failure of the market mechanism. In Britain, the state-owned BSC was used to bail out privately owned steel makers, BL was financed with both state and private capital, and a number of privatized firms have had government Special Shares that subtly yet fundamentally affect their corporate governance. The French state financed the steel firms before nationalization, and afterward devised new public-private capital mixes for them. Even fiercely independent Peugeot (PSA) had recourse to loans in the mid-1980s that were heavily subsidized by the state, while state-mandated changes in the operation of the national financial markets later in the decade allowed PSA to restructure some of the debt that it did carry and gave it new flexible financing options.

In other words, the financing of large firms straddles what is in reality a very blurred boundary between public and private spheres of action and decision making.[6] The distinctions between nationalized and privatized industries are not necessarily as clear as we tend to assume, even with apparently extreme examples such as BSC and Peugeot, and even within Thatcher's Britain. Regulatory issues also straddle the public-private divide where very large firms are involved (Chick 1990). Whether the state gets involved in industrial reorganization, and how, is not just a matter of public or private ownership.

As the public-private divide gets murkier, so the differences between Britain and France lessen. Arm's-length Britain found ways to channel public money to the private steel firms, ways to closely monitor BSC, and ways to actively encourage international auto firms to invest in the country. It is increasingly hard to accurately categorize a government's strategy as regards industrial change, at least in Western Europe. Both Britain and France in the 1980s helped some firms to exit, financed adaptation to a varying extent, and protected some firms by muting the market (protecting trade, allowing cartels, and providing government subsidies). What were important, in both the firms' survival and adaptation and in the particular relationships between government and industry, were the financial structures of the firms themselves, and the national financial markets and policies that they faced.

Nationalization and Privatization

People pay the most attention to government's role in financing industry when a firm's formal ownership is the subject of debate. This is particularly true of Britain and France in the 1980s, where nationalization versus privatization, as ways of ensuring industrial success, were at the forefront of industrial policy debates. Seeing state and private ownership as diametrically opposed strategies for dealing with industrial adjustment, however, is an oversimplification. There are degrees of difference in how far the state is involved, and how much competition is a means of forcing restructuring. More to the point, state and private ownership are not necessarily at the extremes of this continuum, and one strategy is not inherently more likely to mean success (however defined) than another.

Ownership does, of course, matter in the sense that changes in the structure of property rights are likely to have an effect on firm behavior (Vickers and Yarrow 1988), but whether the state is the formal owner of a firm is only one of a number of factors to be taken into account in government-industry relations. The regulatory framework within which a firm operates is at least as important: "managerial incentive structures are determined via a complex set of interactions among factors that include the type of ownership, the degree of product market competition, and the effectiveness of regulation" (ibid., 44). This is another way of saying that the source and form of a firm's capital, and its corporate governance structure, are important factors in government-industry relations.

Given the role of public (i.e., state) and private ownership in these two countries in recent years, it is worth outlining something of the lines of the debate in each country, the approach of each government involved, and some of the outcomes. This will help illustrate the arguments presented here, and will also give some background for the more detailed case studies that follow.

In Britain during the 1980s, privatization was "the boldest stroke of the Thatcher administration . . . sold on principle but underwritten with a calculated and ruthless pragmatism" (Tony Blair, M.P., *Times*, November 10, 1987). The Thatcher governments' privatization program for selling state-owned assets was based (as was nationalization in Britain in the 1940s) on the conception of a radical separation between the public and private sectors. The assumption was that privatization would "free" the firms concerned from the debilitating constraints imposed on them by the state. In other words, as in the 1940s, the assumption was "change the ownership and the problems will go away" (see Prosser 1986, chap. 5). Much of the appeal of Thatcher's version of industrial privatization was due to the long-standing perception in Britain that nationalization had meant government ministers indulging in too much meddling in industrial affairs. Thus government ministers presented privatization as "marking out a new and clear divide between the legitimate public and private domains" (Graham and Prosser 1987, 18).

The sales have had a great impact on Britain's political economy. Both the British cases analyzed here were eventually privatized.[7] The percentage of British GDP attributable to state-owned companies fell from 9 percent in 1979 to 3 percent in 1990, as companies ranging from small high-tech firms to the large utility monopolies were transferred to the private sector. The sales took many different forms, from the quiet hiving off of subsidiaries to the highly publicized flotation of utilities. The size and scope of the sales were the result of many factors, including a lack of unified opposition from the unions or the Labour Party, and few institutional constraints on a determined government. In addition, managers decided (or were persuaded by government) that removal from the public sector was definitely in their interests. The government tended to trade away liberalization or regulatory measures in return for management cooperation over sales. Big industrial companies such as British Steel and British Leyland had been nationalized when near the point of financial collapse. By 1979 they were seen as political embarrassments. The lack of support for nationalization in principle meant no basis for opposition to privatization in practice. With nationalization and privatization seen by all concerned as issues of ownership transfer, debate focused on the preferred owner, with decisions on the technical and financial issues being made without any major parliamentary role, except for ideological arguments.[8]

The government's publicly stated motives for privatization varied from arguments about increased efficiency and freedom to widening share ownership. Whatever the justifications, the government certainly pushed some of the larger sales to reduce the Public Sector Borrowing Requirement (PSBR), as by a peculiarly British accounting quirk, the proceeds from assets sales are counted as negative public expenditure. (In mid-1992 there were reports that the Treasury was planning to sell off debt owed to it by privatized companies, in a bid to trim the government's borrowing requirement, which was again rising steeply [*The Times*, June 15, 1992].) One argument was that the private sector gives industries access to investment funds that they would not be able to obtain as public sector companies. This argument is disingenuous, however, for in many cases it was the government's own strict limits on external financing that severely constrained the nationalized industries' access to capital. Furthermore, it was the Conservatives' own ideology, along with the opposition of the Treasury, that precluded the kind of hybrid stock options mixing public and private capital that were developed in France. After all, there was a precedent for allowing private investment in a publicly controlled company, namely British Leyland (chap. 5), and public-private capital mixes were extensive in the case of the Phoenix schemes (chap. 2).

Contrary to the ideology, privatization did not widen the chasm between the public and private sectors in Britain. The "chasm" was already very narrow at some points. As early as 1967, government involvement in the British shipbuilding industry had blurred the public-private division, with heavy assistance to private enterprises and the creation of hybrid firms.[9] As of the summer of 1992, the British government still held equity stakes—mostly very small—in thirty-three private sector companies.[10] One aspect of the asset sales of the 1980s is particularly worth noting here: the sales of British Steel, British Aerospace, Jaguar, and others included Special Shares, retained by the government, that, if invoked, can block an attempt to purchase more than 15 percent of the company's shares. In some cases, the government share can automatically trigger a repurchase of shares over the 15 percent limit. The government's decision not to invoke its Special Share in December 1989 had a major impact on Ford's takeover of Jaguar (chap. 5). As Graham and Prosser (1987) point out, the Special Share is a novel form of restriction for Britain, providing for compulsory expropriation of property if certain conditions are met. Yet the free transferability of shares is supposedly a basic principle of the nation's company law. Other companies listed on the Stock Exchange have reportedly wanted to include such a restrictive provision in their Articles, but the Stock Exchange has refused to allow this. "Presumably the decision to allow privatized companies this special provision was reached by negotiation between the Stock Exchange and the Government, which is yet another indication that the privatized companies are not ordinary private sector companies" (Graham and Prosser 1987, 38).

In contrast with Britain, the state industrial sector was still very significant in France by 1993. Some state ownership dated from the end of the Second World War, but the nationalizations of 1981–82 greatly increased the size and scope of the public sector. The Socialists believed that nationalization would protect the national economy, and increase jobs and investment. The purchases included five big industrial groups, the steel companies Usinor and Sacilor, a number of previously private deposit banks, and the two finance companies Paribas and Indosuez.[11] In 1986 the center-right government of Jacques Chirac vowed to sell sixty-five state-owned companies. In the event, a Socialist president and stock market problems severely curtailed the government's ambitions and only twelve sizable companies were privatized between 1986 and 1988.[12]

The center-right government wanted to ensure some financial stability for these newly privatized companies, most of which had been nationalized in 1982. Instead of British-style Special Shares, however, the French government, in cooperation with each company's management, organized a kernel of "friendly institutional investors" for each firm. These investors each took a minority equity interest in the firm, with a long-term investment view (Jacquillat 1987). This notion of a core group of friendly equity holders is rooted in French corporate governance practices, and is central to the financial structure of Peugeot SA (chap. 4).

Meanwhile, the Socialist enthusiasm for nationalization waned over the decade. By 1989, Mitterrand's official policy had been dubbed "ni . . . ni . . . "—neither nationalization nor privatization, an attempt to simultaneously appease both sides of the debate. Even so, the 1989 budget contained FFr4 billion for contributions to the capital of the state companies, rising to FFr4.7 billion in 1990.[13] Finding adequate financing for the state companies was still a major problem. For much of the 1980s, the state-controlled banks and insurance companies had helped to fund the firms by subscribing to their rights issues, but the banks and insurance companies began to complain of being strapped for cash themselves. So in the spring of 1991, the government allowed private companies to take minority stakes in government-controlled firms. These partial privatizations were only allowed under strict conditions, and as part of a cooperation accord that included the raising of new capital to which all investors must contribute (*Financial Times*, June 17, 1991). In all cases, the state remained in control of the firm—this was not privatization à la Thatcher. Although this change in policy marked the formal end of "ni . . . ni . . . ," the public-private divide had grown steadily less distinct throughout the 1980s.

The French governments had to find ways to finance their state-owned industries in the 1980s but, unlike the British, they came up with some overt public-private capital mixes to do so.[14] In 1983 the Socialist government passed a law allowing the nationalized industries to issue two new forms of financing, *titres participatifs* and *certificats d'investissement*. The former are nonvoting loan stock, with a return based partly on the going bond rate and partly on some other index chosen by the firm, such as turnover. The latter are nonvoting preference shares. The various nationalized enterprises made extensive use of these new instruments. By the end of 1984, over FFr6.5 billion had been issued, mostly in the form of *titres participatifs*. From June 1988 to June 1990, FFr183.4 billion in fresh capital was supplied to the French public sector companies. Only FFr13.8 billion came from state cash injections and FFr21.1 billion from debt write-offs. FFr34.3 billion came from the financial markets (*Financial Times*, June 26, 1990). By 1990, ten of the state-controlled companies had stock market listings and could raise cash through rights issues (although they were limited to issuing only up to 25 percent of their capital as nonvoting stock [*Financial Times*, October 18, 1989]). In late 1989 the Industry Ministry was denying press reports that the government had approved a FFr40 billion plan to finance foreign acquisitions by state-owned companies (*Financial Times*, October 18, 1989).

There were also a number of equity substitutes and share swap deals between the nationalized firms. Away from the main parent companies, the state sector had been buying foreign businesses and subsidiaries and selling unwanted ones:

> The outcome has been a de facto flexibility in the boundaries of the state sector almost unprecedented since the Second World War, leaving nationalised companies almost as free as their private sector counterparts to expand, and in particular, to expand abroad. (*Financial Times*, November 9, 1989)

However, the picture is changing yet again, following the March 1993 election of an RPR-UDF center-right government with an overwhelming majority in the Assemblé. On May 26, the new prime minister, Edouard Balladur, unveiled a privatization plan that, he said, would both roll back the frontiers of state involvement in the economy and help to finance economic recovery. Twenty-one firms are on the privatization list. Twelve were first scheduled for sale in 1986, including the major banks Crédit Lyonnais and Banque National de Paris, and industrial giants Rhône Poulenc, Elf-Acquitaine, and Bull. The nine new candidates include Renault and the steel giant Usinor Sacilor. The Balladur government is hoping both to restrain public borrowing and to use the funds raised to finance unemployment programs. With the French economy in recession in 1993 and the Paris stock market in the doldrums at the time of this writing, the sell-offs are getting underway only gradually. The government has already made it clear, however, that newly privatized companies will again be protected by *noyaux durs*, with the government encouraging long-term investors to take strategic stakes in the firms. In theory, such shareholder groups will this time be open to foreign investors. Société Générale has already announced that it plans to participate in the new round of share sales by increasing its holding in a number of companies already partially privatized, such as Rhône-Poulenc. The new economy minister, Edmond Alphandéry, summed up the government's attitude succinctly:

> Rather than have control of a company raffled back and forth on the stock market . . . it is far better for its management to have a certain number of shareholders of reference, who know the company's strategy and have an interest in it succeeding. (Interview in *Financial Times*, May 10, 1993.)

If the government's plans succeed, these sales will reduce the economic weight of the public sector from around 18 percent of the total economy at the end of 1991, to near the British level of just over 5 percent (*Financial Times*, March 16, 1993).[15]

To reiterate, one of the arguments underpinning the analysis in the following case studies is that the financing of large firms straddles the increasingly blurred boundary between public and private spheres of action and decision making. When a major manufacturer needs access to huge sums of financing in order to survive, the government gets involved, either directly through outright aid (perhaps by taking on the firm's debts, ultimately by nationalization); or indirectly, by channeling investment through specialized loan schemes, or by encouraging other manufacturers to compensate for a firm's withdrawal from certain markets or regions. The reason for government involvement is obvious—the economic and political repercussions of firm contraction or failure. In fact, the financing considerations for a major manufacturer are never driven by the market alone. Thus local and national politicians were very actively involved in striking financial deals with Peugeot to get the company to locate production facilities in depressed steel regions. This not only lessened some of the impact of steel company closures on the regions, it also gave PSA additional financial resources. In addition, private ownership does not necessarily mean no government control over the structure, commercial decisions, or financing of a firm. In 1978, the Giraud Plan gave the French state significant control over the financing of the major steel firms, although they remained under private ownership. In Britain, ministers liked to argue that a nationalized firm in trouble had "unfair" access to cheap cash—but so did the privately owned Chrysler UK, and the remaining private steel companies. These are all examples of the places at which government, industry, national financial markets, and international economic change meet.

This blurring of the public-private boundary applies not only to privately owned firms, but equally to companies in the state sector. This is clearest in France, where, as described above, public-private capital mixes are increasingly seen as a way of solving the nationalized firms' needs for large sums of investment capital without loosening the state's overt ability to approve the firms' overall industrial strategies. The same has also been true in Britain, however, as illustrated by the Phoenix schemes.

Not only do the public and private spheres increasingly overlap, but, similarly, state and private ownership are not somehow at opposite ends of the industrial policy spectrum. We cannot rely on "nationalization" and "privatization" as labels defining the boundaries of government-industry relations. The extent to which government is involved in any one firm's financial affairs varies over time, whether the firm is state- or privately owned. The distinctions between an activist state that is heavily involved in industrial intervention and a "hands-off" state that sits back and lets the free market determine industrial outcomes, are increasingly incoherent. Despite differing institutional structures and differing ideologies on the part of the governing party, there were remarkable similarities in the ways in which these two states were involved in helping major manufacturers to survive industrial crises and to adapt to changing markets and technologies. In order to clearly understand the workings and the outcomes of government-industry relations, and particularly to explain those national differences that do exist, we must look more closely at the actual workings of the national financial system. And the best place at which to start is with the financial structures of individual firms, since these reflect, are affected by, and ultimately themselves form a part of, the national system.

2. Financial Markets and Financial Policies

National differences in the organization of financial markets and in the pursuit of financial policies go a long way toward explaining key aspects of government-industry relations in Europe in the 1980s. Although capital is the most fungible of goods, financial markets are still profoundly national in character, and are regulated and manipulated by national governments. Such differences affect, among other things, the sources and types of capital to which firms have access. The privatized Jaguar's only major source of outside financing in 1986 was the British stock market, while the French steel firms' primary source, for a long time, was government-subsidized debt. Since the mid-1980s, thanks to government legislation, French firms such as Peugeot can now use new financial instruments to restructure their debts.

There is much more to the workings of a national financial system, however, than basic differences in institutions and structures. For example, Zysman assumes that a capital-market-based system means an arm's length relationship between financial institution and firm, with exit the only means by which shareholders can exercise influence on the firm; whereas in a credit-based system, long-term debt financing means a close, long-term relationship between the firm and its source of finance. But Peugeot SA relied heavily on share capital for much of the 1970s and 1980s, and its major investors neither exited when it got into trouble, nor had an arm's-length relationship with the firm. Conversely, French banks did not take a particularly close or long-term interest in the steel firms they had financed since the 1960s. The reason for this has to do with the workings of the French financial system.

In his study of banking, Pauly (1988) finds that national banking sectors include unique relationships between government and market participants, between the participants themselves, and between the constituencies affected by political change. He also emphasizes the importance of state control over domestic banking markets, and their political architecture and regulation. These points apply equally to other areas of financial markets, such as to the wider equity and debt markets and to issues of corporate governance. Stock exchanges can be very different kinds of institutions—the French Bourse is a relatively young institution, more easily dominated in the 1980s by a big firm like Peugeot. The British exchange is highly developed, and Jaguar was at the mercy of the short-term opinions of traders in volatile markets. The French banks had a very different kind of relationship with the French steel firms than did the British banks with British Leyland.

A national financial system is more than just the institutions used to channel savings to investors. It includes a host of other regulations and methods that affect the ways in which firms can structure their balance sheets and distribute the rights and responsibilities of owners and investors. The broader definition of a national financial system incorporates the many aspects of corporate governance, such as the kinds of voting rights that can be attached to categories of shares; whether most corporate debt is in the form of bonds or direct loans; what kinds of loans can be made, with what conditions attached, and issued and underwritten by whom; the relationships permitted between financial and nonfinancial institutions; disclosure rules for share ownership; the equity-raising activities permitted; the definition of concepts like fiduciary responsibility; the definition and permissible activities of banks; the use of depreciation in company accounting; and so on.

The intention here is not to present a textbook description of either the costs and benefits of debt versus equity financing, or the minutiae of national variations in accepted accounting rules. Rather, it is to illustrate the argument that starting the analysis of government-industry relations and industrial financing at the level of the individual firm—instead of at the level of national institutions and the state—yields not only a richer understanding of how firms try to cope with crises of adaptation and survival, but also a more complete picture of how national financial systems and governments actually operate. We see more clearly where the crucial differences between national financial systems actually lie, because we see the impact of those differences on the manufacturers themselves.

Financing Industry

The analysis of the following case studies is oriented around four main arguments—that the divide between the public and private sectors is often nearly impossible to discern; that the solutions to the financing of major manufacturers at a time of crisis and restructuring were remarkably similar in Thatcher's proprivatization Britain and Mitterrand's pronationalization France; that the financial structure of the individual firm is a crucial component in its survival and adaptation; and, most importantly, that this firm-level financial analysis reveals the actual workings of the national financial systems, as maintained and regulated by government. Making this last step from the firm back to the level of the national financial system means that the analysis must be oriented around one key question, namely, which aspect of the firm's financial structure, broadly defined, matters the most in determining outcomes, and how?

The kinds of finance to which a firm has access are a key factor in (a) whether the firm can *survive* as a manufacturer at a time of intense competition and market upheaval; and (b) whether the firm can *adapt* to new competitive and technological challenges over the long term.[16] This is particularly true of firms in capital-intensive industries such as steel production and auto manufacturing—and doubly so in the latter case, where the development of new products and processes is both time-consuming and extremely expensive. For short-term survival, a firm needs to finance its short-term operating activities and meet its current liabilities.[17] Ideally, it needs relatively flexible financial sources that it can access relatively quickly and easily without jeopardizing its longer-term financial health. Adaptation, however, requires somewhat different financial resources. For this the firm needs long-term, preferably low-cost, and above all stable investment financing. But to grasp the importance and desirability of undergoing a potentially major upheaval for adaptation, the firm also needs some form of coherent leadership, a dominant voice pushing the importance of a long-term plan, focus, or strategy—a single owner, strong and motivated management, or dominant shareholder(s) or other active investor(s). This leadership may, of course, entirely misjudge the nature of the "threat" facing the firm, or focus on the wrong factors, but a management focused only on short-term survival does not augur well for long-term adaptation.

In the following chapters, much of the analysis focuses on the firm's sources of funding, rather than just presenting a summary of annual net profit and loss. As well as distinguishing between proportions of debt to equity on the firm's balance sheet, we must ask whether holders of the firm's debt and/or equity are dispersed across markets and interests, perhaps including overseas interests? Or are there only a handful of—perhaps only one—clearly identifiable dominant stakeholders? Are apparently widely dispersed shares in fact closely held or privately traded? The answers to these questions help to reveal just what it is about a firm's corporate governance and the characteristics of its financial structure that profoundly affects the processes of crisis management. Three possibilities in particular are considered: first, the costs of various forms of financing, such as interest payments and the need to make dividend payments in order to maintain credibility with the equity markets.[18] The second explanation for the impact of financial structure on firm survival is availability. How easy was it to raise the enormous sums of financing needed? Did shareholders take a dim view of the firm taking on additional long-term debt, and if so, what could they do about it? Did turning to one source of financing in particular make other providers more or less likely to finance the firm's needs? The third explanation to consider is the impact on the firm of the providers involved, specifically of their attitudes toward the firm's restructuring needs. Were holders of debt, say, more or less apt to take a long-term view regarding industrial financing than shareholders? What kinds of conditions did the banks, the state, or shareholders place on making funds available?

All of these issues—costs, availability, attitudes of providers—fall under the heading of "corporate governance." All have implications for a firm's ownership structure. All are, in turn, a reflection of the national financial system in which the firm operates and of the individual firm's own organizational, political, and commercial history. The term *national financial system* is thus used here in its broadest sense, to include not only the basic form of market, but also the regulation of ownership and corporate governance. While it is true that any government is, in a sense, constrained by the national financial system, it is also government that mediates, regulates, and occasionally reorders national financial markets and institutions. It is ultimately the government that decides how the financial system will respond to international economic pressures, and how far and in what ways those pressures will be transmitted to domestic firms via the financial system. This is why the politics of financial markets is the place at which state, industry, banking, and international economic change meet.

This brings us to a consideration of the British and French national financial systems. Other aspects of the apparent fundamental differences between the two nations are discussed in part 3. Here, the intention is to further illustrate the variety of ways in which industries can be financed, and the kinds of impacts these differences can have on individual firms and on the wider economy. This discussion also helps to develop one of the themes of this book—that governments are, in many ways, profoundly involved in trying to provide major firms with access to financial resources.

National Financial Systems

> When Versailles was being built, Colbert founded a state-owned glass manufacturer because he feared that the Venetians, who dominated glass making, might do to the mirror business what Japan has recently done to the motor industry. (*Economist*, June 1, 1991, 75)

Economic nationalism on the part of governments is not a recent invention. There are numerous examples of states protecting, promoting, even founding, particular industries. As has been argued above, however, the role of the state in financing industry is usually considered only in terms of a firm's formal ownership. Public fights or scandals may also force the financial side of government-industry relations into public view, as with the bankruptcy of

Creusôt Loire in 1984 (chap. 3), or the government's manipulation of financial "incentives" to ensure the sale of Rover to British Aerospace (BAe) in 1988 (chap. 5). Otherwise, industrial policy and financial policy are usually seen as quite separate. Reality is, of course, far more complicated.

France

One of the most obvious differences between the French and British financial systems is that the state's financial role is discussed more frequently and directly in France than in Britain, and successive French governments have argued the importance of the financial dimension of industrial policy. The form of financial restructuring undertaken in the Giraud Plan for French steel, for example, depended on the existence of institutions and government-industry financial relationships that did not exist in Britain.

State influence over banking in France goes back to at least the middle of the nineteenth century. After the Second World War state savings institutions were established, along with various funds to channel investment capital to industry through the private banking sector. The emphasis on getting enough finance to industry is still reflected in the institutional makeup of government departments. A number of new institutions were also established to create an elite core of technically trained administrators to run and plan the nation's economy. The graduates of the École Nationale d'Administration (ENA) and École Polytechnique took their ideas about economic management and long-term planning into the Ministry of Finance and the Planning Commission (Stevens 1985). Through the tradition of *pantouflage* these *grand corps* members often take up senior management positions in public and private corporations, as did Peugeot's Calvet, or enter politics.

Since the late 1940s, the main agent involved in making funds available for industrial development or restructuring has been the Ministry of Finance. The Ministry, until late in the 1980s, controlled all direct public investment, most of the banking system, including the central Banque de France, and virtually all of the financial incentives used to implement the National Plans. When the Balladur government made the Banque de France formally independent early in 1994, it marked an important shift in power away from the Finance Ministry and, in particular, from the Trésor. The Trésor is the core of the Finance Ministry, with enormous influence over financial affairs. It sanctions the nationalized industries' investment programs; intervenes in the national economy with loans and transfer facilities; and supervises specialized financial intermediaries, including France's largest financial institution and largest institutional investor, the Caisse des Dépôts et Consignations (CDC), which in mid-1992 managed assets of some FFr1.6 trillion, not including mutual funds, and had an equity portfolio of FFr4.3 billion (*Euromoney*,

September 1992).[19] The range of instruments that has been used by the state to fund industry is impressive. In 1982, a Commissariat Général du Plan (CGP) report found that there were some 300 industrial policy mechanisms available that year, including 150 different forms of industrial subsidy.[20] One of the most important funds is the Fonds de Développement Economique et Social (FDES), a committee directed by the Trésor. The Trésor also controls the Interministerial Committee for Management of the Industrial Structure (CIASI), which brings together officials and bankers for industrial rescues.[21]

Each new problem identified in industrial financing has tended to result in yet another state-sponsored fund. In 1983 the Socialist government set up the Fonds Industriel de Modernisation (FIM) to help with industrial modernization. The Fund receives part of its resources from the Compte de Développement Industriel (CODEVI), a savings vehicle set up in 1981 to channel finances to industrial firms, and to borrow in domestic and international markets. In 1984 FIM had a total of FFr7 billion with which to support technological modernization programs by French firms such as Peugeot. Peugeot's 1984 loan, like others from FIM, was approved by the Ministry for Industry and guaranteed in full by the government (Balassa 1985). There have also been a number of very specialized loan institutions that draw on the private market with implicit or explicit state backing. The Groupement de l'Industrie Sidérurgique (GIS) was created in 1948 and endowed with the ability to make loans to the nation's steel industry. It also floated bonds on the securities market and distributed the proceeds among its members for investment (chap. 3). Despite this impressive array of controls and instruments, a 1982 report commissioned by the government concluded that the various national financial instruments did not play an effective role in national economic and industrial planning.[22]

Apart from a brief period in the mid-1980s when bullish international stock markets and high interest rates encouraged firms to turn toward securities issues, banks have long been the principal source of finance for French industry (table 1). At the start of the decade, according to one source, some firms relied on banks for up to 71 percent of their external financing (Emmott 1991). Between 1982 and 1986, securities issues tripled their share of total funding (*Financial Times*, November 2, 1989). By the end of the decade, firms had turned back to debt as their principal source of funding. In the first half of 1989 Banque Nationale de Paris's corporate lending rose by 15 percent; Paribas's by 21 percent (*Financial Times*, November 2, 1989). It is often claimed that this reliance on long-term debt from the banks gives them a detailed knowledge of industrial affairs and considerable influence over firms' actions (Hall 1986). It can certainly make firms vulnerable to economic downturns and particularly dependent on state-subsidized credit. The expansionist appetites of many of the largest French companies in the boom years of the

TABLE 1. Structure of Financing of Nonfinancial Enterprises (as percentage of total flow of net resources; excluding Grandes Enterprises Nationales)

	Self-Financing	Share Issues	Bond Issues	Borrowing		
				Short-Term	Long-Term	Negotiable Notes
1974–79	39.3	7.6	0.8	39.5	12.8	0.0
1980	34.8	9.4	0.7	39.9	15.1	0.0
1981	29.8	11.4	2.3	44.6	11.7	0.0
1982	33.6	8.4	1.6	41.4	15.0	0.0
1983	34.6	11.6	1.8	30.8	21.1	0.0
1984	36.9	12.0	3.6	31.4	16.1	0.0
1985	54.4	20.4	0.5	12.9	10.9	0.7
1986	57.9	30.6	−0.1	2.7	5.3	3.6
1987	47.4	25.5	0.3	12.4	12.2	2.2

Source: Data adapted from OECD Economic Survey: France, February 1989.

mid- to late-1980s meant a steep increase in debt levels across all industrial sectors. French corporate debt was close to 170 percent of value added in 1980. This had fallen to around 155 percent by 1986 but was close to 175 percent again by the end of the decade (*Financial Times*, December 27, 1990.) Both Peugeot SA and Usinor are cases in point. The reliance on debt also means that corporate debt/equity ratios tend to be higher in France than in Britain or the United States, but not as high as in Japan and Germany, where the banks play an even more dominant role in industrial financing (see table 2). But until very recently the role of the banks was rarely as investors in their own right.

Until the late 1980s, the majority of French banks financed state expenditures and loans, rather than actively participating in national industrial devel-

TABLE 2. Debt/Equity Ratios of the Nonfinancial Corporate Sector

	1974–79	1980	1981	1982	1983	1984	1985
France	1.33	1.23	1.40	1.55	1.56	——	——
U.K.	1.38	1.13	1.23	1.03	1.87	0.74	0.70
U.S.	0.96	0.77	0.92	0.87	0.78	0.90	0.83
Germany	3.36	3.85	4.13	4.11	3.48	3.42	2.39
Japan	3.31	3.14	2.91	2.92	2.68	2.11	1.82

Note: Figures are liabilities, excluding equity and trade credit, as a proportion of equity at market prices, except for France, where equity is at book value.
Source: Data adapted from OECD Economic Survey: U.K., 1987.

opment. Most banks preferred loans for other sectors such as agriculture or energy (Bellon 1985). Government reports often criticized the banks for not understanding the economic realities of industry, and being "insufficiently oriented towards industrial development."[23] The relationship between the banks and industry is now changing, however. The 1982 report on the banking system, which was highly critical of the amount of overcentralization and credit control, was embraced by the Socialists (Green 1986). By the mid-1980s there were signs that the government's campaign to change banks' attitudes toward industrial investment risks was beginning to pay off.

Some of France's larger banks are wholly or majority-owned by holding companies with sizable industrial connections. The bank holding companies do, however, tend to keep their ownership participations in commercial firms below 50 percent. The formally private Crédit National (the director and two subdirectors are appointed by the government, but the board is elected by shareholders) has been a particular source of industrial finance since 1946. It lends directly to industry, uses its funds to guarantee other banks' medium- and long-term loans to industry, and also manages and supervises funds that the government lends or grants, such as the FDES (Zysman 1983). Crédit National was one of the major financial interests involved in the financial restructuring of the French steel industry in the late 1970s (chap. 3). The three major deposit banks in France (Banque Nationale de Paris, Société Générale, and Crédit Lyonnais) were all publicly owned in the postwar era, and helped manage government industrial funds. In 1982 the Socialist government nationalized the remaining private shares in the three, along with thirty-six smaller banks, and the two investment banks, Paribas and Indosuez. The aim was to better control the flows of finance to industry and social investment, but in most respects nationalization did not radically alter the structure of French banking (Green 1986).

A new banking act in 1984, however, extended the already broad powers of the banks. Deposit-taking institutions had been allowed to take shares in non-bank companies since 1966, but few did so, seeing this as the preserve of the *banques d'affaires* Paribas and Indosuez. Since 1987, however, Banque Nationale de Paris, Société Générale (privatized in 1986), and Crédit Lyonnais have built up large portfolios of shares in French companies. With the capitalization of the French Bourse rising rapidly since the October 1987 crash, such investments are increasingly lucrative. By the end of 1990, the combined equity portfolio of the banks was FFr179 billion, up from FFr124 billion at the end of 1989 (*Financial Times*, June 17, 1991).

There are signs that French bankers are hoping to strengthen the system whereby one bank usually provides most of a firm's commercial and investment banking needs. They are said to envy German counterparts such as

Deutsche Bank, which has an intimate relationship with German industry (*Economist*, August 4, 1990). However, German banks are allowed by law to vote on behalf of other shareholders at annual general meetings, the source of much of their influence, which power the French banks lack. The French banks do not expect to start controlling firms, or sending in managers and directors: "What they want is business . . . as a first option. In that way, the French banks are trying to be Japanese, to set up a community of interest between themselves and their clients" (Emmott 1991, 41).

An even greater impact on industrial financing in France in the 1980s came from the comprehensive reforms of the capital and investment markets over the course of the decade by the late Pierre Bérégovoy, finance minister in the Socialist governments and prime minister from April 1992 to March 1993. With extensive legislation, the segmented and subsidized credit circuits that financed specific sectors of the economy were trimmed. France moved from being one of the most highly regulated markets in Europe to one of the most deregulated. By the end of the decade, the French stock market possessed one of the most efficient trading systems in the world, and one of the most liquid government bond markets. The state also withdrew in other areas from its direct role in industrial finance. For example, in early 1991 the state guarantees enjoyed by government-controlled borrowers when they borrowed on the international capital market were removed.[24]

A number of new markets were also created in the 1980s, with "resounding success" (Price Waterhouse 1989). The second market (*second marché*) was started in 1983, for smaller companies. In 1986, trading began in interest rate futures on the *marché à termes des instruments financiers* (MATIF). In 1988, MATIF absorbed the Paris Commodities Exchange. In 1987, trading began in put and call options on the *marché des options négociables de Paris* (MONEP). In addition, firms were permitted to float commercial paper for the first time in French history (Melitz 1990). A *société anonyme* (corporation) may also now take out a subordinated loan (*prêt participatif*) from any financial or commercial enterprise, including banks and insurance companies. This is a legislatively created form of debt financing that ranks above equity but below all other debts, and is considered as equity for accounting purposes.

Still, there are difficulties with raising long-term capital. First, France does not have the kind of state pension fund reserves, or private pension funds, found in the United States and Britain. In 1988, total pension fund assets in France amounted to just 3 percent of GDP, compared with 46 percent of GDP in Britain. There are pressures to encourage the creation of private pension funds, not least the growing annual deficits in the state pension system. Plans to introduce private funds in 1992 were stymied by union opposition, but with the mounting strain on the public system, the center-right government may decide to bite the bullet and introduce legislation to encourage company pension funds. This would have an enormous impact on the structure of the French financial market.

The second difficulty with raising long-term capital is that, although equity market capitalization has increased substantially from 9 percent of GDP in 1978, at 26 percent of GDP it is still far behind the United States at 53 percent, and Britain at 89 percent (*Financial Times*, June 17, 1991). Foreign equity trading in Paris in 1990 was less than $10 billion (*Economist*, May 18, 1991). The majority of the capitalization and transactions on the French stock market have tended to involve bonds (Price Waterhouse 1989). Furthermore, as so many listed companies are controlled by other listed companies, the total capitalization figure of FFr1,688 billion includes much double counting (ibid.). The market is also considerably more concentrated than that of the U.K. (see table 3). Again, the Balladur government is hoping to encourage changes that could end the traditional liquidity problem of the Paris Bourse, by abolishing investment tax on small investments and encouraging investors to switch some of the billions of francs now invested in bank-administered savings funds into equities.

Despite the last decade of deregulation, and the development of new markets, the state has continued to play a dominant role in industrial financing, albeit less overtly than before. Through their equity holdings, the state-owned banks, the state-controlled savings institution and investor Caisse des Dépôts, and state-owned insurers together "represent the far from invisible hand of the state on French industry" (*Economist*, June 1, 1991). The implication is that the state now controls the capital for industrial investment via equity holdings, rather than through loans and controls over the credit markets. The control is certainly less direct, but it still allows the government to exercise considerable influence over the financial affairs of major manufacturers in trouble.

TABLE 3.   Market Capitalization at December 31, 1988 (U.S. $billion)

	Capitalization	% of World	Top Ten Stocks	Top Ten's % of Market
United States	$1,958.2	29.8%		
Japan	2,964.6	45.1		
U.K.	569.9	8.7	$167.2	29.3%
France	152.1	2.3	71.5	47.0
Germany	200.4	3.1	125.4	62.6
Italy	96.2	1.5	62.5	65.0

Source: Data adapted from Drexel Burnham Lambert, International Equity Research report January 25, 1989.

Finally, despite all of the changes in the capital markets, there still isn't an active takeover market in France. The shareholding rules that apply to the *société anonyme* make hostile bids very hard to win. There are a number of different kinds of shares, with different levels of voting rights. These include nonvoting preferred stock, shares with double voting rights, restrictions on voting rights, and stock warrants that can be converted in the case of a bid (Peugeot issued such warrants in the mid-1980s when the family sought to protect the firm against possible hostile takeover—see chap. 4). A small group of shareholders can have preemption rights over one another's shares, and companies under attack are allowed to issue new capital. Many major companies "have created a barrier of holding companies to shield their businesses" (*Economist*, June 1, 1991). Peugeot is a case in point.

In addition, any foreign company buying over 20 percent of the capital of a French firm needs official clearance (*Economist*, June 1, 1991). The distrust of American-style takeovers was underlined by Mitterrand in 1989:

> I want to put the French on their guard against this takeover mania, against this gangsterism. . . . I want to protect French producers . . . [and] entrepreneurs from this roving, predatory money which grabs everything without effort. (Quoted in *Financial Times*, November 2, 1989)

New takeover legislation came into effect early in 1990, requiring any investor who acquires more than one-third of a listed company to launch a bid for at least another third. In addition, shareholders must declare their holding once it reaches 5 percent of voting rights, rather than the old threshold of 5 percent of shares. As shares can have double voting rights, the new rule gives additional protection to target companies.

In theory, a "capital structure consisting mostly of equity . . . carries substantial risks of inviting a hostile takeover or other threats to management control" (Jensen 1989, 62). In practice, the structures and practice of corporate governance in France are such that this statement is not necessarily true at all.

Britain

In contrasts of French and British policy-making, Britain often comes off the worst, its policymakers said to abdicate responsibility for industrial affairs, and its governments to remain isolated from industry (Dyson and Wilks 1983). Without the Gallic efficiency of central direction, British policy decisions supposedly get lost in a maze of ambiguous consultation and red tape.[25] It is often assumed that the French are in a much better position to tackle industrial problems, with their *dirigiste* traditions and belief in industry's economic importance. However, British governments can be just as interventionist, and discretionary, on certain issues.

The policy of British government toward industry is typically characterized as being "arm's length," with a fundamental emphasis on consensus and consent. Since at least 1918, governments have said that industries facing economic change should rationalize themselves, with government cajoling rather than coercing.[26] It is often argued that there is an unbridgeable gulf between the financial and industrial sectors in Britain, the latter tending historically to be self-financing, the former to be heavily involved in overseas lending. This gulf apparently widened in the 1980s, as London consolidated its position as one of the world's major international financial centers. By 1989, London handled about one-fifth of the world's international banking business (*Financial Times*, November 9, 1989). In 1988, the invisible earnings of Britain's banks, brokers, and insurers were large enough to cover the nation's car imports (*Economist*, August 5, 1989).

During the 1980s, the Thatcher governments were consistently criticized by businessmen for insisting that the City could adequately meet industry's financial needs. Stephen Walls was director of Plessey before it was swallowed by GEC in a hostile takeover in 1988:

> What scuppered us was a number of factors. The political climate was not right, with a government that would not intervene to support anything that looks like an industrial strategy; and everything was running in favour of free marketeering, stock-market-dominated solutions to industrial restructuring. (*Financial Times*, October 20, 1989)

The Thatcher government ended forty years of exchange controls in October 1979, making U.K. residents completely free to invest and borrow abroad, and giving nonresidents access to the U.K. credit markets. The subsequent outflow of British investment capital overseas, and the equally high levels of inward investment from overseas, led to charges that British industry had inadequate access to stable sources of domestic capital. London is the biggest foreign equity market in the world, and at £150 billion, foreign equity trading accounted for nearly half of London's total turnover in 1990 (*Economist*, May 18, 1991). Other areas of the financial markets also prospered in the 1980s. The London International Financial Futures Exchange (LIFFE) opened in 1982, and has taken over the London Traded Options Market (LTOM). In May 1991, the Futures and Options Exchange opened, the world's first property-futures market (*Economist*, May 18, 1991).

There are no actual laws prohibiting nonfinancial firms from owning banks, but the Bank of England's policy is to keep the banking and commercial (i.e., industrial) sectors apart, to lessen potential conflicts of interest and to prevent problems spreading from the commercial to the banking sector. Also, unlike in France, there is some separation between financial institutions providing banking services and those providing securities services, although a bank may use a securities subsidiary to underwrite corporate debt (Federal Reserve Bank of New York 1987). Despite the general rule that British banks have little involvement in the affairs of industry, there have been a number of notable exceptions in recent years (see chap. 5).

Britain had something of an industrial takeover boom between 1985 and 1989, with plenty of bitterly contested hostile bids. Between 1980 and 1988, 75 percent of the leveraged buyouts in Europe were located in Britain. The next biggest share belongs to France, at just 9 percent of the buyout total (*Financial Times*, October 24, 1989). Junk bond financing never attained the prominence that it had in the United States, however. Also unlike the United States, Britain has a "voluntary but powerful" Takeover Code (Emmott 1991). It bans maneuvers that attempt to limit the transfer of ownership, but it also makes takeovers harder in that an offer must be made to all shareholders at the same price, once a firm has accumulated 30 percent of the target's shares. Repeat bids are not allowed within one year, and bidders must not act "in undisclosed concert" with others (ibid.). Firms are also banned from frustrating a bid by overburdening themselves with debt or by taking poison pills. Other aspects of takeovers are more formally regulated. For example, any stockholder owning more than 3 percent of shares must disclose the fact (until 1987, the disclosure limit was 5 percent).

By the turn of the twentieth century, the shape of the banking system was basically established, dominated by the Big Five clearing banks, with the Bank of England as lender of last resort. Retail, wholesale, and discount banking were seen as distinct parts of the industry, each looking after its own affairs through a central committee or association (Capie 1990). Since 1979, the Bank of England's responsibilities as supervisor and regulator have been gradually extended, and the role of the old restrictive "clubs" markedly reduced. The Bank of England itself has been under state control since 1946 but preserves its independence from the government, maintaining close ties to the concerns of the financial institutions known as the City.[27] Yet the Bank lacks clear formal powers. The cliché is that the Bank represents the Treasury in the City and the City in the Treasury. Whereas the French Trésor once clearly dominated the Bank of France, the Treasury's relationship with the Bank of England is ambiguous, and largely dependent on the chancellor of the exchequer and bank governor involved.[28]

As described above, the securities market and investing institutions dominate the financial markets in Britain. British industries, in contrast with their French counterparts, are in general more likely to use retentions, equities, and short-term loans to finance their investment, rather than long-term bank loans (see table 4). At the turn of this century, the fledgling British auto industry actually turned to the stock market for financing rather than to the British banks, who were reluctant to provide long-term funds (Lewchuk 1986). Firms seeking long-term money are still apt to go directly to the bond markets themselves, rather than to the banks. They tend to finance expansion from savings and, in the case of large firms, from the sale of equity, not from credit (Zysman 1983; Cox 1986).

Finally, the Thatcher governments encouraged structural changes at the London International Stock Exchange, in order that the U.K. securities industry might better compete in domestic and international markets. In 1983 the government exempted the Exchange from the Restrictive Trade Practices Act, and had subjected the Exchange to its own specific rules and trading arrangements by the end of 1986. These changes included new ownership rules allowing outsiders to acquire majority participation in Exchange member firms, and domestic and foreign corporate membership (*Economist*, April 30, 1988).

Despite its predominance, however, the London International Stock Exchange has not necessarily been an effective means of raising industrial finance. It is "primarily a market for trading existing securities; its role as a device for raising new money for industrial development is very much a secondary function" (Cox 1986). The high levels of institutional share ownership mean the Exchange is "more geared to the buying and selling of securities than as a source of long-term equity ownership in particular companies" (ibid.). About 70 percent of U.K. equity is owned by financial institutions and funds, around one-half by life assurance and pension funds alone (OECD 1987). The proportion of equity held directly by individuals had declined from more than one-half in the 1960s to less than one-quarter by 1990.

The dominance of institutional investors may also be one explanation for British companies' apparently unbreakable habit of paying out hefty dividends, even during a recession. The causes and consequences of this habit are another subject of much debate, but it could be argued that a dividend is worth

TABLE 4.   Sources of Funds in the U.K. Company Sector (percentages)

	1977	1978	1979	1980	1981	1982	1983	1984	1985
Shares & Loans[a]	6.0	9.9	3.3	4.1	10.4	0.1	0.7	9.9	8.0
Short-term[b]	16.4	16.0	25.6	16.8	31.3	33.8	31.7	24.0	−0.6
Self-financing[c]	77.6	74.1	71.1	79.1	58.3	66.1	67.6	66.1	92.6

Source: Data adapted from Central Statistical Office 1988.
[a]Receipts from issues of share and loan capital.
[b]Increase in amount owed to banks, short-term lenders, and creditors.
[c]Gross income.

more to a pension fund than the capital gains that theoretically would result if the company retained its cash, strengthened its balance sheet, and boosted its share price. If British companies know that their major investors look askance at a cut in dividends, they may be even less likely to send out such a negative market signal when times are tough. In any event, in 1991—definitely a recession year for the British economy—the dividend payments of industrial firms rose 5.3 percent (*Economist*, January 25, 1992). When British Steel suggested it might cut its final dividend payment in November 1991, the company's shares promptly plunged 20 percent (see chap. 2).

There is also a long-running debate within Britain over the concept of shareholders' preemptive rights, and whether these put British companies at a competitive disadvantage. Unlike in the United States, where new shares usually can be sold, theoretically, to whoever wants them, in the United Kingdom a company must almost always offer new shares to existing share-holders first.[29] This is intended, in part, to protect shareholders against involuntary dilution of their stake in a company. In France, shareholders with preemptive rights can waive them selectively, and very frequently do so. In Britain, 75 percent of the shareholders must waive the preemptive right, and rarely do so (*Economist*, October 26, 1991).

By the end of the 1980s, the Exchange was not a very popular institution with many British industrialists. Critics spoke of the "wild west" elements prevalent in Britain's financial framework, with over 5,000 companies listed on the London International Stock Exchange (*Financial Times*, October 6, 1989).

The previous pages have given a sense of each nation's financial system, of the kinds of differences that exist between them, and of the variety of financial sources available to large firms in each country. In France, a major source of external industrial financing has been debt, channeled through the banking system, and often directly provided or indirectly subsidized by the state. Despite extensive financial sector reforms in the 1980s, and the creation of a number of new capital markets, there are still difficulties with raising long-term capital in France, and the state still plays a dominant role in industrial financing, albeit far less overtly than in earlier years. Companies with publicly traded shares can protect themselves from hostile bids with the assistance of a core group of friendly investors. In contrast with the relatively underdeveloped French Bourse, the London International Stock Exchange plays a dominant role in the nation's financial market, and firms are more likely to raise capital through equity issues than are their French counterparts. Hostile bids and leveraged buyouts were far more common than across the Channel in the 1980s. The British government has not historically played as public a role in channeling investment to industry.

Each national financial system, as outlined here, affects not only the general shape of industrial financing in that country, but also the forms of corporate governance found at each individual firm. By exploring the implications of this for major manufacturers such as British Steel and Peugeot SA, the case studies illustrate the argument that a firm's financial structure is a key component of its survival and adaptation, and of broader government-industry relations.

The first part of this chapter dwelt on the argument that the financing of large firms straddles what is in reality a very blurred boundary between public and private spheres of action and decision making. This section gave the background to the argument that financial structures at the national and the firm level are not politically neutral or technical issues, but rather are crucial components of industrial restructuring and of wider government-industry relations. This brings us to the third major theme of this analysis—that in Thatcher's Britain and Mitterrand's France, the solutions to the problem of financing major manufacturers at a time of crisis and restructuring had far more in common than is generally supposed. This only becomes apparent when we begin the analysis of government-industry relations at the level of the firm, rather than at the level of state institutions and characteristics.

Despite the many differences that do exist between the French and British financial systems, it is wrong to conclude that France is an aberration, the Gallic odd-one-out in an Anglo-American world where politics, the financial markets, and the affairs of industry are distinctly separate spheres. Industrial policy and financial policy are always and everywhere intertwined. A government's macroeconomic and fiscal policies have an obvious and acknowledged impact on industry. But the government also regulates and mediates the broader financial system, including forms of corporate governance and ownership, giving rise to national differences that have a profound impact on industry and on individual firms. The state also has the power to alter the structure of the financial market, through legislation and regulatory moves.

The rapid development of new and complex financial instruments during the 1980s has revolutionized corporate finance, particularly for those major firms that can tap into the international markets as well as their own domestic ones. By the end of the decade, currencies, commodities, and government and corporate bonds were being issued and traded twenty-four hours a day, around the world. The capital liberalization policies of numerous governments ushered in this explosive growth in international finance. Freed from old regulations and patterns of segregation, brokers and sellers discovered new ways to combine old forms of finance and investment, creating complex swaps, options, and various forms of hedging. Traders discovered a myriad of new things to trade and new ways to trade them.

However, even big, internationally oriented industries still look first to their national governments for favorable legislation, and primarily to their national financial markets for funds. Profound differences still remain between the various national financial systems. Concerning the industrial performance and short-term survivability of auto firms, for example, Womack concludes that the United States' financial system scores badly on both counts; that the continental Europeans have high scores on survivability but poor scores on industrial performance; and that the Japanese system seems to do well on both counts.[30] How many of these national differences remain, and for how long, will depend on the responses of national governments.

The fact that such nationally specific variations do remain is often attributed to historical and other fundamental differences between Britain and France. To reiterate, such underlying differences do, indeed, exist and have had (and continue to have) profound effects on each nation's political economy. The argument here, however, is that the "fundamental differences" are not necessarily the ones that appear to be most obvious to the casual observer, nor even the kinds of differences focused upon by the "institutional and structural constraints" literature in political science. Many of these apparently profound differences are actually not as important as one might think, when government, finance, and international economic change meet, at the level of the individual firm. The really fundamental differences lie, instead, in the realm of corporate governance, and the impact of firm-level financial structures on industrial survival and adaptation.

3. Comparing Britain and France

For Margaret Thatcher . . . what she supported tended to happen. What she neglected or opposed tended not to happen. What she permitted, but did not support, might happen, but only in a context where she had openly distanced herself from the consequences and therefore assisted in the enfeeblement of what she allowed others to do. (Young 1989, 464)

President [Mitterrand] himself has asserted his dominant position within the executive, both in day-to-day business and in longer-term policy-making, through a personal style which is both activist and interventionist yet discreet. . . . This has considerably reinforced presidential oversight and control over both the legislative and executive decision-making processes. . . . (Cerny 1985, 29)

Thatcher and Mitterrand were the dominant political leaders of their nations in the 1980s. Both pronounced very strong views on government's relationship with industry at a time of crisis and change. For different reasons, both the Thatcher and Mitterrand governments also had significant political capacity to intervene in the troubled steel and auto industries in the 1980s. Both benefited from a great deal of governmental centralization. Both faced weak opposition with unions, parliamentary opponents, and industrial organizations all fragmented (Smith 1989). Both had a powerful impact on their party's political platform. Most interestingly for comparative researchers, their ideological views and policy pronouncements were diametrically opposed, particularly where government-industry relations were concerned.

In 1979 Britain elected a Conservative government with Margaret Thatcher as prime minister. Under the general rubric of monetarism, bringing down the high inflation rate was the major macroeconomic concern of the 1980s. The size of the Public Sector Borrowing Requirement (PSBR) became a primary indicator of economic health, leading to stringent financial controls over nationalized industries such as BSC. Reliance on rigid monetary indicators subsequently waned during the 1980s, but the overall economic policies and objectives did not change (Riddell 1989). The post-1979 Conservative governments in Britain claimed that their method of dealing with industrial problems was to stay out of the market and let price signals drive industrial change. Thatcher stressed that "there is no limit to the harm that government intervention can cause" (Norton 1989, 2), and declared that "industry is responsible for its own destiny" (DTI 1988a: cmnd 278). Ending state ownership and creating "the right conditions for enterprise" became the mainstays of Conservative Party ideology in the 1980s. Industrial policy was reoriented toward measures affecting the fiscal and regulatory climate in which industry operates, but the government still remained very involved in some areas of industrial policy.

In contrast with the British political scene in 1979, the French political parties were divided, not on the issues of liberalism versus state involvement in industrial affairs, but rather on the degree and form of active state intervention. The center-right Barre government (1976–81) spoke a great deal about market forces, but was closely involved in the affairs of industry, singling out promising national champions. The lion's share of assistance went, however, to declining industries such as steel. The 1981 elections brought first a Socialist president, then a Socialist majority in the Assembly. The new government's objectives were diametrical to those of the first Thatcher government then in power. The Parti Socialiste pledged to tackle unemployment with Keynesian reflation, to reindustrialize France, and to expand the public sector. The government increased total investment in industry,[31] and the Ninth Plan (1983–88) laid out a system of contracts between the state and specific industries (see chap. 3, on Usinor and Sacilor).[32] However, the Socialist experiment didn't last. By late 1981 reflation was precipitating a massive balance of payments crisis, and 1982 brought an austerity policy of devaluation and domestic deflation with an emphasis on improving the balance of trade, holding down wage increases, and strengthening industry's profits. These policies continued through the 1986–88 center-right RPR-UDF government under Prime Minister Jacques Chirac and into the 1988–93 Socialist administration.

Thatcher and Mitterrand were instrumental in making some dramatic changes in long-standing government-industry relationships and institutions in their countries. In France, major manufacturers and financial firms were taken over by the state; the rights of trade unions were encoded and extended;[33] the financial markets were extensively reformed; and decentralization of the administrative system was begun. In other areas, the state decreased its ability to intervene in the affairs of individual firms. Traditionally, the tax authorities held long negotiations with firms as to their annual tax liabilities. It was rumored that large firms such as Peugeot could even negotiate reduced taxes in return for actions in line with government objectives (Bayliss and Butt Philip 1980). Since 1981, the whole system of incentives and credits has been increasingly codified and corporate tax rates lowered (Inland Revenue 1987). Between 1978 and 1984, the complex system of postwar price controls was also gradually abolished,[34] increasing the commercial freedom of major private manufacturers such as Peugeot.

Meanwhile, in Britain, a large proportion of state-owned industry was returned to the private sector, the rights of trade unions were severely curbed,[35] the financial markets were further liberalized, and the administrative system was further centralized. The Department of Trade and Industry's size and scope lessened considerably as the budget for various industrial support schemes shrank and privatization further eroded the Department's role in industrial affairs.[36] By 1987–88, the DTI's annual budget was down to £1.1 billion a year from its 1981–82 peak of over £3.2 billion, and the Department's focus had shifted to more passive, facilitative activities such as regulation and competition policy (Wilks 1987). On the other hand, the operation of competition policy actually became increasingly discretionary (Utton 1986). Regional aid schemes, historically the primary form of financial assistance to British industry, were steadily reduced in scope and funding, and from 1988 assistance was granted selectively, at ministerial discretion. In 1984 the whole system of corporate taxation was overhauled and the tax rate reduced,[37] while some areas of tax allowances were increasingly subject to the discretionary definitions of the Secretary of State for Industry (Kay and King 1986). Tax policy is no longer "more important than selectively administered funds" for British companies (Zysman 1983, 222).[38]

The difference between the Thatcher and Mitterrand governments showed up most clearly in their attitudes toward state ownership of industry. The British political Right argued that public ownership of industry was inherently inefficient, led to bloated bureaucracies, and distracted both government and industry from the best performance of their proper tasks. The French Left, in contrast, argued that only the state had sufficient will and resources to ensure that industry remained competitive.

This perception of the two nations as very different cases goes deeper than their styles of policy-making, however, or the particular governments and leaders of the 1980s. Following Gerschenkron (1962), many have argued that the historical timing of their initial industrialization accounts for differences in contemporary British and French government-industry relations and particular industrial policies (Moore 1966; Shonfield 1969; Elbaum and Lazonick 1986). Britain's early industrialization around the textile industry required relatively small amounts of start-up capital, easily mobilized by individual entrepreneurs. The lack of direct state involvement in industrialization established a pattern of "arm's-length" relations that continues today.

British commentators frequently note that industry tends to have a low priority in policy-making under any government, and that there is even a traditional "contempt for production" (Wilks 1986b).[39] Throughout the decade, writers from across the political spectrum compared the economic fortunes of Britain and other EC nations, bemoaning the former's decline. In the particular area of government-industry relations, comparisons were often made between Britain and France by those who advocated some form of national industrial policy for Britain. Thus Elbaum and Lazonick (1986) argue that industrial planning by firms, financial institutions, and government is important for international competitiveness and economic growth. Such authors cast a wistful eye at France as a centralized state committed to national planning.[40]

In contrast, the post-1945 French state developed a close relationship with industry in general, based on government control of credit financing. Almost every theorist who tackles the French political economy deals in some respect with the importance of the French state, a continuity of focus that sets France apart (Keyder 1985). Many would still agree with the following finding:

> Today French policy-makers of all political persuasions are more likely to approve of a dirigiste style of intervention than their British counterparts . . . even French businessmen have been socialized into such views. When a sample of French employers was asked "who should be the decision-makers for very large investments," two-thirds chose the state, either alone or in conjunction with corporate management, and only one third chose the market or corporate management alone. (Hall 1986, 279)

For all these undoubted differences, closer analysis of government-industry relations in the 1980s throws up some uncomfortable counterexamples. The Thatcher governments strongly opposed subsidies for state-owned industries and intervention in industrial affairs, yet agreed to massive financial aid for British Leyland, intervened heavily in BSC's finances, and bailed out private sector steelmakers. One of Zysman's (1983) arguments is that in a liberal, market-based system the financial markets act as a barrier to state influence in industry, and if the state attempts to be more interventionist, it will face conflict over the sanctity of markets. But in Britain in the 1980s—an archetypal market-based system dominated by a passionately pro–free market Conservative Party—the state had enormous influence over many aspects of industrial adjustment, and even fundamentally altered the rules of the market with Special Shares in privatized firms, without seeking any special authority to do so, and without arousing the wrath of financial institutions or its own party. In France, the first Socialist government abandoned expansionary Keynesianism for austerity policies and, in effect, began privatization of some state-owned industrial concerns. The supposedly *dirigiste* French governments of the 1980s took a long time to come to grips with the problems of the steel manufacturers, but did eventually oversee a rapid retrenchment in the industry. More fundamentally, the Parti Socialiste instituted a systematic withdrawal of the state from direction of the nation's credit markets.

In fact, both governments were involved in the survival and restructuring of their major steel and auto manufacturers. And it is in the form of this involvement that we find some surprising similarities between the actions of these two supposedly very different governments. Both the arm's-length British and the interventionist French found the means and mechanisms of financing to back the firms' restructuring plans, rescued the near-bankrupt, assisted the small producers involved in each sector, and encouraged more private capital involvement in the industry. The two governments gave their policies very different labels, to be sure. The British said that they were taking government out of the affairs of private industry, and reducing manufacturers' overall recourse to state aid. The French said they were using the powers and resources of the state to improve private allocations and market responses. Each government's argument looks coherent from the point of view of their own rhetoric, and each set of actions can be interpreted in ways that are quite consistent with arm's-length and *dirigiste* characterizations of the two nations' government-industry relations. But when we look at the level of the actual firms themselves, at what these governmental actions meant in terms of the firms' ability to survive and even to adapt, the two governments' apparently very different actions and motivations turn out to be basically the same in many cases. In contemporary Western Europe, states are playing an ever more active role in domestic industrial adjustment. In particular, governments of varying political persuasions are involved in providing companies with access to financing, both for short-term survival and for longer-term adjustment and investment. The outcome is that supposed divisions between public-

and private-sector adjustment strategies, between market-driven and state-led change, are becoming increasingly indistinct. Recognizing the similarities, and focusing on firm-level financing, allows us to understand more clearly what the real sources of differences were between the various cases.

States intervene to deal with the failure of the market mechanism. For large manufacturers facing rapid technological, competitive, and market changes, much of this failure can lie in the ways that the financial system did or did not respond to the firm or industry's needs in the first place. Differences in national financial systems and policy are therefore a major part of the explanation of the survivability and adaptability of major manufacturers. These differences are thrown into high relief by the events of the 1980s (and also, to some extent, by the changes wrought by the creation of a single market in the European Community from January 1993). Even as the differences become clearer, however, they may actually be declining. As the four case study chapters will show, differences in the national financial systems meant big differences in firms' options for survival and longer-term adjustment. Yet despite these differences, when the state got involved in one way or another in financing the firms, the public-private division became very murky. It became hard to discern the apparently big differences in government-industry relations between a liberal Britain and interventionist France. Both governments had to ensure, at the very least, that the big manufacturers could survive, yet both had very constrained budgets with which to do so. Both therefore ended up using a variety of techniques that crossed the market-interventionist divide.

4. The Steel and Auto Industries

Large manufacturers are, in a sense, in a constant state of adjustment. There are very few irrevocably doomed or "sunset" industries, in the sense in which we usually understand the term.[41] Some subsectors of a specific industry may be declining in importance, or be overtaken by technological developments elsewhere in the industry—for example, major car manufacturers are starting to challenge the craft-based specialty carmakers in their ability to custom-produce cars to order. Most of the so-called sunset industries, which is how many people still think of the steel and auto industries, are, in fact, meta-morphosing into something new, not simply dying out. The new steel mini-mills and specialty steelmakers have evolved out of the old firms, or the earlier technologies, but are in many ways a new kind of firm, exploiting new technologies for a new market. A sector or segment in decline is one in which there are no possible significant changes in product or process by which firms can regain a competitive advantage, and one in which demand for the industry as a whole is stagnant (Zysman 1983). Neither of these requirements apply to the contemporary steel or auto industry. Rather, both industries are in dynamic transition, involving deep and basic changes in firm organization and industry structure. In both auto and steel manufacturing, the 1980s (and on into the 1990s) saw the emergence of new firms, the reorientation or death of old ones, and a loss of labor and change in work skills.

There are three dominant aspects to the tale of the steel and auto industries over the past fifteen years. First is the huge financial cost involved in restructuring plants and firms, and in keeping up in the research and development race. Second is the relentless international competitive pressure on firms across Europe and the United States. The third aspect is the industries' high political profile. Despite changes in their international markets, and their declining share of European countries' GDP, these are two industries that still have an enormous impact on domestic economies in terms of employment, investment, links to other sectors, exports, and so on. That is where their similarities end, however. The two industries differ in a number of fundamental ways. Both are encountering international economic shifts and new overseas competitors, but the impacts of those changes on the two industries, and the kinds of response needed, are quite different. For the auto industry, the presence or absence of foreign firms with domestic manufacturing facilities is a crucial aspect of industry structure and of competitive pressures. In the steel industry, however, we rarely find foreign firms with significant domestic manufacturing facilities. The international competition problem for steel is usually one of imports.

The process of internal differentiation in the two industries also differs. After the Second World War, the auto industry underwent an increase in mergers and consolidation as mass producers sought to capitalize on economies of scale. Although economies of scale are no longer as important as they were twenty or thirty years ago, new entrants to the market still need enormous investments, even if they are only going for a niche market. By the end of the 1980s, the small specialist producers such as Jaguar were almost all under the direct or partial ownership of multinational mass producers. In the steel industry, on the other hand, the increases in mergers and consolidation of earlier decades are now giving way to new entrants or to spin-offs from the old heavy steel producers. The 1980s saw the rise of smaller mini-mills, especially in the United States, that take advantage of the new production technologies and can respond to the new demand for very precise products and a close relationship between customer and producer.

In the auto industry, there are a few small specialty makers but the typical firm is a big national producer that dominates at least the home market, and is also very active in one or more of the world's major regional markets. Most of these firms have joint research and development interests, and even equity stakes in one another, to reduce their phenomenally high research costs. There are growing differences in industrial organization between the American and European mass producers, and those located in Japan—differences that go a long way to explaining the great success of the latter in recent years (Womack, Jones, and Roos 1990). In every country with one or more big carmakers the firms have a high economic and political profile. In the steel industry, in contrast, there are usually one or more big national producers who dominate the home market (five, in the case of Germany), but there are an increasing number of smaller producers as well. Links between major firms are nowhere near as extensive as in the auto industry, although there are growing links between the European firms, who are buying up one another's plants and buying into one another's distribution channels, while Japanese firms have been taking equity stakes in steel companies in the United States.[42] Finally, the differences between the steel producers in various regions and nations are mostly in terms of the kinds of technology used, not in terms of fundamental industrial organization.

Both industries have forward and backward links to the rest of the national economy, but the auto industry's are in many ways far more extensive. The industry has had a profound impact on industrial organization as such, being the conduit by which first mass production techniques, and then lean production techniques, were spread globally. A car contains, on average, up to 10,000 individual parts, most of which are produced by other components manufacturers. These, in turn, may be either large differentiated manufacturers or firms that are highly dependent on the auto industry, even on just one manufacturer. It is in auto manufacturing that we are now seeing the development of "flexible manufacturing," or "agile production," whereby the same production line can turn out not just variations of the same model, but completely different cars. In the ferociously competitive environment of carmaking, manufacturers use virtually every available technology in industrial design, development, and production. The industry is on the cutting edge of high technology developments that then spread to other industries, both in terms of the end product itself (such as the development of fuel injection systems, the lightweight plastics used in car bodies, and complex electrical systems), and in terms of manufacturing techniques (such as CADCAM, and the use of robots and automated production systems). Auto manufacturers also have backward linkages to the energy and steel producers. In contrast, although the steel industry has backward linkages to the energy and raw materials sectors, these are decreasing in national importance. The industry has not generally been the conduit by which new technologies or production processes spread to other industrial sectors. Its customers are, however, major economic actors in the national economy, such as the auto and construction industries, and white-goods manufacturers. Steel producers are thus very vulnerable to downturns in manufacturing demand in general. The industry's high political profile is based on the general assumption that steel production is the backbone of national industrial competence.

Against this background of fierce competition and rapid technological developments, the European Community has played an increasing role in the relationship between government and industry in its member states in recent years. Following the collapse of the international steel market, the European Commission declared a "manifest crisis" and invoked its unique powers to regulate steel production in Europe. In the case of the auto industry, EC involvement has been in the form of trade agreements and controlling state aid to the industry. The intent in the next few pages is not to discuss the role of the EC and its state aid regime in any depth. There is a significant body of literature devoted exclusively to the workings of the Community and its impact on national industries.[43] Rather, this section sketches out the European crisis and the state and EC intervention in these two industries as a background to the subsequent case studies. It also illustrates the kinds of common international and economic pressures facing the two national economies and their major manufacturers during the 1980s.

Evolving Patterns of EC Intervention in the Steel and Auto Industries

Steel

By 1900 the European steel industry had absorbed large portions of the manufacturing labor force, was geographically concentrated, and was closely tied to other sectors in national economies. Steel had become politically significant. Governments saw it as strategically important for domestic economic development and for international trade. The formation of the International Steel Cartel (ISC) in 1926 confirmed the dominance of politics over economics in the world steel trade (Jones 1986). Like the national cartels that preceded it, the ISC sought to stabilize the industry through production quotas and price controls.

The European Coal and Steel Community (ECSC), founded by the Treaty of Paris in 1952, replaced the ISC, but was committed to expansion. The treaty grants to the Commission of the European Communities the means necessary to shape the structure and conduct of the steel industry.[44] The Commission can issue directives controlling prices, mergers, and non-EC imports, and under Article 58 has broad regulatory discretion if the industry is afflicted by a "manifest crisis." Under Article 54 investment projects over a certain size have to be notified to the Commission before construction commences. The Commission cannot prohibit investments, but can refuse to lend money in their support and can recommend that others withhold funding. This range of powers is wider than for any other sector except agriculture.

The ECSC had originally hoped to reorganize the steel industry across international boundaries. By encouraging mergers, large investments in new capacity, and structural reorganization to improve the industry's competitive position, however, it drove the firms more closely toward their own governments (Zysman 1983). By 1980 steel in Europe had become "an industry of increasingly large national oligopolies" (Messerlin and Saunders 1983, 63).

After 1952, as European steel production grew rapidly, the ECSC's price-control system set limits on competition between member countries. When production began to stagnate in the early 1970s and Europe's share of world output fell, the system could not control the steel market (Messerlin and Saunders 1983, 63).

There were many causes for the crisis that hit the international steel industry in the mid-1970s. The overall slowdown of economic growth was a major factor, but three others were also crucial—the decline in big steel-using industries such as shipbuilding; new technologies allowing smaller inputs of high quality steel and the development of alternatives such as plastics;[45] and the rise of new competitors. The increased competitive pressures were felt quickly in Western Europe, not just in import penetration but, more importantly, in the protectionist responses triggered in major markets such as the United States. Similar crises had hit the industry before, but the period after 1974 was different in "the extent, the persistence, the duration, and the increasingly detailed nature of the interventions" by governments (Mény and Wright 1987, 24).

In 1976 the Commission's Simonet Plan recommended voluntary sales quotas. The 1977 Davignon Plan (named for then EC Industry Commissioner Etienne Davignon) set mandatory minimum prices for some steel products, along with a series of protectionist measures to temporarily shield the industry from cheap imports, in order to begin restructuring. Despite the trade restrictions, imports from non-EC members rose to 12 percent in 1980 (from 3 percent in 1961), while exports from the EC to the rest of the world rose slowly.[46] In 1978, the Commission introduced voluntary production quotas and raised steel prices by 50 percent. In November 1980, with capacity utilization at an all-time low of 58 percent, prices collapsing, and little compliance with the voluntary restrictions, the Commission invoked Article 58 of the Treaty of Paris for the first time and declared a manifest crisis. Compulsory production quotas were imposed, with inspections and fines, that covered 60 percent of the European steel industry's output. There was widespread recognition that the rush to invest in large plants in the 1960s had led to serious overcapacity with demand falling. As aid to industry for specific purposes is prohibited under the Treaty of Paris, aid rules were devised in 1980 to permit state assistance to the steel industry. Aid could be used only for restructuring, not for propping up firms, and had to be approved by the Commission. The further collapse of demand kept European steel output down to less than two-thirds of capacity in the first half of the decade. In addition, the United States threatened to impose import duties on EC steel in 1982 on the grounds that the sale of subsidized steel amounted to dumping. The duties were dropped when the EC promised to cut exports to the United States.

In late 1987, with the European industry still in crisis, the Commission proposed further cuts. Forty million tonnes of steel capacity had been cut annually in the previous seven years, along with some 200,000 jobs. The 1987 plan cut another thirty million tonnes of annual capacity and 80,000 workers over the next two years. The Commission threatened to lift production quotas immediately if national ministers would not agree to the plan. It was passed, extending production controls on most products for a few more months. The quota system ended July 1, 1988, when the twelve EC countries refused to agree to cut at least 75 percent of the remaining thirty million tonnes of excess capacity. The voluntary restraint agreements covering the import of steel products from non-EC countries continued, but the EC pledged to phase these out by March 1992, when the United States was also due to end voluntary restraint agreements on steel imports. In the event, the end of seven and a half years of quota protection for the United States producers has triggered the filing of eighty-four charges of dumping and unfair trading practices by the American firms, against producers in twenty-one countries. In November 1992, the United States Department of Commerce decided to impose punitive duties (i.e., tariffs) on steel imports, many from the EC.

By the end of the 1980s, following three years of sustained growth in the industry, the situation seemed considerably better. The Commission had prohibited further state aid to the industry after 1985, except for specific research projects or pollution control. When the statutory quota restrictions were lifted in 1988, the strong growth in all of the European steel markets meant that the effect was not as traumatic as many producers had feared. However, this relief proved short-lived. With overcapacity still running at around thirty million tonnes in the EC steel industry, the economic slowdown in 1991 and 1992 forced the major producers to once again cut prices drastically in an attempt to hold onto market share. By the end of 1992, virtually every major steel company in Europe was losing money; and the combination of overcapacity, cheaper imports from Eastern Europe, an imminent steel trade war with the United States, and the long-term downward trend in steel consumption, are again leading to talk of a crisis in the industry. Despite all of the upheavals of the 1980s, the talk around the industry by 1993 seemed every bit as pessimistic as in 1979.

Against this sense of impending crisis, and with "urgent appeals" from its fifteen largest steelmakers, the European Community proposed a new steel plan. This is not, however, son of Davignon—no one is seeking to resurrect the "manifest crisis" measures of ten years ago. Under the plan approved by EC industry ministers in February 1993, steel output in the Community will be reduced by some 20 percent (up to thirty-five million tonnes), and some 50,000 jobs will be eliminated out of a total of 370,000. The brunt of the adjustment is expected to fall on Germany, Italy, and Spain. In addition, the ministers approved the negotiation of higher levels of steel imports from Eastern Europe, but subject to increased tariffs once certain levels are reached—this despite the fact that steel imports from Eastern Europe totaled less than five million tonnes in 1992, equivalent to barely 4 percent of total EC production (*Economist*, March 6, 1993). In return for the production cuts, steelmakers could get up to Ecu450 million of central funding between 1993 and the end of 1994 to cover redundancy and other restructuring costs (Ecu900 million, if member states will match the EC funds).

The EC thus had a high profile in the steel industry in the 1980s, arbitrating among national members to restructure the European industry and to restore its international competitiveness. There have long been disparities in costs and competitive positions among the Community industries. Such disparities, along with the industry's evolution into a group of large national oligopolies, have meant closer ties between national firms and their governments. Governments try to protect their steel producers and producers press their governments to obtain favorable terms from the Commission. Much of the politics of restructuring were, and still are, played out at the national rather than the European level.

There is one further development in the international steel industry that has yet to make an impact on the European producers—the rise of the so-called mini-mills. These mills, rapidly becoming well established in the United States and Japan, make steel in plants one-quarter the size of those of the big, integrated producers such as Usinor. They use cheap scrap, not iron ore and coke; are much less labor intensive; make a narrow range of the most popular products; and are built to last for only a decade or so. All in all, only some 30 percent of their costs are fixed, compared with 70 percent, on average, for the major, integrated producers in the EC. Apart from a few smaller producers in northern Italy, such mills have yet to establish themselves in Europe, but it can only be a matter of time. Technological improvements are allowing the mini-mills to start production for the massive market for flat-rolled steel, even as the integrated producers of the EC are resorting to sporadic price wars to try to retain their shares of a shrinking market. With such high fixed costs, compared with the mini-mills—and with former integrated producers in Eastern Europe eyeing the new technologies as a cheaper way to survive in the 1990s—the likes of Usinor and British Steel will be under even greater pressure to find the financing to maintain their massive plants.

Meanwhile, in 1990, the European Commission decided to revise gradually the Treaty of Paris in the twelve years leading up to its expiration in the year 2002. While the latest restructuring plan was being thrashed out, the Commission also decided to wind down the Ecu750 million financial reserves of the treaty, or to absorb them into other EC funds, over the next ten years (*Financial Times*, November 24, 1992). So in theory, and whatever "crises" may arise during the 1990s, the European steel industry is slowly losing its special status under the ECSC.

Autos

The auto industry is the world's largest and most complex manufacturing activity, oriented by the late 1970s around three regions—North America, Europe, and Japan. By 1986, Europe had overtaken the United States as the world's largest auto market. While European car and component manufacturers have cut their labor forces drastically in recent years, they still directly employ over 1.7 million people across the EC. As in the United States, the 1970s brought falling demand, increased competition and debt burdens, and massive employee layoffs for the European auto industry, along with new technologies. The 1980s brought still further technical advances, and new relationships between suppliers and manufacturers and between the manufacturers themselves. By the late 1980s, Japanese imports had captured some 10 percent of the European Community's market, while EC cars had only 2.5 percent of the Japanese market.

The European Community has four medium-sized auto manufacturers, Renault and Peugeot in France, Volkswagen in Germany, and Fiat in Italy, as well as two American multinationals, General Motors (GM) and Ford. In the spring of 1990, the prospect of a huge domestic market in Eastern Europe "hypnotized" Western Europe's carmakers (*Economist*, March 17, 1990), and over the next two years the larger producers set up joint ventures in a number of these nations, with Peugeot at one point hoping to assemble its new luxury car in the then USSR. In the event, shrinking household savings and the pain of economic restructuring in Eastern Europe mean that car consumption there is unlikely to pick up significantly until the middle of the decade. Meanwhile, the Western European car market hit the skids in 1992 and slumped further in 1993. As in the 1980s, the industry's high political profile is again leading to international trade disputes.

By the 1980s, the EC's role in the industry was focused around the regulation, by the European Commission, of trade agreements and of state aid to the industry. In 1983, the EC as a whole reached its first voluntary restraint agreement with the Japanese producers. Among other things, this included an agreement to keep Japanese exports to a "moderate level," around the prevailing 9 percent market share. In 1988 the Commission asked Japan to continue to limit its auto exports to the EC after the abolition of internal trade barriers in 1992, to transfer more technology to the European plants, and to increase the percentage of local content in the final products. This was formalized and expanded in 1991, with an EC-Japanese voluntary export restraint (VER) agreement limiting direct imports into the twelve EC nations until the end of 1999.

The 1991 agreement replaced the bilateral market restrictions that had been imposed by the United Kingdom, France, Italy, Spain, and Portugal, but by holding Japanese imports to a constant market share it assumes that these five markets will remain just as restricted to the end of the decade. The Community and Japan must now closely monitor developments in the European auto market, and agree on an annual limit for Japanese imports based on the expected outlook for new car demand for the year ahead. At the time of writing, this system is still quite new but already there are signs of friction. The 1993 review had initially forecast a 6.5 percent fall in auto sales in the EC for the year, and Japan had agreed in April to limit exports to the whole Community to 1,089,000 vehicles, an 8.1 percent decline from the previous year. By June of 1993, with figures showing auto sales in January–April down by 17.8 percent from 1992 levels (and down 20 percent in France), the forecast was revised to show an annual sales slump in double digits. Only two months into the 1993 agreement, the EC formally requested a downward revision in the Japanese export quota. Maintaining the VER agreement in adverse market conditions is not going to be as easy as in the relative boom years of the late 1980s.

Meanwhile, in the run-up to the creation of a single market for goods, services, capital, and people across the Community by year-end 1992, the Commission took an active stance against industrial subsidies by national governments. The Treaty of Rome prohibits the European Commission from favoring or discriminating against state-owned companies and also outlaws state aid that distorts competition. The vast discretionary powers awarded the Commission had previously allowed it to ignore this contradiction for decades. However, the impending single market led to a tightening up of such contradictions.

In 1988 the EC drafted tough new rules for its auto industry, which would clamp down on state aid, and abolish technical barriers to free European trade. Since 1989, all government investments in the auto industry worth over Ecu12 million (around $14.5 million at December 1992 exchange rates) that include any element of subsidy must be cleared by Brussels. In the summer of 1989 alone, the EC told the German and Spanish governments to scrap or alter forty-seven state-aid packages to their auto industries, each worth more than $13 million (*Economist*, August 5, 1989). These rules have had a considerable impact on government-industry relations in both Britain and France, with the Commission intervening over government aid to the Rover Group (chap. 5) and altering the formal status of France's nationalized champion, Renault, in ways that could profoundly affect the financial resources available to Peugeot SA in the 1990s (chap. 4).

The EC is also attempting a more general harmonization of the auto market, but this is proving to be tricky. The pretax price of a single car can differ by up to 30 percent between EC countries,[47] while each nation has its own technical, emissions, and noise standards. In November 1992, the EC Competition Commissioner Leon Brittan announced that manufacturers, importers, and dealers will not be allowed to keep the EC car market segmented by national boundaries, but with a new downturn in the industry, governments and producers are bound to try harder than ever to protect "home" manufacturers and their market shares.

By 1992 it was apparent that the recovery of the late 1980s had been short-lived. Simultaneous weaknesses in the economies of North America, Europe, and Japan have hurt all of the major producers. Once again there is talk of serious worldwide overcapacity, and firms across all three regions are closing plants and laying off large numbers of workers. The upheaval is the worst, however, in Europe. Unlike in 1982, Toyota, Honda, and Nissan now have plants within the Community's borders, producing cars for the European market.[48] Demand is thus dropping just as large-scale investment in new production facilities is coming on-line and more investment is under way. Nissan opened a plant in Spain in 1993, while Suzuki is working on production facilities in the same country that will begin operations in 1995.

EC intervention in government-industry relations has thus evolved a great deal in the past two decades, but the pattern is uneven. In the case of the crisis in the steel industry, the Commission could call upon significant powers of intervention from the 1952 Treaty of Paris. In the case of the auto industry, however, the Commission's role has emerged through a series of rules and regulations governing discrete areas of industrial policy. The Commission has had a major impact on state aid to the industry, but it has not been able to overcome jealously guarded national differences in technical standards or taxation.

Introducing the Four Cases

In Britain and France, both the steel and auto industry had become dominated, by the late 1970s, by a few large firms. Therefore, each of the following case-study chapters is focused on one particular firm, with additional analysis of related firms in each industry to illustrate the themes of the argument. In the auto industry, British Leyland (BL) was chosen out of the British mass-market auto firms because it is the only one that (at the time of writing) is still mostly owned domestically. Peugeot SA (PSA) was chosen as the focus of the French auto industry case, rather than the state-owned Renault, in order to balance the study with a firm that has always been privately owned, and one that illustrates particular aspects of the French systems of industrial financing and corporate governance. PSA is also rarely covered in the political economy literature, and is worthy of greater study. I chose not to focus on the auto multinationals from the United States or Japan, as much (even most) of their survival and adaptation concerns the decisions and/or finances of the parent company in the home country. Choosing the two steel-industry cases was much more straightforward. By the late 1970s, the British Steel Corporation (BSC) was clearly the dominant steel producer in that country, while a series of mergers and joint ventures had established Usinor and Sacilor as the principal steel groups in France.

In most respects, the political contexts involved in the cases of French steel, BSC, BL, and Peugeot were very different. In the case of French steel, a powerful trade association saw its influence in steel policy rapidly decline, while the state took more direct responsibility for the firms' affairs. There were detailed and passionate public debates about location, manning levels, and technology in the industry. The early rounds of plant closures sparked violent uprisings in the steel regions, and governments constantly feared a repeat of this grass roots unrest.

The speed and timing of BSC's restructuring after 1979 was due to the election of a Conservative government, specifically one led by Margaret Thatcher. The rigid External Financing Limits imposed on the corporation were a purely Conservative instrument, born of a commitment to reducing the Public Sector Borrowing Requirement. Retrenchment had begun under the previous Labour administration, but under Thatcher the cuts at BSC occurred earlier and faster than at any public or private EC steel firm. Yet the resulting job losses did not spark the kind of national political debate that occurred in France. The Thatcher government focused on inflation rather than unemployment as the economic foe, and the moderate steel unions were not organized to fight a national campaign.

The political contexts involved in the case of the two auto industries were wholly different again. There had long been widespread agreement between the French government and auto industry on many issues, particularly concerning protection of the domestic market—although by 1990, the government's growing support for the single European market was arousing the very public ire of M. Calvet of Peugeot. However, there were often bitter labor relations at Peugeot plants, in large part due to organization by immigrant workers protesting inequitable treatment.

The debate surrounding the fate of British Leyland, now the Rover Group, was the most politicized and contentious of these four cases. As a major producer that must compete with multinationals in its home market, its position has long been ambiguous. Since 1980, BL's overseas competitors have been actively encouraged to establish new production sites in Britain. Secret plans to sell parts of BL to American multinationals stirred up considerable nationalism among the back-bench M.P.s of the House of Commons. However, the job losses entailed by BL's retrenchment did not spark the degree of industrial unrest found at Peugeot, even though BL had been the source of much militant unionism in the mid-1970s. Recession, the speed of retrenchment, and changed work practices significantly diminished auto union activity in Britain.

Between them, these firms are good examples of the issues raised by the debates over industrial nationalization and privatization in Britain and France in the 1980s. They also illustrate the role of different firm financial structures, and of national financial systems, in industrial survival and adaptation. In addition, BSC was a privatization pioneer, hiving off business units and forming joint ventures with private sector firms. Usinor played an important role in the development of new financial instruments for getting private capital into the nationalized industries in France. Peugeot used, and encouraged the development of, new financial instruments and markets as liberalization snowballed in France in the 1980s.

Above all, the tale of each firm's experiences over the past fifteen years is illustrative of the role of governments and national financial markets in industrial survival and adaptation.

CHAPTER 2

The British Steel Corporation

In 1979 the state-owned British Steel Corporation (BSC) had 135,000 employees and annual losses of £500 million. By 1993 it had metamorphosed into British Steel, a private sector company of 41,400 employees, with 100 percent of its shares quoted on the London International Stock Exchange and pretax profits in the April–September half-year of £27 million. Supporters of former Prime Minister Margaret Thatcher trumpeted the story of BSC as an example of what strong management and free market principles can achieve, while industry ministers in the late 1980s liked to emphasize the government's role in "forcing" BSC to get its act together. At the time of writing, British Steel publicizes itself as one of the world's lowest-cost steel producers; the third largest steel manufacturer in Europe, producing 75 percent of Britain's liquid steel output at four large plants; and Britain's sixth largest exporter. However, British Steel has also just suffered a before-tax loss for two fiscal years in a row; its share price is still below the value at privatization in 1988; and its management, along with other EC steel companies, is pushing for EC restructuring plans, and complaining bitterly that state-owned rivals are unfairly subsidized by their governments.

The tale of the British Steel Corporation is usually told as an example of a "typical" British nationalized industry, with debate centering on how much control the arm's-length government really exercised over the firm, and on the role of the post-1979 Conservative government and its ideological agenda. The reality was, of course, more complex. A close analysis of the 1978–80 restructuring of the corporation's balance sheet and the government's subsequent role as dominant stakeholder in the company, the various stages of privatization, and the little-studied Phoenix schemes, reveals a different picture. Many aspects of government-industry relations around BSC transcended the political divide between the Labour and Conservative administrations, while the boundary between public and private capital and ownership was far from clear in a number of cases. Most important, an analysis of firm-level financial issues shows that the financial structure of a nationalized company is a key component of government-industry relations, and not merely a technical side issue irrelevant to the politics of the relationship. For most of the 1980s, the relationship of the promarket, antinationalization Thatcher governments with the state-owned BSC was decidedly not arm's-length. In strong contrast with the case of British Leyland and of the French steel industry, the British government was closely involved in the direct financing and restructuring of BSC, essentially playing the role of a supportive dominant stakeholder. To explain why, we must look to the firm's own financial structure and form of corporate governance.

The bulk of this chapter focuses on the financing of British Steel and on the blurred public-private boundary. Part 1 provides the background to this analysis by describing the late 1970s' steel crisis and subsequent restructuring of BSC, and the political context of government-industry relations around the steel industry in the United Kingdom.

1. The Restructuring of the British Steel Corporation

When mass production of steel first began, Britain assumed a commanding technological and competitive lead. By 1913 competition from the United States and Germany had reversed that lead, causing the British steel industry to enter "a spiral of competitive decline from which it has never fully recovered" (Elbaum and Lazonick 1983, 51). In the interwar period, it was generally recognized that some form of major structural reorganization was required in the industry, but the interests of individual firms, unions, and banks were fragmented. Consensus on reorganization simply wasn't forthcoming (Tolliday 1987). The 1949 Iron and Steel Act of the postwar Labour government nationalized the industry, but did not abolish the identity of the ninety-six companies affected. The industry bitterly resented the state takeover and resisted the government's plans at every step (Abromeit 1986).

The Iron and Steel Corporation of Great Britain, established in 1951, was essentially only a holding company. The Conservatives promptly returned the partly nationalized industry to private ownership in 1953, although subject to some price controls.[1] Some of the privately owned firms' investment decisions were also dictated by political expediency. The classic example of this came in the late 1950s, when the Welsh firm, RTB, and the Scottish firm, Colville's, each sought to build a new strip mill. With a general election imminent, the Conservative Macmillan government announced in November 1958 that both mills would be built, despite doubt from the companies that sufficient demand existed for two mills. The government supplied £70 million in aid to RTB and £50 million to Colville's, thus committing the industry to large-scale development at both Llanwern in Wales and Ravenscraig in Scotland. These developments subsequently cost more than anticipated, the demand for their output was not forthcoming, and both firms "were brought to the verge of bankruptcy" (Richardson and Dudley 1986, 312).

The steel industry's health worsened during the 1960s. When Labour returned to power with renewed determination to nationalize this "command-ing height" of the economy, the industry was neither unified enough, nor strong enough financially, to argue that it could organize itself for recovery. The 1967 Iron and Steel Act created the British Steel Corporation by nation-alizing the fourteen biggest steel companies that employed 70 percent of the industry's labor force and accounted for some 90 percent of its total produc-tion. The act left decisions on organizational structures and the reorganization of production to the corporation. The corporation's board had day-to-day control over BSC and basic commercial freedom, while the ministers at the Department of Industry approved the board's investment and production plans.

Retrenchment

In 1973, BSC embarked on an ambitious modernization strategy, with major state investment, to focus production on a few, large integrated plants using then state-of-the-art production techniques—in the midst of which, the full effects of the first oil crisis hit the British economy. As the international crisis in the steel industry mounted, so did BSC's losses. In 1978 a Labour govern-ment White Paper acknowledged that, given the state of crisis in the industry, BSC would have to adopt a more aggressive approach to closing older plants and that it needed a substantial capital reconstruction. With its own future looking tenuous, however, the government was in no position to act deci-sively on BSC. By 1979 the corporation was losing £5 million a day, and its chairman began a restructuring plan of plant closures and job cuts at a scale and speed then unique in the EC.

In 1980 the new Conservative government appointed Ian MacGregor as chairman of the corporation. He quickly drew up a short-term corporate plan (the Survival Plan), which aimed to restore BSC's competitiveness by reduc-ing effective crude capacity to just fourteen and a half million tonnes. Mac-Gregor has come to be associated with the restructuring of BSC, but his predecessor, Villiers, had already overseen 75,000 job losses and accepted a capacity target of fifteen million tonnes per annum by the time he retired in June 1980.[2] In 1970 BSC was based around twenty-one integrated sites. By 1980 it had just five major production facilities—the strip mills at Port Talbot and Llanwern in south Wales and at Ravenscraig in Scotland, and the general steel plants at Scunthorpe and Lackenby (Teesside) in the north of England.

Between 1980 and 1983, some 43 percent of total steel employment was cut, reducing the number of employees to 63,000. As in France, the early steel firms in Britain had developed around the availability of raw materials, principally coal and iron ore, and around transportation needs. Although most ore was imported into Britain by 1979, over 50 percent of BSC's employment was concentrated in Wales, Scotland, and the north (Morgan 1983). The effects of the retrenchment on some regions were devastating. In the eighteen months to January 1983, some 10,000 jobs were cut from the public and private steel industry in the North England area of Sheffield and Rotherham alone. Unemployment rose to over 14 percent in Scotland and 16 percent in the north of England. With the closure of the Consett steelworks, unemployment in Derwentshire reached 24.6 percent by 1982. BSC employment at Llanwern was more than halved, from 9,353 in 1979 to just 4,139 in 1983, while Ravenscraig's job total fell from over 7,000 to under 4,000 (Trade and Industry Committee reports, various). In October 1982 MacGregor revealed a new three-year plan of closures aimed at BSC capacity of even less than fourteen and a half million tonnes (Trade and Industry Committee 1980–81, HC 336-I). The associated redundancy costs increased BSC's annual financial losses. It had planned redundancy costs of £178 million for 1981–82, but by March of 1982 the actual costs were £209 million and rising (Trade and Industry Committee 1981–82, HC 308). The closures continued into the mid-1980s. Meanwhile, MacGregor also reorganized BSC by product specialization, abolishing the old regional divisions and making each group a separate profit center. By the mid-1980s, management and pay bargaining were largely decentralized to the plant level, exacerbating old work-force rivalries between regions and plants (Hudson 1986).

The recession and high interest rates of the early 1980s hit the British steel industry very hard. Some two-thirds of BSC's sales go to the capital goods sector, one-third to the consumer goods sector. The strength of the steel market is thus linked not only to the level of manufacturing activity in general, but also to the level of capital investment, particularly in the auto industry (Trade and Industry Committee 1983–84, HC 344).[3] The corporation, along with other manufacturers, also protested the government's exchange rate policies. Raw material prices in steel are dollar denominated, while European steel prices are critically affected by the strength of the German deutsche mark, making the British steel industry's competitiveness doubly sensitive to exchange-rate movements. In July 1988 Chairman Scholey said that one of the reasons for BSC's increase in profits in 1987 was that the value of the pound fell to DM3.1. "When the rate was DM4:£1, it gave us a pretty tough time" (Trade and Industry Committee 1987–88, HC 631).

The European Commission also played a role in the restructuring of BSC. The corporation planned its financial needs after 1981 in terms of the Commission's objectives of ending state aid to the steel industry by December 1985. Plant cutbacks and closures were carried out with one eye on the EC's capacity reduction requirements, with the EC giving minimum figures for particular product categories, and BSC and the government deciding which plants would be affected. In 1980, Britain was allowed a maximum production level of 22.84 million tonnes (13.5 percent of the EC total), with a total four and a half million tonne cut in capacity mandated for year-end 1983. The rules on EC aid also had a profound impact. In 1980, the Ravenscraig complex in Scotland could be considered BSC's most advanced facility. When the EC ruled that firms could only continue to receive aid if they improved their steel plants, BSC used the opportunity to modernize its Welsh facilities, installing a new hot-strip mill at Port Talbot and converting steel making there and at Llanwern to the continuous-casting process already in use at Ravenscraig.

The Political Context

Apart from the defence and strategic reasons, looked at its very worst, there is no fundamental reason why the United Kingdom should have a steel manufacturing industry. . . . (Mr. Rawlins, Executive Director, National Association Steel Stockholders 1984, HC 344: 579)

Few observers would agree with Rawlins's observation. Steel is seen as so integral to the manufacturing base and industrial image of any nation that the desirability of maintaining indigenous steel-making capacity is often seen as an indisputable given. Decisions involving steel manufacturers and their workers thus carry intrinsic interest for the public and the press. In the case of BSC, the political context of its fate in the 1980s was dominated, in the eyes of the public and the press, by two issues: a bitter thirteen-week strike in early 1980, and the campaign to keep open the Ravenscraig plant in Scotland, an issue that simmered throughout the decade. Behind the scenes, however, another story was taking place—a profound shift in the relationship between the corporation and the government, begun by the new financial arrangements permitted by the Iron and Steel Act of 1975, and formalized in the 1981 Iron and Steel Act. This shift marked the final stage in the government's evolution from the role of nationalizer of a fragmented industry in 1967 to dominant stakeholder in a unified, if crisis-riven, corporation in 1981.

The 1980 strike was called over the annual pay negotiations. The two sides eventually accepted an arbitrated pay increase of 11 percent nationally. However, the unions saw job losses and wages as separate issues, and the Trades Union Congress (TUC) Steel Committee focused the strike entirely on an increased pay award. The local social crises triggered by the mass steel redundancies never became translated into a national political forum, as in France. The moderate Iron and Steel Trades Confederation (ISTC), the industry's largest union, had adopted a "realistic approach" to the restructuring proposals, and although it eventually joined with the ten other unions concerned to argue that the costs of plant closure could far exceed the planned savings,[4] labor opposition to the plans was fragmented by interregional and interplant rivalry, and became a series of separate campaigns to save threatened plants. Although the strike was directed at wage levels, it nevertheless had very political overtones. It was widely rumored that the Conservative Party had targeted the steel unions since 1978 as public sector workers that a Conservative government could defeat in an industrial confrontation. Chairman Villiers claimed he had warned the government that a low pay offer and abrupt announcement of mass redundancies would trigger a strike. He concluded that either the government was indifferent, or it actually wanted a strike (Downing 1981). There is evidence that the government vetoed Villiers's initial plans to offer the unions a pay increase of 10.5 percent to 14 percent in 1980 (Granada TV 1980). According to Hugo Young (1989, 195) "The steel dispute was to be prosecuted to its bitter end to achieve, as one minister told me with grim relish at the time, 'a demonstration effect.'"

The fate of the Ravenscraig complex in west Scotland pitted the government and the workers against the management of the corporation in a number of confrontations that began in 1982 when MacGregor hinted that he wanted to close the Ravenscraig strip mill (Trade and Industry Committee 1980–81, HC 336-II). The Scottish Office (led by then-Scottish Secretary George Younger), local Scottish interests, and labor groups, immediately launched a major, and ultimately successful, lobbying effort, directed at the Department of Trade and Industry.[5]

> Ravenscraig is of vital importance to the Scottish economy, and for the sake of the Scottish nation we shall state categorically and quite simply that Ravenscraig must remain intact. (Councillor C. Gray, Strathclyde Regional Council, Scottish Affairs Committee 1982–83, HC 22)

The Committee on Scottish Affairs was convinced that there would be "something of an industrial holocaust if Ravenscraig closes" (Scottish Affairs Committee 1982–83, HC 22). The Department of Trade and Industry (DTI) concluded that it would be wrong to close any of BSC's integrated plants on the basis of forecasts made during a recession, and instructed BSC to keep all five plants in operation for the next three years (Trade and Industry Committee, 1983–84, HC 181). Government aid had helped to establish the plant in 1957 and regional aid was used to attract domestic and multinational companies to the region. By 1981 BSC had invested over £400 million in the Ravenscraig complex, with a government contribution of £65.4 million in regional development grants (Scottish Affairs Committee 1982–83, HC 22). It is therefore not surprising that every time the prospect of curtailing or ending production at Ravenscraig was brought up, the DTI resisted, arguing for "flexibility" and a commitment to retain all five integrated sites.

When the steel market began to pick up in late 1985, Ravenscraig won a temporary reprieve, and in 1987 British Steel (BS) promised to keep the complex open until 1994, "subject to commercial requirements." In the event, the combination of privatization and a new steel-market downturn doomed Ravenscraig. BS had begun to focus its research and development on the Welsh sites and Ravenscraig's plant was becoming increasingly out-of-date. The Ravenscraig hot-strip mill was closed in April 1991. In January 1992, British Steel announced the entire complex would be closed down by year-end and steel making concentrated at the two modern plants in Wales. Local politicians condemned the company's "betrayal" of the local community. Prime Minister John Major called the closure a matter of "very great regret." British Steel said it was no longer feasible to keep Ravenscraig operational.

The Ravenscraig complex became a symbol, both to the Scottish and labor groups who sought to maintain Scotland's historic role in steel making, and to those who saw private ownership as inherent to making British Steel more commercially efficient and less subject to political pressure. Less noted than the Ravenscraig debate, or the earlier steel strike, but even more important to the political aspect of BSC's story in the 1980s, was the shift in the government's relationship with the corporation. The debate in Britain over whether governments could exercise much control over the nationalized industries is a long-standing one. In fact, the autonomy of nationalized industries varied, not only from industry to industry but, more importantly, depending on the particular issue at stake. At BSC, the post-1975 steel crisis brought an end to the ostensibly arm's-length relationship.

For most of the 1980s, the government worked hard to distance itself from BSC's plans, reiterating that the decisions on closures were ultimately those of the chairman. The government was aided by MacGregor's abrasive and brusque public persona. As then-Industry Minister Lamont concluded in 1983, "Mr. MacGregor had a very tough challenge in getting the capacity reductions, the demanning. I am not sure that could easily have been achieved through a more emollient style of management" (Trade and Industry Committee 1983–84, HC 344). Industry ministers stated that their role was to react to the corporation's proposals: "when we see the Corporate Plan we decide whether or not it is acceptable" (Jenkin, Trade and Industry Committee 1982–83, HC 212, 251). The Trade and Industry Committee concluded in 1981 that "the appraisal of the Corporate Plan was in the main an exercise to allow the Department to continue to fund the Corporation" (HC 336-I, para. 28). As the closures and cuts got under way, however, the 1981 Iron and Steel Act fundamentally altered the relationship between the state and BSC.

The act abolished the corporation's statutory duties, which, though vague, had stipulated its public purpose of promoting the efficient and economical supply of iron and steel products and "furthering the public interest."

More important, it placed BSC under the direct control of the minister for industry, removing any notion of an arm's-length relationship. The minister gained the specific power to "discontinue or restrict any of [BSC's] activities or to dispose of any of their property, rights, liabilities, and obligations" (quoted in Abromeit 1986, 128). This enabled the sponsoring minister to order the sale of any of the BSC's plants and businesses at any time, previously a prerogative of Parliament, and without the need to consult Parliament first—an important consideration in the subsequent privatization, between 1981 and 1987, of some forty BSC subsidiaries, shares, and overseas interests. With the additional introduction of close monitoring of BSC through monthly reports, the corporation was monitored more often, and in far more detail, than ever before (Richardson and Dudley 1986).

Privatization

When BSC became the private-sector company British Steel in December 1988, it was the fourth largest world steel producer (behind Nippon Steel, Usinor-Sacilor of France, and Siderbras of Brazil), with 82 percent of its production continuously cast (up from 22 percent in 1981). The sale was straightforward and popular with investors, with none of the public debate or rancor of the later sale of the Rover Group (chap. 5). Even before the 1988 flotation, however, BSC had been a pioneer in the field of privatization, thanks to what became known as the Phoenix schemes. A private steel sector has always existed alongside the BSC, mainly in specialized steel production. Until the late 1970s, these firms prided themselves on their resiliency compared with BSC. When the steel crisis of the late 1970s hit, however, the privately owned firms began to look for ways to off-load their excess capacity and debts, while reducing the degree of "production overlap" with BSC. The government ruled out BSC taking over private-sector assets and encouraged BSC and the private companies to find ways to pool or exchange their assets to create new companies. The corporation and some of the private companies had already approached the DTI with proposals for the formation of private companies jointly owned by BSC and the private firms, and these proposals eventually became the Phoenix schemes. The private sector's goal for the schemes was clear—to rescue themselves from imminent collapse and bankruptcy. The secretary of state formally approved the first Phoenix company in mid-1981. As events unfolded in unexpected ways, the government's desire to prevent any of the private companies from going bankrupt led to a number of its own guidelines being waived, and to some highly unusual outcomes. The subsequent blurring of the public-private boundary is analyzed in part 3 of this chapter.

This is the basic history of BSC during the 1980s. It is a case that has been analyzed by political scientists a great deal over the years, usually as a typical example of a British nationalized industry. The debates have tended to focus on how much control the government really exercised over the firm, and over the privatization process. Yet the picture of government-industry relations at BSC is not as clear as these analyses usually suggest. The government's relationship with the corporation was not at all arm's-length when it came to the terms of the 1981 act, the close monitoring of BSC after 1981, the orders to keep the Ravenscraig complex open, and perhaps also the conduct of the 1980 wage negotiations. On the other hand, the role of the government in the Phoenix schemes (instigated by the private sector firms and BSC, with the government's own guidelines frequently waived), and in the final privatization of BSC (very much on the company's own terms), looks quintessentially arm's-length and uninvolved. Once we look more closely at firm-level financial issues, however, the reasons for these varied outcomes become clearer.

2. The Financing of British Steel

This analysis of financial issues at BSC falls into four parts—the 1978–80 financial restructuring, the financing of the corporation after 1980, the privatization process, and the fortunes of the private British Steel. From this firm-level perspective, the case of BSC and its private-sector successor is illustrative of the workings of the British financial system. It also reveals some aspects of government-industry relations that are remarkably similar to relations in France. Most important, the tale of the financing of BSC and British Steel illustrates the relative importance of the availability and costs of various forms of financing, and of the attitudes of the providers of that finance, for a major manufacturer during a time of crisis and adaptation.

The 1978–80 Financial Restructuring

The financial restructuring of BSC actually began under the Labour government of Prime Minister Callaghan. Until 1978, 45 percent of BSC's financing requirements were met by loan capital from the National Loans Fund (NLF) and foreign loans, and 55 percent by subscriptions of Public Dividend Capital (PDC). The large loans were intended to meet the fixed capital requirements arising from the corporation's 1973 Development Strategy and to finance operating losses. Both the NLF and overseas borrowings carried interest payments.

By 1978, when the government released its White Paper on the state of the industry, it was clear that BSC would need a substantial capital reconstruction, but given the volatile state of the international steel market (and its own political vulnerability) the government was unwilling to commit to a detailed reassessment of the corporation's capital structure. It did, however, decide not to issue further interest-bearing loans from the NLF or more Public Dividend Capital. Instead, BSC's financial requirements were now to be met solely by subscriptions of capital—labeled "New Capital"—under section 18(1) of the Iron and Steel Act of 1975. This act empowered the secretary of state, with Treasury approval, to pay to the corporation "such sums as he sees fit." The government admitted at the time that it did not expect any dividend on this New Capital until after reconstruction (HMSO 1978). Table 5 illustrates the breakdown of BSC funding sources from 1975 through 1980.

Both PDC and New Capital were essentially nonrepayable, and remuneration (in the form of dividend payments) was discretionary. They served as forms of equity financing, where the government put up investment funds and in theory received some dividend return on its investment. The major difference between the two was that the decision to disburse New Capital involved only the secretary of state and the Treasury. In each case, however, the government formally or informally waived dividend payments. Chairman MacGregor was later to call this form of financing a public corporation "a sort of fairyland in which somebody gives you presents" (Trade and Industry Committee 1980–81, HC 336-I, para. 56).

Some of the outstanding NLF and overseas loans were repaid in the 1978–79 and 1979–80 financial years (April–March), but the amounts were significantly less than the disbursements of New Capital received from the government. Under the 1981 Iron and Steel Act, the outstanding NLF loans (some £510 million) were written off, along with some £3 billion of New Capital.[6] The Conservative government continued the financial restructuring begun under Labour, reducing the balance sheet value of the corporation's fixed assets by £1.141 billion between April 1979 and March 1980. In December 1982, the government wrote off an additional £1 billion of BSC's capital, making a total write-off of £4.5 billion in public money. All future

TABLE 5.   BSC, Source of Funds, 1975–76 to 1979–80 (£ million)

	1975–76	1976–77	1977–78	1978–79	1979–80
Long-term funds					
PDC	344	490	445	——	——
New capital	——	——	——	850	905
NLF	131	161	216	(161)	(209)
Foreign loans	184	214	133	(8)	(35)
Short-term bor-					
rowings	(1)	66	7	34	(94)

Source: Data adapted from Trade and Industry Committee, 1980–81, HC 336-II.
Note: (Negative number denotes net repayment).

financing of the corporation was to come from New Capital, thus completing the replacement of the corporation's interest-bearing debt with interest-free capital. By 1984, the corporation's annual interest costs had fallen from £100 million to £60 million, or 3 percent of capital employed (Trade and Industry Committee 1983–84, HC 344). Although there was some attempt to itemize the amounts of assistance intended for specific extraordinary items, the methods used to arrive at the final aid figures were never made public. How the money was actually to be used was a matter between the corporation and the Department of Trade and Industry.

After the reconstruction of its finances in 1979–80, BSC was left with £630 million in foreign debt. Unlike British Leyland's ongoing relationship with private banks (chap. 5), these were one-off loans that had been negotiated with Treasury approval in the early 1970s. BSC also had just £320 million in short-term debt. The corporation wanted all of its outstanding debt to be replaced with New Capital but the Treasury preferred otherwise, arguing that writing off the foreign borrowings would have involved either government negotiations with the lenders to get agreements on early repayment, or the transfer of the loans from BSC to the government. Unlike the French government, the British government was not prepared to negotiate directly with the steel firm's creditors. Instead, the government pledged BSC to repay its outstanding foreign loans by June 1985, replacing them with New Capital. All of this left the corporation with a very comfortable debt:equity ratio of about 33:67. Table 6 provides annual financial details on BSC from 1978–92.

The restructuring of BSC's finances was not a partisan issue. It was Labour who first converted the corporation's debt into government equity, and the Conservatives who finished the process. It had become apparent that state "loans" with their attendant interest payments were becoming too costly for the firm in the face of a mounting worldwide steel crisis. Nor was this restructuring unique to British steel. As we shall see, a similar debt:equity conversion and debt write-off occurred in the cases of French steel and British Leyland.

The Financing of BSC after 1980

We accept the decision to continue funding BSC. The national interest undoubtedly requires an efficient and viable steel-making industry—both and private—to supply the majority of the domestic market. (Trade and Industry Committee 1980–81, HC 336-I, 30)

The 1981 Iron and Steel Act, and the conversion of the bulk of the corporation's debt into equity, essentially confirmed the government as not just the nominal owner of BSC, but also its primary stakeholder. No other institutions—in

TABLE 6.   BSC Financials, Fiscal Year Ending March 31 (£ million)

	Profit/(Loss) before Tax & Exceptionals	Exceptional Costs	Net Profit/(Loss)	Long-Term Debts
1978–79	(309)			
1979–80	(545)		(1,784)	1,297
1980–81	(660)		(1,020)	1,150[a]
1981–82	(358)		(504)	651[b]
1982–83	(869)	(483)		
1983–84	(256)	(79)		
1984–85	(383)	(264)		
1985–86	42	(34)	38	
1986–87	177		178	172
1987–88	419	(36)	411	114[c]
1988–89	593	(140)	562	
1989–90	733		564	
1990–91	254			
1991–92	(55)	(100)[d]		

Source: Trade and Industry Committee Reports, various issues; Moody's International, various issues; Financial Times, various issues.

Note: Exceptional costs = Plant closures, redundancy payments, etc.

[a]£509m due to government, March 1995; £616m foreign loans; £25m other.

[b]£569m foreign loans; £82m other.

[c]£2m bank loans; £53m foreign loans; £59m lease obligations.

[d]Largely related to the closure of the Ravenscraig steel plant in Scotland.

either the state or the private sectors—had what could be called an ownership or financial stake in BSC. This is in strong contrast to the case of French steel where, as we shall see, a plethora of institutions across the public-private sector divide were holders of steel company debt; and it is also different than the case of British Leyland, which continued to have access to huge lines of credit from private-sector banks. BSC's only significant source of financing after 1980 was the state, and specifically the Department of Trade and Industry.

The post-1979 Conservative government developed a new method of controlling the finances of the nationalized industries—External Financing Limits or EFLs. The use of EFLs differed from the methods used by earlier governments in that they were frequently set below the amounts requested by the nationalized industry, in order to act as a form of financial discipline. Thus the government's macroeconomic policy to reduce the Public Sector Borrowing Requirement (PSBR) became the determinant of its relations with the nationalized industries. BSC's External Financing Limit was set by the DTI, which depended heavily on the corporation itself for the information on which its decisions were made, while the Treasury disbursed the funds. As early as July 1979, however, the DTI had begun to monitor BSC's finances on a month-to-month basis, an unprecedented level of detailed monitoring of a British nationalized industry that became even closer after the change in BSC's status brought about by the 1981 act.

BSC's financing was now made up of subscriptions of New Capital, the amount negotiated annually with the DTI. BSC didn't always get the amounts for which it asked, but even with the extraordinary amount of control exercised by the secretary of state over BSC's finances, the government was frequently forced to increase the corporation's funding limits in the first half of the 1980s. Immediately after the 1979 election, the new secretary of state for industry, Sir Keith Joseph, had announced that the government would not finance BSC's losses after March 1980. The government then backed down slightly, announcing that BSC would be required to break even in 1980–81, and that its EFL would be set at a firm £450 million. Circumstances dictated otherwise. As BSC's losses continued to mount, the new secretary of state found himself in what was for him an agonizingly uncomfortable position— bailing out the steelmaker to the tune of over £1 billion. After the government directive to keep Ravenscraig in operation, the EFL for 1982–83 ended up being far greater than the £365 million originally negotiated. Having committed itself to saving the firm, the government felt it had no choice but to keep coming up with the money.

There were years when the government successfully reduced the amount of aid requested. In 1981–82, MacGregor requested an EFL of £750 million, but the Department of Industry revised the figure downward. Similarly, for 1983–84, BSC requested an EFL of £425 million, based on a projected operating loss of £131 million, and contingencies of £150 million (£131 million of which was to cover closures and redundancies). The government reduced the proposed contingency provision and set an EFL of £321 million. Meanwhile, the government was pushing BSC to break even ahead of the EC's 1985 deadline for nationalized steel firms to be economically viable, stipulating that the corporation "break-even before interest in 1984–85 and thereafter to earn a real return on its capital" (HMSO 1983–84, 3.42). What is certain is that, without state aid, BSC would not have survived to the mid-1980s.[7] See table 7 for a listing of British Steel's EFLs between 1976 and 1985.

In its negotiations with the government in the early 1980s, BSC was clearly pushing for as much funding up front as it could get. In 1983–84, for example, the operating loss was calculated after charging depreciation of £90 million and interest of £72 million, thus reducing an expected £31 million gross profit on operations to a loss of £131 million. Such high depreciation is inherent in a very capital-intensive industry such as steel. In addition, BSC was investing a great deal in modernizing the Port Talbot facilities, while also aware that as of 1985, no more state aid would be permitted under EC rules, except for purely restructuring costs.

TABLE 7.   British Steel's EFL, 1976–77 to 1984–85 (£ million)

	Nominal £	1982–83 Prices
1976–77	949	1,938
1977–78	806	1,447
1978–79	752	1,222
1979–80	579	805
1980–81	1,119	1,311
1981–82	694	740
1982–83	568	568
1983–84	321[a]	
1984–85	275[a]	

Source: Data adapted from Trade and Industry Committee, 1983–84, HC 344.
[a]Estimates.

The attempts to limit BSC's financing levels whenever possible did have some negative consequences, such as a delay in starting the Port Talbot modernization scheme (Trade and Industry Committee 1983–84, HC 344, 373). The steel unions in particular condemned what they called "management by cash limits." BSC senior management, however, were reportedly very much in favor of the EFL limits, seeing them as a simple and healthy discipline that still left them free to decide on the specifics of restructuring (Abromeit 1986). They also felt that EFLs "tighten the discipline within the machine" (ibid., 173)—in other words, effectively strengthen central management's position vis-à-vis the corporation's divisions and subdivisions. This may have been an important consideration, given that middle management openly supported the Trade and Industry Committee's criticisms of BSC's inaccurate financial forecasts in 1981.

Privatization

> We want, whatever the ownership is, freedom to operate commercially in the market. (Chairman Scholey, Trade and Industry Committee 1985–86, HC 539)

In mid-1988, the government was anxious to find an uncontentious state-owned industrial candidate to sell to the private sector. The privatization program had ground to a halt over the complex and politically unpopular proposals to sell the water and electricity industries. The government needed a smooth and high-profile sale to reassure the public and the City before embarking on the more complex sales. When the British Steel Corporation turned a healthy pretax profit of £419 million in 1987–88, it moved up in the industrial-privatization queue. A key factor in BSC's favor was that Chairman Scholey was cooperative and enthusiastic about the whole idea—in large part for financial reasons.

BSC was not the only nationalized industry for which financial concerns played a major role in management's attitudes toward privatization (Marklew 1989). Although the corporation had usually received the minimum funding it required from the government, its external financing limits were becoming increasingly tight as the 1980s progressed and its financial health improved. In 1987 the corporation was given a negative EFL for 1988–89 of £100 million, based on estimates of its likely future profitability. BSC management began to speak of the desirability of access to "more flexible" private capital. (The same management incentive of negative EFLs was subsequently used on some of the water boards prior to their privatization.) After flotation, British Steel's capital expenditure did indeed increase, from £253 million in 1987–88 to £307 million in 1988–89 (*Financial Times*, June 16, 1989), although this may have been due as much to the improvement in the industry as a whole, as to the firm's new-found access to private capital.

The company could have been broken down into component parts such as its five major production facilities, but it was apparent that Chairman Scholey was very much in favor of retaining BSC in its existing form after privatization. The government was in no mood to argue, and saw no reason to challenge Scholey's contention that only a company of this size could compete in the recovering European market. BSC was duly floated on the London International Stock Exchange in December 1988. The flotation proved popular. The company had set aside 452 million shares for the British public, but increased this number at the expense of institutional and overseas allotments when public applications for more than 1.5 billion shares came in. The total sale price came to £2.5 billion, making it the fourth largest sale, in terms of revenue, to that date.[8] British Steel itself spent £20 million on the flotation (*Financial Times*, November 22, 1989).

The sale was swift and not open to outside input or public debate. Information about the company was given in its prospectus for sale, of course, but decisions such as the retention of all five integrated sites in one company, the share offer price, the timing of the sale, and the creation of a government Special Share (see part 3) were all made without discussion even within Parliament. Major groups such as the British Independent Steel Producers' Association and the various trade unions were not consulted.

At the time of its flotation in December 1988, BSC had accumulated debts of about £1 billion (*Times*, December 4, 1988). The government was not able to write off any of BSC's debts prior to flotation, due to EC rules governing aid to the steel industry. However, although British Steel took on all of the corporation's financial liabilities, BSC's debt levels were very low for a mature steel company emerging from a severe cyclical downturn and restructuring. They had, of course, been substantially reduced already, with the capital restructuring and debt write-offs of the early 1980s.

The actual form of BSC's privatization is also telling. Given the political symbolism of steel manufacturing, sale to a foreign competitor was absolutely out of the question. While British Aerospace could step in and purchase Rover (chap. 5), there was no equivalent firm for whom it made commercial sense to take on all five of BSC's integrated production sites as a going concern, or who was willing or able to do so. The level of capital required to purchase and then to operate a major firm in a highly capital-intensive industry was beyond the scope of an employee or management buyout.[9] Stock market flotation was the only viable financial option.

Financing the Private British Steel

> Life would be easier if we had Deutsche Bank behind us. (Sir Robert Scholey, Chief Executive of British Steel. *Financial Times*, December 28, 1991)

In its first two years in the private sector, British Steel saw its before-tax profits increase—from £419 million in 1987–88 to £593 million in 1988–89 and £733 million in 1989–90. Then the picture took an abrupt turn for the worse. With the onset of recession at home, a slowing of the European economy, and another crisis of overcapacity and cheap competitive challengers for the European steel industry as a whole, British Steel found itself once again in a severe cyclical downturn, and less than popular with investors.

In November 1991, British Steel announced a 94 percent plunge in its pretax profit for the first half of 1991–92, to £19 million, compared with £307 million in April–September 1990. Management announced that the firm would maintain its interim dividend at 3 pence per share, but warned that the final dividend was in doubt. As noted in chapter 1, the London International Stock Exchange is dominated by large, institutional investors, for whom dividend payments are an important consideration. Following the dividend warning, British Steel's share price promptly plummeted 25 percent in two days to around 85p, its lowest level since privatization at 125p. The company's share prices fell even lower, to 60.5p, in June 1992, when the firm reported a £55 million pretax loss for 1991–92 and cut its final dividend from 8.75p to 4.5p per share. November 1992 brought still gloomier news—the company declared a pretax loss of £51 million for April–September 1992, and became the first privatized company to omit its interim dividend. British Steel shares fell to a new all-time low of 46.5p. In addition, net borrowing increased from £11 million at the end of 1991 to £196 million at the end of 1992, as exceptional items, including closures and redundancy costs, contributed to a £108 million net cash outflow.

It was in the aftermath of the November 1991 final dividend warning that Sir Robert Scholey, in an interview with the *Financial Times*, made the above quote referring to Deutsche Bank. He had been discussing British Steel's failure to move into eastern Germany, noting that talks with the German Treuhand privatization agency had ended because the company was put off by the very high social and environmental costs associated with taking over former state-run steel works in the east. The company's institutional shareholders would be unhappy if profits failed to appear and share prices fell. "British Steel cannot do what it wants. . . . Life would be easier if we had Deutsche Bank behind us." A similar lament was heard some years earlier, from the chairman of then-independent luxury carmaker Jaguar (chap. 5).

The June 1992 reporting of a pretax loss, coming just a week after the ending of steel making at Ravenscraig, overshadowed an equally important announcement from management concerning a linkup with Swedish stainless steel company Avesta. The joint venture established a new company, Avesta Sheffield, as the largest stainless steel maker in Europe and second largest in the world behind Usinor-Sacilor of France, with net assets valued in June 1992 at £547 million. British Steel holds 40 percent of the equity in the new company while the other main shareholders are Swedish companies that hold a majority stake in Avesta. Avesta was to issue 55.3 million new shares worth £164 million and a £35 million loan note to British Steel in return for its stainless steel business. The Avesta deal marked a major cross-border venture in the European steel industry, aimed at reducing overcapacity and increasing both firms' ability to survive the cyclical downturn.

3. The Blurred Public-Private Boundary

The previous section described in detail the financing of the nationalized BSC and the private British Steel. The assessment of the firm-level financial issues is given in part 4. This section discusses the blurring of the public-private divide in the case of BSC. It is more extensive than the comparable sections in the other case-study chapters, for two reasons. First, the Phoenix schemes have been studied very little in the literature on government-industry relations in Britain. Writers have tended to focus on BSC, and to skim over the various Phoenix ventures as side issues to the central tale of the nationalized giant. The Phoenix schemes were a major development in the British steel industry, however, and a very interesting aspect of government-industry relations in general. Second, the Thatcher governments of the 1980s supposedly maintained a clear divide between the public and the private sectors—in contrast both to earlier, more interventionist governments in the United Kingdom and to the practices of successive administrations in France. Yet the Phoenix schemes were an overt example of state aid being used to bail out faltering private companies, and to subsidize fledgling industrial concerns—even though they were claimed by the Conservative government as an example of returning assets to the private sector. In addition, the Special Share held in British Steel, like that in other privatized companies, challenges the view that privatization places large manufacturing concerns on the other side of an impenetrable public-private divide.

The Phoenix Schemes

Since 1967, the private-sector steel firms had prided themselves on their relative health compared with the state-owned giant.[10] They had lower overheads, depended less on the large manufacturers as customers, and those who were members of diversified groups had access to additional financial resources. Yet overall, the private producers had close commercial ties with BSC, although competing private firms did occasionally conflict with the corporation over prices. Since 1967, governments had been mostly concerned with BSC, seeing the private sector as a minor niche within the industry. Things changed abruptly in the early 1980s, however, as the severity of the recession hit the private producers.

As the steel crisis deepened, the British Independent Steel Producers Association (BISPA) lobbied the government heavily for some assistance. BISPA complained that government aid to BSC allowed MacGregor to pursue a very aggressive pricing policy that they could not match. "The Secretary of State and his colleagues . . . are in imminent danger of being the instruments of the collapse of the private sector" (Trade and Industry Committee 1980–81, HC 336-II). The argument was evidently persuasive. In December 1981 the government introduced a private-sector steel scheme designed to help companies (mostly those covered by the ECSC Treaty) to rationalize and restructure their operations.[11] Assistance under the scheme totaled nearly £50 million, and was on a case-by-case basis, subject to approval by the Treasury and the EC. BISPA's main concern, however, was that BSC production in areas that overlapped with the private sector be removed from BSC's business as soon as possible, one way or another. This concern led to the Phoenix schemes.

Certain plants had long been in joint ownership between the public and private sectors. At nationalization in 1967, the major steel companies were transferred into BSC along with their assets, subsidiaries, and shares in other companies. BSC thus inherited a stake in a number of companies who otherwise belonged to the private sector, putting it in the position of competing with some of its own subsidiaries. Around 20 percent of BSC's production overlapped with the private sector by 1980–81 (Abromeit 1986). Yet BSC refused to sell any of the plant that it wanted to be rid of to the private sector outright, for fear of competition (Young 1986a). An interesting example of this reluctance was given by Bill Sirs, general secretary of the ISTC, when he made the following claim to the Trade and Industry Committee (1983–84, HC 344, 133) about BSC's London Works:

> . . . an industrialist wanted to purchase it. He did not want it to be known who he was. He asked me to deal with it and see if BSC would come across. They would not. They did not want a competitor. I wrote to Margaret Thatcher and she said, "It is in their hands, not mine." There you can have this Government which believes in competition and a person willing to buy that plant and have it as an on-going plant and we had a refusal.

By late 1980 the worsening steel crisis was threatening many of the smaller private companies and there was little likelihood of the larger ones obtaining the financing from their parent companies to maintain their existing scale of operation. Failure of these companies would have led either to an enlargement of the public sector, or to increased import penetration. The former was anathema to the new Conservative government; the latter would have made the recovery of BSC harder. BSC and a number of private companies approached the DTI with proposals for the formation of viable private companies, to be jointly owned by BSC and the private-sector firms. The private sector's goal for the schemes was clear—to rescue them from imminent collapse and bankruptcy.

The DTI promised to "urgently consider" any such proposals, drawing up guidelines by which to consider them (see table 8). The government ruled

TABLE 8.   Government Guidelines for Considering Phoenix Proposals

(a)	BSC should not have majority equity ownership or control;
(b)	the new ventures should be free-standing companies without recourse to parent guarantees;
(c)	the new ventures should be commercially viable from the outset (i.e., with low gearing, or debt levels, and relief from obligations incurred prior to foundation);
(d)	working capital requirements should be channeled through BSC;
(e)	the finance required should be significantly less than would be required to finance BSC's business if it remained in the public sector;
(f)	the valuation of assets should reflect their contribution to the new venture.

Source: Adapted from Committee of Public Accounts, 1984–85, HC 307.

out BSC taking over private-sector assets and instead encouraged the two sides to find ways to pool or exchange their assets to create new companies. Such schemes had the added benefit of introducing private capital into parts of BSC's business in line with the government's developing ideas on privatization. The DTI also ruled out imposing any rationalization schemes on the industry, instead seeking proposals from the businesses themselves. "The Government informed the companies that they had no strategic "blue-print" for the UK steel industry and did not propose to lay down guidelines on which capacity should remain open and which should close" (Comptroller and Auditor General 1985, 1.5).

The secretary of state formally approved the first Phoenix company in mid-1981. As events unfolded in unexpected ways the government's desire not to allow the private-sector companies to collapse meant that a number of its own guidelines were waived. It was helped by the 1981 act that allowed BSC to "acquire, form and hold interests in companies only with the consent of . . . the Secretary of State" (Committee of Public Accounts 1984–85, HC 307). The DTI could consider and justify each Phoenix proposal individually. From 1980 to 1984 seven Phoenix schemes were approved, each one part capacity reduction and part market rationalization. The new ventures all received some form of "compensation payment" from the government via BSC—in other words, financial aid to make the ventures work. The following summary of the first three schemes illustrates the financial arrangements and politics involved.

Phoenix One: Allied Steel and Wire
The first proposal was submitted by the private-sector firm GKN and BSC in December 1980, to establish a jointly-owned company, Allied Steel and Wire (ASW). GKN had been both a competitor and major customer of BSC for many years, and the two had been discussing a merger of their overlapping interests in the wire sector since 1978 (Abromeit 1986). The government was brought in when it became apparent that the new company would need public money as starting capital—the private sector was simply "too broke to pay BSC an adequate price for the assets they want to part own" (*Economist*, March 5, 1983). A tentative proposal was made to the DTI in December 1980. It was revised somewhat by the DTI,[12] and the new company started trading on June 29, 1981. GKN provided 71 percent of the new company's fixed assets. BSC provided 29 percent of the assets and also ASW's initial and future cash requirements. The DTI estimated that if BSC and GKN remained in competition in this sector, it would mean annual losses for BSC of £5.5 million to £50 million and might even endanger BSC's operation at Scunthorpe. By 1986 ASW was Cardiff's largest private employer, with an annual

profit level over £13 million and 3,200 employees (BISPA 1986). The firm was eventually sold in a management buyout.

Phoenix Two: United Engineering Steels
Phoenix Two, however, was a much messier affair. In late 1980 GKN and BSC also discussed a joint venture for manufacturing and selling engineering steels. Buoyed by the successful establishment of ASW, the government encouraged the potential private-sector partners (Duport, Tube Investments Ltd., Hadfields, and GKN) to bring forward proposals. But BSC and GKN concluded that the market for engineering steels was too unstable at that time to structure such a joint venture. However, the Duport Group and Tube Investments (TI) were in dire financial straits. Duport wanted to off-load its steel subsidiary altogether and TI wanted to withdraw from Round Oak Steel Works Ltd. (ROSW), a company it already jointly owned with BSC. TI wanted to sell its share to BSC, but was prepared to put ROSW into liquidation, if necessary (Committee of Public Accounts 1984–85, HC 307).

BSC argued that the Duport operations and order loads would be a good fit for Phoenix Two, so the secretary of state authorized BSC to acquire as much of Duport's steel interests as would be useful. BSC took over all of Duport's steel assets and assumed £25 million of Duport bank debt, converting it to a ten-year loan. The DTI estimated that the purchase cost BSC £21.2 million net, but benefited its operating results by £10 million a year. Duport, on the other hand, got out from under its steel losses and associated bank debt, was rescued from possible bankruptcy, and went on to earn a pretax profit of £2 million in 1983–84. Meanwhile, the DTI felt that it would be "improper" to allow ROSW, a company 50 percent-owned by BSC, to go into liquidation. It consented to BSC's acquiring the TI share in May 1981 for a nominal £1. BSC also took over ROSW's borrowings from banks and from TI. When the market took a further nosedive in late 1982 Round Oak's losses soared and BSC closed the plant altogether in 1983. The acquisition of ROSW cost the corporation twice that of the Duport purchase. BSC claimed that buying the two Phoenix Two companies had benefited its operations to the tune of £32.5 million up to March 1984, but these figures were not separately identified in any way in BSC's accounts.

Negotiations on Phoenix Two continued between BSC and GKN. A formal proposal was made in February 1984 for a jointly controlled engineering steel group, United Engineering Steels Ltd. (UES). The proposal involved merging four BSC Sheffield plants with GKN's Brymbo plant and reducing capacity some 40 percent by closing two of the plants. Compared with the smaller schemes pursued to that point, this one had a major effect on the final shape of the corporation (BSC Chairman Haslam, Trade and Industry Committee 1984–85, HC 474). UES is 61 percent-owned by British Steel and 39 percent by GKN, but is run as a 50–50 joint venture. By 1989 it had become Britain's second biggest steelmaker and one of Europe's largest suppliers of steel to the auto industry, and plans were under way to float UES on the stock exchange. UES also established a private-sector monopoly in engineering steels: "This is a result fraught with paradox, since it is in direct contradiction to the aims of denationalization as expressed by the Prime Minister . . . to increase competition and improve efficiency" (Trade and Industry Committee 1983–84, HC 344, 34).

Phoenix Three: Sheffield Forgemasters
Phoenix Three, in the open-die forgings and heavy-steel castings sector, was first proposed by Johnson and Firth Brown (JFB) in December 1981. A ten-year market-sharing agreement between BSC and JFB was due to expire in 1982. JFB knew the corporation had no intention of renewing the agreement, while the JFB group as a whole had seen its performance slump in 1981. Unsecured creditors began pressing the group to dispose of its steel operations, one way or another.

JFB offered to contribute 71.4 percent of net assets to the new company, and BSC 28.6 percent along with a cash contribution. Both sides were incurring losses on these operations, and the government feared that the collapse of JFB would mean "leaving BSC to pick up the pieces, which was unacceptable to the Government" (Comptroller and Auditor General 1985, 4.3). The secretary of state accepted BSC's calculation that the effects on its profit-and-loss account would be about the same whether or not Phoenix Three went ahead, and approved BSC's acquisition of an equity stake in the new company, Sheffield Forgemasters Holdings plc. The DTI also agreed to the provision of selective financial assistance, on the grounds that the scheme would mean a reduction in capacity, the creation of a viable company, and the retention in Britain of an important industry. By October of 1984, however, it was obvious that the new company was in danger of going into liquidation, as its losses rose. In December, the company and its bankers reached a settlement whereby BSC provided £5 million in trading facilities and guaranteed a £5 million loan for further restructuring (Committee of Public Accounts 1984–85, HC 307).

Other less ambitious schemes continued into the mid-1980s (see table 9), including BSC's acquisition and closure of the Alphasteel strip mill in 1985. A number of smaller ventures, involving primarily joint BSC plant ownerships with GKN and Firth Brown, were also started. These deals involved "new and different links between the government and private steel" (*Economist*, March 5, 1983). BSC shares in these firms ranged from 25 percent to

TABLE 9. Other Phoenix Operations,
up to March 1984

Companies	BSC Involvement	
British Bright Bar	40% stake, plus loan stock	
Clyde Shaw	50% stake, plus loan stock	
Seamless Tubes	75% stake	
Cold Drawn Tube	25% stake	
Hadfield Holdings	37.5% stake	
	Total BSC Contribution, at inceptions:	
	Assets	£71.9 million
	Cash[a]	£57.7 million
Further Commitment/Liability		£102.0 million

Source: Adapted from Committee of Public Accounts, 1984–85,
HC 307; and Trade and Industry Committee reports, various issues.
[a]includes debts retained and realized by BSC.

74.5 percent. In other European countries, the joint-venture, public-private hybrids created under these schemes would have been called mixed-economy undertakings, and would almost certainly have been counted as public enterprises (Abromeit 1988).

The myriad links inherited by BSC from prenationalization days help explain the relative ease with which BSC became involved in such complex public/private deals. Also, the Phoenix schemes were not the first time that rationalization of BSC had also involved the private sector. Private steel plants were purchased and closed by the corporation in the early 1970s, as part of the postnationalization Heritage Programme of consolidation and rationalization. In 1970, BSC bought Wellington Tube Works at Tipton for £3 million, and closed it in April 1971. It also chose to close the Birchley rerolling mill at Warley in 1973–74, rather than sell it to the private steel companies who were reputedly interested in buying the mill for £1 million (Heal 1974).

Neither Parliament nor other government departments had much access to financial information about the Phoenix companies or information on the process of establishing BSC subsidiaries. The comptroller and auditor general's office relied on information from the DTI for its assessment of the Phoenix schemes (Committee of Public Accounts 1984–85, HC 307). Still, based on the information to which they did have access, both the comptroller and the Committee of Public Accounts felt that the first three major Phoenix schemes had disproportionately benefited the private-sector partners involved:

"not only were they relieved of the need to finance their loss-making activities but the assets concerned were transferred to the joint companies on favourable terms" (HC 307, 32). One M.P. concluded that the schemes:

> are nothing to do with profit or loss. They are really to do with ideology: either to keep the private sector going or alternately to prevent the state sector expanding. . . . We have no idea of the costs that are likely to be involved. . . . In the uncertain circumstances of the time they could have gone either way; one has gone into profit and the other is still making some losses and one does not seem to have come into fruition at all. It is a rather unusual situation. . . . (Eric Deakins, M.P., HC 307, 1591)

The government claimed that one of its overriding objectives was to decrease public funding of industry. It wanted the Phoenix companies to become wholly private with no recourse to public money from the DTI or from BSC. So when ASW was set up, the department agreed to advance a large sum of money to the firm to meet its financing needs for the first few years of operation. It turned out that ASW did not need the extra cash at the times agreed for its provision, but under the agreement it got it anyway. The DTI didn't want to advance money according to market conditions, as this would have entailed a degree of monitoring control inconsistent with the notion of private, intervention-free firms (HC 307). When GKN argued that its assets were not worth their net book values because of competition from the publicly subsidized BSC, the DTI backed off from judgment, saying that the value placed on the physical assets was a matter for negotiation between BSC and GKN (HC 307).

At no time did the DTI draw up a balance sheet to show whether the completed Phoenix operations as a whole met the guideline requirement that the government financing be less than if the business had remained in the public sector. The government's control over the schemes was the negative role of rejecting proposals it did not like or ruling out unacceptable options. In fact, the very lack of precise institutional responsibilities involved in the Phoenix schemes allowed the DTI to fudge many of the details of the deals with impunity, and to exercise a great deal of de facto flexibility. Regarding the purchase of assets for the Phoenix Two scheme, the DTI gave the Committee of Public Accounts different versions of the purchase prices at different times (HC 307, 34). When the cost of Phoenix Three turned out to be much higher than originally envisaged, the DTI claimed it was actually about the same as if the scheme had not gone ahead, and that the guidelines for evaluation were in any case not firm rules (ibid.). The DTI could bend its guidelines as events dictated, and argue that, whatever the specific methods used, the outcome still fulfilled the overall mandate to get government out of the affairs of private industry.

BSC's advancement of cash to ASW effectively provided backing for additional bank borrowing by the company; the additional financial support for Sheffield Forgemasters came entirely from its public-sector partner; and BSC supplied steel to ASW at a special rate. The government argued that none of this amounted to public guarantees for private-sector firms, but in effect the British government did the same as the French under similar circumstances—provided financing on favorable terms to private manufacturers in trouble.

The Postprivatization Special Share

The time is now right for the Corporation to be free to manage its own affairs and to take business decisions on a commercial basis free from political interference. (Kenneth Clarke, Minister of Trade and Industry, *Times*, February 13, 1988)

The other major example of the blurring of the public-private sector divide in the U.K. steel industry is that of the government's retention of a Special Share in the privatized British Steel. The European Community had already challenged Britain over the 15 percent limit on foreign ownership placed on the privatized Rolls-Royce, a restriction that fell foul of EC trade law. So the government turned to Special Share provisions to control takeover bids in privatized companies.

British Steel's Special Share is incorporated into its Articles of Association. It gives the government a blocking share in the company for five years. No organization or individual is allowed to take more than a 15 percent stake in the company without government approval. If this limit is breached, the directors are required to serve notice calling for a disposal of shares to bring the person under the 15 percent limit. If the notice isn't complied with, the company is required to dispose of the shares at the best reasonably obtainable price. This is a very clear example of what Graham and Prosser (1987) call the unique status afforded privatized companies in the United Kingdom. The state has retained the right of compulsory expropriation of property if certain conditions are met.

The decision to retain a Special Share in British Steel was apparently the product of economic nationalism, as was the original decision to nationalize the industry in 1949. British Steel dominates the steel industry in Britain, and none of its private competitors are large enough or financially stable enough to pose a serious takeover threat. Allowing ownership of a major part of the industry to pass overseas, however, is judged a threat to national security. The auto industry has not been granted the same importance in the national economy (at least, not in Britain). As noted in chapter 1, the workings of the ECSC crisis cartel in the early 1980s also helped to push national steel industries closer to their respective governments. If the chairman of any privatized company believed that such a 15 percent limit was desirable, it would not be too hard for him to argue the case to a government concerned about national autonomy in a key industry and desirous of a smooth sale.

In December 1989, the late Nicholas Ridley, then trade and industry secretary, stated that the government now had reservations about holding Special Shares with a limited lifespan, when investment decisions were increasingly seen in an international, and particularly a European, context (*Financial Times*, December 14, 1989). The Special Share in British Steel is due to expire at the end of 1993. As the case of Jaguar shows (chap. 5), the timing of such a share's expiration, and the decision on whether or not to invoke it at a given juncture, can have a major impact on a firm's financial health and on the workings of the stock market.

4. Assessment

BSC and the National Financial System

The tale of BSC and its private sector successor, British Steel, illustrates two particular aspects of the British financial system. First, the institutional limitations on, and government aversion to, overt public-private capital mixes; and second, the dominance of the stock market in the financing of industry and the attitudes of the market's investors. When the smaller, private-sector steelmakers ran into financial difficulties in the early 1980s, the government decided that they could not be allowed to go bankrupt. Anything that smacked too obviously of nationalization was ruled out for ideological reasons, but the state's ability to channel investment funds to the private sector in any other way was limited. Hence the Phoenix schemes. It is clear from the above descriptions that public and private capital were, in fact, mixed freely in these firms, but in the case of the steel industry, the most obvious—if not the only—way to do so was by using BSC in a bailout operation. When the government had earlier used External Financing Limits to "discipline" the nationalized industries, the Trades Union Congress had argued that the firms should be allowed access to private capital markets for their borrowing needs, as subsequently happened in France, and had condemned "management by cash limits" (NEDC 1981 (81), 28). The British do not have a long history of government-initiated financing schemes that draw on both public and private pools of capital, however. There are few institutional structures that would allow private investment vehicles to easily become involved in channeling funds to industry. It is this aspect of industrial financing in Britain, rather than some notion of privatization as an antidote to state ownership, that marks one of the key differences between government-industry relations in Britain and those in France.

When it came to privatizing the remainder of BSC in 1988, the only viable financial option was to turn to the stock market. The Exchange allowed British Steel to access a potentially vast pool of capital in the heady days of 1988–1990, and the firm's levels of capital investment did increase. But the reaction of British Steel's investors when the company announced a reduced dividend in 1991–92, and then no interim dividend in 1992–93, is an example of the pitfalls that also come from reliance on an institutionally dominated and highly capitalized stock market for financing major manufacturers. As chapter 4 shows, Peugeot's experience with the French stock market was very different, thanks to a different system of corporate governance.

Similarities between Britain and France

There are four aspects of the case of British Steel that, as we shall see in the next chapter, also turn up in the case of French steel. These give a similarity to the cases that one would not expect in two countries with such different institutional and financial systems and with such ideologically different governments in power. In each case, the initial crisis in the steel industry prompted a conversion of debt into equity. In each case, the government subsequently used its national champion to rationalize the whole of the domestic steel sector and to bail out private steel firms. And in each case, the government also used borrowing limits as a means of enforcing rationalization on the dominant firm. In this sense, each government attempted to act as a dominant stakeholder— sooner in the case of BSC, but much later, as we shall see, in the case of French steel. Finally, by the late 1980s, each government was also beginning to search for alternatives to direct state provision of financing for the dominant steel firm. Although the causes were the same, however (EC directives limiting state aid to the industry and government desire to limit the rising costs of support), the outcomes were quite different.

Firm-Level Financial Issues

The first chapter argued that the characteristics of a firm's financial structure and its form of corporate governance profoundly affect the processes of crisis management. Although BSC was taken over by the state in 1967, this does not mean that these issues then became irrelevant for the firm until its privatization in 1988. The availability and costs of financing still had an impact on BSC, as did the attitudes of the provider(s) of that finance.

First, availability. Clearly, when it was state-owned, BSC's only major source of finance was the state, a source with very deep pockets. In the early 1980s, the government stumped up the cash to keep BSC going to a degree that no British private-sector investor would have done at that time. The private-sector firms turned to BSC, and hence also, ultimately, to the state, for financial assistance. BSC's management looked forward to privatization in 1988, as this would make more "flexible" sources of capital available to them, but the only viable private-sector source of financing available for a major, capital-intensive manufacturer in the United Kingdom was the stock market.

As to the costs of financing, the financial restructuring of 1978–80 was basically a conversion of debt into equity. Debt may be a preferable form of financing in good times, but servicing that debt becomes a crippling expense in a time of crisis. As a firm operating in a highly cyclical industry, BSC was also anxious to reduce its debt load as much as possible in the early 1980s. Part of the reason why the company looked so appealing to investors in the immediate aftermath of privatization was the fact that its debt burden was low for a major steel manufacturer. Access to cheap capital was also clearly an important consideration for the private steel companies seeking a bailout via BSC, and for their Phoenix offspring in the early years of operation. Finally, the cost of maintaining its dividend in 1992 proved too high for British Steel—but, as we saw, it had the option to waive payment.

What, then, of the attitudes of the providers of financing to BSC and British Steel in the period described? Between 1967 and 1979, the state had consolidated its position as the owner of BSC. From 1980, the state issued equity to the company in the form of New Capital, and acted as a majority shareholder, approving the board's actions, approving or denying further equity financing, and exercising overall control. The 1981 Iron and Steel Act finalized the state's role as the corporation's dominant stakeholder—an actor with a clear if limited goal for the company (survival, and ultimately financial independence from state aid by 1985), able to dominate the agenda relevant to that goal, and willing to cede control over other issues to the firm's management. We can't take the dominant stakeholder analogy too far: a government is still a political animal at heart, pursuing diverse political ends. Hence the decision to keep the Ravenscraig complex operational through the 1980s, and the intervention in the 1980 wage negotiations and subsequent strike. But the analogy does serve to make clear one of the key differences between this case and that of French steel in the following chapter, where a multitude of holders of the steel firms' debts were involved in the firms' financial health and restructuring, and where the government's ability to act decisively to support longer-term goals for the major firms was initially severely limited.

In the case of the private steel firms, there are two points to raise about providers' attitudes. In the early 1980s, the creditors of some of the small private-sector companies wanted them to pull out of steel making altogether. They were not willing (or just not financially able) to provide the kinds of financing needed to tide over the steel-making ventures of firms such as Johnson and Firth Brown. Second, the institutional investors in British Steel's equity took a very negative attitude—even in a recession—toward the firm's unwillingness, or even outright inability, to make dividend payments. This could pose a major obstacle to British Steel's ability to raise additional investment funds from the market in the near term.

For British Steel, whether nationalized or private, the costs of financing were clearly an important factor in the firm's restructuring process, but the attitudes of the providers of that financing—specifically, the presence or absence of a dominant stakeholder willing to support management and to see the firm through the enormous financial costs of restructuring—were the most crucial financial issue. However, the state isn't necessarily able to take on a dominant stakeholder role so easily—as seen in the next chapter, on French steel, and in chapter 5, on British Leyland, where firm-level financial structures were very different.

CHAPTER 3

The French Steel Industry

In 1977 all of the major French steel firms, both individually and collectively, faced bankruptcy. By 1992, the French steel sector was dominated by one firm, Usinor Sacilor, the largest steel manufacturer in Europe with twenty-three million tons of annual production, and the world's second largest after Nippon Steel of Japan (28.6 million tons annually). After three successive years in profit, however, Usinor Sacilor's balance sheet slipped into the red again in 1991, and provisional results for 1993 showed a FFr8.5 billion loss for the year, as domestic demand slumped. As in the previous case of British Steel, the role of the state in the initial turnaround was crucial, both in ensuring that the steel firms received enough cash to survive the initial crisis, and in getting them access to sufficient capital to begin to adapt over the longer term. As in Britain, the government sought to recapitalize the major firms, provided them with access to private capital sources with overt or covert state backing, and used some form of borrowing limits to enforce rationalization. In addition, the French government during the 1980s had, like its British counterpart, significant political capacity to intervene in the industry's affairs. Both faced weak opposition—fragmented parliamentary opponents in the British case, fragmented unions and industrial organization in the French case. And although the French Socialists were dependent on a coalition with the Communists and unions, the coalition was a weak one that the Socialists could dominate. This meant there was no opposition to the Socialist leadership's rationalization program (Smith 1989), just as there was no opposition to the British Conservatives. The political context was not irrelevant.

Behind these striking similarities, however, there are also some crucial differences between the two cases. The previous chapter described how, in the case of the British steel industry, BSC was the dominant producer by the late 1970s and firmly under government ownership. Through the 1980s, the Thatcher government (ostensibly one driven by a very promarket and anti-nationalization ideology) not only directly financed BSC but was also very closely involved in directing its restructuring and adaptation, essentially trying to play the role of a dominant stakeholder, supporting the firm's reorganization and controlling its sources of capital accordingly. In contrast, the French government found it extremely difficult, in its relationship with the steel sector, to take on the role of a dominant stakeholder. The reason has to do with financial issues at the level of the individual firms. By the late 1970s the firms' principle source of capital was in the form of debt, and many interests—public and private—were involved in those debts. Furthermore, the industry became polarized around two major producers, with conflicting and bitterly contested views on the future of the industry and its preferred production strategy. It was very difficult for the government to deal with this rivalry, in large part because of the form of financing that the steel firms had received up to the late 1970s.

Before turning in part 2 to the financing of the French steel industry, part 1 describes the postwar concentration of the industry, the restructuring of the 1970s and 1980s, and the political context of government relations with the steel industry.

1. Crisis and Concentration in the French Steel Industry

Where the tale of British steel in the twentieth century is one of relative competitive decline, that of the French industry is one of slow development punctuated by intense periods of expansion and reorganization. In 1949, the industry was composed of a myriad of medium- and small-sized firms, but production and investment levels had been collectively managed for many years. The various companies were linked in a web of financial holdings and presented a united front through the steel trade association, the Chambre Syndicale de la Sidérurgie Française (CSSF). The state, through its control of the newly nationalized deposit banks, allocated funds such as the Marshall Plan to industrial development projects. The steel industry was seen as pivotal to national reconstruction, and as the firms were unable to finance new investment themselves steel became the first industry to be closely involved in the national economic plans, accepting price and investment controls in return for access to cheap credit.

Concentration and Restructuring

The postwar period was marked by a series of mergers among the various steel companies. The first came in 1948 when Denain-Anzin merged with Forges et Aciéries du Nord et de l'Est, and nine Lorraine-based producers united into a financing cooperative called Sollac (la Société de Laminage Continu). In 1951 Sollac became Sidelor, joining with de Wendel in 1964 to form la Société des Aciéries de Lorraine and build a new plant at Gandrange. In 1966, Denain-Anzin and Forges et Aciéries du Nord et de l'Est absorbed Lorraine-Escaut, and in 1979 Chiers Chatillôn. Meanwhile, Sidelor and Wendel regrouped into Wendel-Sidelor in 1968, becoming Sacilor in 1973 and adding Marine-Firminy in 1975. Through this increased concentration of ownership, two companies dominated steel production in France by 1973. Usinor (L'Union Sidérurgique du Nord de la France) had most of its plants in Nord-Pas-de-Calais, around Valenciennes, and in the Lorraine, around Longwy, with Dunkerque as its modern coastal plant. Most of Sacilor's (Société des Aciéries et Laminoirs de Lorraine) plants were in the Moselle region of Lorraine, although it had followed Usinor in building a modern coastal site, at Fos (Ministère du Travail 1981; Gendarme 1985).

During the period of mergers, financial interconnections were formed horizontally between firms, so that concentration meant the creation of larger holding companies. According to Hayward (1986a), the prime motivation for these intricate financial interconnections was the preservation of family control. In addition, the biggest producers owned their own mineral and coke-mining operations in regions such as the Lorraine and although the more modern coastal plants imported their iron ore and coking coal, the older inland plants continued to use the Lorraine region as their source. There were also a number of special steel producers not allied with the big two. By 1978 most of these were themselves controlled by large holding companies. Thus Creusôt-Loire, the engineering subsidiary of the Empain-Schneider empire, had a special steel division.

Obsessed with proving their relative strength compared with the West Germans, and buoyed by a state that saw a thriving steel industry as crucial to postwar development, French producers had initiated a massive state-supported investment program in the late 1960s to increase their tonnage output. As with the late-1960s capacity investments in Britain, these came on-line just as the international steel crisis of overcapacity and falling demand hit in the mid-1970s (Lévy 1986). By 1977, the major French steel firms faced bankruptcy. The government assumed responsibility for most of the industry's medium- and long-term debts, replacing the financial holding companies as principal shareholder (part 2).

There had been capacity cuts and closures at various French steel firms throughout the 1960s and early 1970s but it was in 1977–78 that industrywide cuts were first implemented. The 1977 government-industry steel agreement (*plan d'acier*) included a number of closures and the loss of at least 16,000 steel jobs over a two-year period, in return for FFr1.3 billion (FFr1,300 million) in state-supported loans for the industry. The agreement marked a turning point in government-industry relations in French steel, entailing close government supervision in the hope of getting the major producers back to financial health by 1981 (Ministère de L'Industrie 1979). After the 1978 general election, the government announced further agreements with Usinor and Sacilor for massive cuts. The 1979 *plan d'acier* resulted in 22,000 job losses over a two-year period, including 12,000 from Usinor and 8,500 from

Sacilor. As in Britain, the effects of job losses were felt strongly in regions where the steel industry was entrenched in the local economy (see table 10).

Soon after coming to power, the new Socialist government embarked on a wide-ranging program of nationalization. The first manufacturing concern affected was the steel industry, specifically the two giants, Usinor and Sacilor. After a period of intense review of the industry the government announced yet another *plan d'acier* in June 1982, based on the Judet Report. The report had posited three hypotheses for the French steel industry in 1986. The government used the most optimistic one, rejecting the low scenario of 20 million tonnes production and the middle scenario of 21.8 million tonnes production. The highest scenario assumed highly productive investments, especially by the nationalized industries, vigorous exports, and the recapture of the domestic market (Hayward 1986a). Hence the 1982 plan was based around expansion from 19 million tonnes of crude production in 1981 to a planned 24 million tonnes by 1986. In addition, 12,000 jobs were to be shed, but contraction would be more gradual than in the late 1970s. The government hoped the commitment to expansion in the industry would diffuse worker resentment at the job losses. The unions called Industry Minister Mauroy a traitor when the plan was unveiled, but overall they hesitated to embarrass a left-wing government.

By the end of 1983, however, Mitterrand's austerity program was making itself felt. The severe squeeze on public spending forced the government to cut back the billions being consumed by the nationalized industries. The financial losses of the two large steel industries alone had climbed to ten billion francs a year in 1983 (Lévy 1986). In addition, the EC continued to order production cuts. France had been limited to a maximum steel output of 26.9 million tonnes in 1980, and by 1983 had been ordered to cut a total 5.3 million tonnes of capacity. So in the spring of 1984, yet another government plan for the steel industry was announced—the fourth in seven years—as part

TABLE 10.   Restructuring of French Steel, 1978–87

	Total Steel Employment	Regions		
		North	East	Center
1974	158,000	40,900	80,600	14,700
1978	131,000	32,000	56,300	12,000
1980	105,000	28,500	45,800	11,300
1983	90,600			
1987	57,600	21,300	23,900	8,600

Source: Data from Chambre Syndicale de la Sidérurgie Française, various annual reports.

of a larger plan involving the shipbuilding and coal industries. This plan was intended to restore the steel industry to profitability by 1987, a year later than the EC deadline for an industry independent of state aid, through more closures and cutting another 25,000 jobs. Production would be maintained at the 1984 level of 18.5 million tonnes. Investment in new plants was canceled, in favor of developing the two modern coastal sites at Dunkerque and Fos (*Financial Times*, April 18, 1984). The unions, the Communist Party, and the workers protested the planned cuts and the Confédération Générale du Travail (CGT) called for a Lorraine-wide steel strike (Howell 1988). Popular mobilization against the plan was fragmented and localized, however (Smith 1989).

1984 also marked the final stage in a larger process. Over the course of a decade, the geography of steel production in France altered radically. What started as the closure of the most out-of-date plants in the old steel regions ended as a total restructuring of the industry, based around modern, integrated sites on the coasts (see table 11). Not all French observers saw this as a positive change:

> Under the cover of financial rationality and modernization, an unprecedented geographic redeployment of an entire industrial sector is going on under our eyes. Never before has a unilateral techno-political decision by the State so dramatically affected the economy of an entire region. What has become of the laudable principle of the March 2nd 1982 law, making the region a privileged place of synthesis and dialogue? (Gendarme 1985, 102; my translation)

The 1984 plan also called for increased cooperation between Usinor and Sacilor, but stopped short of merging the two into one nationalized group like BSC. Joint operations were formed in engineering steels (Ascométal) and long products (Unimétal), with plant closures included in a rationalization plan.[1] Sacilor got majority stakes in both of the joint operations, as compensation for canceling investment in its Gandrange mill (*Financial Times*, April

TABLE 11.   Regional Steel Production
as Percentage of National Production
(thousands of tonnes)

	1974	1984
East	57.6	33.5
North	29.0	37.1
Other	13.4	29.4

Source: Data from Masson 1986; Gendarme 1985.

13, 1984). The creation of Ascométal and Unimétal removed a major source of the two groups' rivalry. The new Président-Directeur Général (PDG) of Usinor, M. Loubert, said "the director generals of Sacilor and Usinor, my friend Claude Dollé and myself, are convinced that the fight to return French steel to profit can only be fought and won in a spirit of cooperation in all areas . . . " (*L'Usine Nouvelle*, November 1, 1984; my translation). In November 1984 Dollé and Loubert wrote to the minister of industrial redeployment at the Ministry for Industry, proposing fusion (Hayward 1986b).

When the Center-Right government was elected in 1986 it, too, produced a report on the steel industry (the Gandois Report). Despite the apparent timing, this was not an original RPR-UDF plan, but rather the implementation of the Socialists' plan to merge the two into a single firm. Francis Mer was appointed joint managing director of Usinor and Sacilor. His brief was to oversee the merger and return the firm to profit, with a view to eventual privatization (Roume 1986). However, Usinor and Sacilor were not on the list of public enterprises earmarked for privatization by the 1986–88 government.

Further rationalization measures led to yet more factory closures and in the two years of Chirac's government some 20,000 steel jobs were cut. By early 1987 merger of the two had been completed, creating Europe's largest steelmaker and the world's second largest after Nippon Steel of Japan.

The Political Context

Both the government and the industry saw steel manufacturing as central to the post–Second World War economic planning efforts in France. Successive governments had a great deal of influence over the industry through the steel planning commission, pursuing their objectives by negotiation through the Ministries of Industry and Finance. Negotiation often involved a variety of carrots and sticks. One of the carrots was the corporate taxation system: "Traditional enterprises in mature industries enjoyed substantial and evident tax advantages" (Adams 1989, 97). Although the rate of taxation on income was set across all industries, the division of cash flow between income and expense varied enormously, primarily due to differences in the magnitude of depreciation allowed. Even after allowing for capital intensity, steel corporations were taxed relatively lightly (ibid.). The nationalized transportation and coking-coal industries were also a source of leverage, as the government could threaten to raise or promise to lower the cost of these for the steel companies.[2]

In addition, until 1986 the government enjoyed broad authority to regulate prices across the economy, with different degrees of control for different sectors. The steel sector was regulated especially assiduously as a stabilization measure, restraining the industry's investment enthusiasm in periods of boom and overcoming its pessimism in periods of recession (Adams 1989). Price controls affected the industry's ability to finance its investment with internal funds. As the government controlled access to many of the external funds too, governments had the opportunity to curb investments they did not favor. So, for example, steel prices were kept low in the mid-1960s, forcing the companies to seek financial credit—which was made contingent on the companies making the mergers desired by the government (Adams 1989).

On the other hand, the steel industry did not see itself as at the mercy of capricious state planners. The industry "pretentiously described itself as 'the profession,'" identifying its sectional interest with the general interest (Hayward 1986b, 503). Even in the face of mounting debts and a collapse in the European steel market in the late 1970s, the Barre government could not force the steel producers to modernize their plants or prevent them from abandoning restructuring investments for which they had already received state loans. The most famous example of this was Usinor's abandonment of investment in the steel plants it had already constructed at Thionville and Longwy. Unlike the British steel industry, the various French producers had a powerful and united trade association, the Chambre Syndicale de la Sidérurgie Française (CSSF). The association acted as an intermediary between the Ministry of Finance and the industry, helping to ensure financial flows and government favor. It engaged in economic forecasting and collective bargaining, and through the Groupement de l'Industrie Sidérurgique (GIS) floated bonds on the securities market and distributed the proceeds among its members for investment (part 2).

Finally, as in the United Kingdom, the investment decisions of the private steel firms were subject to considerable political pressure. For example, in 1978 Usinor decided to build an oxygen plant at Neuves-Maison rather than at Longwy. The affair turned into an intense bidding battle, involving trade unionists and local and national politicians. The Socialist and Communist opposition pressed for the building of both plants. The UDF mobilized in favor of Neuves-Maison (primarily due to the efforts of three senior members, who were deputies from the region) and had a decisive role in the final decision (Masson 1986).

From 1978, however, the state gradually took a more direct role in the industry's affairs, lessening the CSSF's position as intermediary. Nationalization was an even greater blow, giving the government the power to appoint and dismiss the Président-Directeur Générals (PDGs) of the nationalized enterprises, and to appoint two-thirds of the members of their *conseils d'administration* (boards). In the case of manufacturing industries such as steel, these powers rested with the Ministry of Industry (Delion and Durupty 1982). The final metamorphosis in government-industry relations came with the 1984 steel plan, worked out in secret by the Council of Ministers and containing for the first time a government-drawn blueprint for the structure and development of the industry. Mitterrand himself stepped in and canceled the proposed mill at Gandrange, illustrating the increasing role of prime ministerial and presidential decisions in the industry, at the expense of the CSSF's sponsor, the Ministry of Industry.

Against this background of increasing state dominance over the industry there were two further important aspects to the industry's political context—the rivalry between Usinor and Sacilor, and labor resistance to plant closures. The rivalry of the two main steel groups was partly geographic (Valenciennes and Dunkerque versus Moselle and Fos), partly financial as they competed for access to state-subsidized credit, and partly strategic. Usinor favored moving production facilities away from the old bases in the Lorraine and toward new, integrated coastal sites; Sacilor favored developing the existing inland sites. Nationalization increased the already fratricidal antagonisms between the two steel giants, as they competed for state aid. The reactions of labor to plant closures were of more immediate concern to successive governments. At each stage of retrenchment in the industry, both the Socialist and Center-Right governments were reluctant to authorize plant closures. It was not direct pressure from the unions as such that they feared. The unions were only superficially involved in the planning process, and had little control themselves over their fragmented memberships.[3] Rather, the governments feared the electoral repercussions in areas dominated by the steel industry. In 1967 the announcement of four hundred job losses in the Lorraine iron mines had triggered strikes and protests that paralyzed the entire region's steel industry within a week.

The 1977–78 cuts triggered violent resistance on the part of steelworkers in the steel towns of the Nord and the Lorraine. The most spectacular events occurred in Longwy in 1979, where the revolt against the closures was organized around *coups de poing* (punches) designed to rouse public opinion and to pressure the government into action. Small groups of militant workers organized in secret to block roads and rail lines, occupy local administration buildings, sabotage facilities, and even attack the local police stations. The workers succeeded in their aim to get mass-media attention with these dramatic and sudden actions, but interunion rivalry between the Communist Party-affiliated CGT and pro-Socialist CFDT undermined the movement against steel closures. In addition, the local CGT Metalworkers and the national organization in Paris differed over whether the protest should be kept focused on the steel industry, or expanded into a broader political movement against the government. The CFDT was also divided between the central leadership, who favored negotiated closures, and those organizing the protest, who were willing to support nontraditional actions outside the plants. In March 1979, tactical disagreements over a march on Paris destroyed the fragile unity between the CGT and CFDT metalworkers, making it easier for the Ministry of Industry to deal piecemeal with the steel unions and workers (Ross 1982; Eisenhammer 1986). Opposition to the closures was eventually effectively neutralized by substantial severance awards of FFr50,000 in cash from the government for workers who voluntarily left the industry. Immigrant workers were "assisted" in returning to their countries of origin, and various schemes encouraged early retirement.[4] The government justified its role in these schemes on the grounds that the industry couldn't cope with the inevitable consequences of job losses on its own (Ministère de l'Industrie 1979). The governments of the 1980s were also naturally anxious to avoid repetition of the events of 1977–78.

Usinor-Sacilor

In 1988, the merged Usinor-Sacilor reported net profits (of FFr4.5 billion) for the first time in fourteen years (*Financial Times*, April 26, 1989). "Même la sidérurgie est prospère et pousse ses avantages à l'étranger. Qui l'eût cru?" (Industry Minister Fauroux, *Le Monde*, June 6, 1989.) It then embarked on a number of production and merger agreements with other European steel producers, creating international linkages with Belgium's nationalized Cockerill Sambre, with the Italian-based Riva Group, and with Luxembourg's Arbed. The biggest venture was a controlling stake in the German steelmaker Saarstahl. Usinor-Sacilor took 70 percent of a new holding company that owned Saarstahl and Usinor's subsidiary in the Saarland, with the state of Saarland holding the remaining 30 percent. The acquisition was of enormous symbolic importance, as it involved the French steel industry's old arch-rival, the Germans.

Then came the new downturn in the European steel market and in 1991 Usinor, like British Steel, found itself once again in the red, with a net loss of FFr3.1 billion. In 1992, the net loss narrowed slightly, but widened sharply to FFr5.8 billion in 1993 (see table 12). The company blamed a combination of world economic difficulties, weak domestic demand, and a fall in prices that,

TABLE 12.   Usinor-Sacilor Net Operating
Profit/(Loss), 1988–93 (FFr million)

1988	4,600
1989	7,600
1990	3,500
1991	(3,100)
1992	(2,400)
1993	(5,800)

Source: Data from *Financial Times*, various issues.

it said, were worsened by "massive" cheap steel imports from eastern and central Europe (*Financial Times*, October 23, 1992). In addition, Saarstahl went under in May 1993, causing Usinor to take extraordinary costs of FFr2.2 billion relating to the failure. The company also began to complain that overcapacity in Europe was aggravated by other national governments (principally Italy and Spain) continuing to subsidize their loss-making companies, arguing that the EC "cannot ask us to lose money and restructure while it showers loss-making competitors with state aid" (*Economist*, November 21, 1992).

Nevertheless, the company's aggressive international strategy has continued into the 1990s, including the FFr3 billion takeover of Edgcomb, one of America's largest steel merchants; the purchase of American steel company J&L Specialty Products; the buildup of a 49 percent stake in Italy's Lutrix; the takeover of a German stockist Ancofer Feinstahl; the purchase of a big British steel distributor, ASD, in May 1991; and in April 1992, a production-sharing deal with Hoogovens of the Netherlands. In 1989–90 alone, Usinor-Sacilor spent $1.6 billion on acquisitions and minority stakes, most of it abroad (*Economist*, September 14, 1991). During the same period British Steel, in contrast, made very few foreign deals or purchases, and complained that its French rival could go on a shopping spree thanks to the deep pockets of the state.

This is the basic history of the French steel industry from the late 1970s to the present. The story is usually seen as a prime example of the *dirigiste* role of post-1945 French governments in industrial planning and of the country's intimate government-industry relations. State involvement in the industry was indeed extensive, with price controls, steel plans, and subsidized credit making for extremely blurred public/private-sector boundaries even before the crisis of the late 1970s. This description raises two major questions, however. Why were all the major French steel producers bankrupt by 1977–78, when the government had supposedly played such an active role in nurturing the industry for so many years? Why did it take a *dirigiste* and intimately involved state such a long time, to 1987 at least, to restructure the industry? The answers to these questions become clear once we look more closely at firm-level financial issues, and particularly at the large number of institutions that held steel industry debt in the postwar period.

2. The Financing of French Steel

After the Second World War, the French steel industry became heavily dependent on medium- and long-term debt for the majority of its financing. This debt burden necessitated a major financial and organizational restructuring in 1978, known as the Giraud Plan. After formal nationalization in 1981, the government used a variety of methods to channel funds to the industry. Meanwhile one firm, Creusôt-Loire, balked at closer state involvement in its restructuring, and went bankrupt. As in the previous case of BSC, notions of state versus private ownership are not adequate explanations of these events. Rather, the details of the various aspects of financing a major manufacturer during a period of crisis and restructuring illustrate the actual workings of the national financial system; and also some unexpected similarities with the British case. Once again, when we look to the firm's own financing and form of corporate governance, we find that while the availability and cost of financing played a major role in the restructuring process, the crucial factor was the attitudes of the providers.

Debt Financing Post-1949

After the Second World War, many French steel firms were joined in a web of financial cross-holdings, with collectively managed levels of production and investment, and a common voice in the form of the Chambre Syndicale. As already mentioned, the industry became closely involved in the postwar national economic plans, accepting price and investment controls from the state in return for access to cheap credit. The many firms defined their relationships with each other and with the state in financial terms. These relationships were conducted primarily through financial institutions such as the Trésor, the big state-owned lending banks such as Crédit Nationale, state-directed funds such as the Fonds de Développement Economique et Social (FDES, a state fund under the direction of the Trésor), and specialized loan institutions. Of these latter groups, the most important for the steel industry was the Groupement de l'Industrie Sidérurgique (GIS).

The GIS was a group-borrowing association set up by the CSSF and the steel firms. Since the equity market was relatively underdeveloped in France at this time, the steel firms' access to capital in the postwar period was limited to investment funds such as the FDES and to the private credit market, which the firms tapped primarily via the unique institution of the GIS. The GIS allowed the entire industry to borrow at the going rate by launching bond issues that would have more attractive terms than companies could secure on their own. According to one estimate (McArthur and Scott 1969), by the mid-1960s the GIS was the source of well over half of the industry's borrowing in the private-capital markets. The GIS accumulated a reserve with which it guaranteed particular loans, and could cover possible default in any particular case. Thus, firms that would have been hampered by their status as high credit risks were able to borrow at the going rate under the all-encompassing protective umbrella of the GIS. In addition, the GIS guaranteed steel firms a regular place on the financial calendar, ensuring bonds could be issued on the capital markets, access to which was tightly regulated by the Ministry of Finance.

The president of the CSSF was president of the GIS, while the GIS's staff and board of directors were drawn entirely from the leading steel companies and the staff of the CSSF. The GIS (and hence the CSSF and the major steel companies) reviewed both applications from individual companies and the investment program of the industry as a whole. In order to get a portion of the GIS borrowing, the individual company's plans had to be scrutinized and approved by the GIS. Then, the actual annual GIS borrowing had to be approved by the Ministry of Finance, while the individual companies' share of the borrowing had to be approved by the Steel Directorate in the Ministry of Industry. "This pyramiding of authorizations to borrow money opened the way for negotiations at each level. . . . In steel the financing of major investments was anything but a confidential affair between a company and its banker" (McArthur and Scott 1969, 200–201).

In practice, however, the CSSF's presentation of a united, orderly industry was a screen that kept the intergroup rivalries and firm weaknesses hidden (Gendarme 1985). Since financial issues were the basis of the government-industry relationship, as long as government was apparently effective in its goal of financing the industry, it had no reason to look beyond the representations made by the Chambre Syndicale. The two sides had unequal access to information, since the GIS and CSSF had detailed knowledge of the financial picture of individual firms and of the industry as a whole, whereas the government's information came primarily from the GIS and CSSF. In addition, the various government agencies were rarely united themselves as regards the details of policy. Even after nationalization in 1981, the committee of ministers and advisors set up to coordinate planning and investment decisions for the two was stymied by industry rivalries, and by clashes between the Ministry of Finance and the Ministry of Industry over spending levels (Hayward 1986b).

The 1978 Giraud Plan

> Any industry that suffers from heavy debt and structural crisis is bound to be susceptible to government pressure. (Lévy 1986, 64, PDG of Usinor, November 1981 to June 1984)

Until the late 1970s, the CSSF continued to act as intermediary between the Ministry of Finance and the steel firms, presenting itself as the representative of a united industry, able to juggle the individual firms' demands and investments, and to play the various government agencies off against each other, while keeping the intergroup rivalries and firm weaknesses hidden. When the industry began to collapse under its burden of debts in the mid-1970s, these divisions and rivalries came to the surface. By 1977, the government was faced with a steel industry that was bankrupt, fragmented, and more concerned with blaming each others' contrasting investment plans than with tackling the long-term problems of the industry as a whole.

In 1977, the Barre government took a more active role in controlling the finances of the largest steel groups. De Wendel and Usinor had to hand over part of their shareholdings to the state funding institution, the Caisse des Dépôts, as a guarantee that they would fulfill certain restructuring promises made to the government (this was the 1977 Steel Plan). But the crisis accelerated so rapidly that these moves did little more than allow the government to survive the 1977–78 election period (Hayward 1986a). By mid-1978, the industry's debts had risen to 115 percent of sales (see table 13), and financial and structural reform were imperative if the steel giants were to survive. The government at that time was ideologically opposed to the solution of nationalization, but had already become implicitly involved in guaranteeing the companies' financings, since so much of their debts came ultimately from the FDES and the state banks. So under the Giraud Plan of September 1978 the government assumed responsibility for a large proportion of the medium- and long-term debt of the industry, effectively replacing the old financial holding companies as principal shareholder. The plan involved some complex redistributions of the companies' debts, the government being anxious to avoid the appearance of de facto nationalization as much as possible.

The 1978 financial restructuring did not cover a number of smaller companies or the specialty-steels sector. Five major steel entities were involved: Usinor; Sacilor; Sollac (a subsidiary of Sacilor); Solmer, controlled 95 percent jointly by Sacilor and Usinor; and Chatillôn-Neuves-Maisons, wholly owned by the industrial conglomerate Chiers-Chatillôn. These five together produced some 75 percent of French steel and accounted for about 60 percent of sales.

TABLE 13.   French Steel: Medium- and Long-term Debts, and Net Losses

	1975	1976	1977
Debts			
Million FFrs	28,300	33,900	38,000
As % of sales	100	104	111
Net losses			
Million FFrs	3,700	4,000	6,100

Source: Data from Ministère du Travail 1981.

There were two aspects to the 1978 plan; a restructuring of the firms' debts, and a reconstruction of their equity to create two major steel firms. The financial measures were concerned with redistributing the firms' outstanding loans. These broke down into three distinct categories—outstanding loans made by the FDES and by the state-owned bank Crédit Nationale; outstanding credits extended to the firms by private French banks; and other private debts, including those amassed via the GIS (see table 14).

First, the FFr9 billion that the steel groups owed to the FDES and the FFr1.2 billion owed to Crédit Nationale, were transformed into "special participatory loans," with repayment dates deferred to 1983 and an extremely low interest rate of 0.1 percent. These loans would be reviewed in 1984, "depending on the groups' situation at that time" (Masson 1986). Next, the government negotiated a series of measures with the private banks, which it called their participation in the cleanup operation for French steel. Of the FFr9.4 billion in credit extended to the steel groups by the banks, FFr600 million was converted into equity. In this way the banks subscribed to the capital in the new financial holding societies set up by the government. The banks also had to forgo the interest owed on the nonconverted part of their claims (some FFr400 million at FFr80 million annually to 1983). Finally, the banks were instructed to keep the credit lines to the steel groups open, as revolving credits that would not be called in.

The third group of debts involved FFr11.9 billion owed via the GIS and four other special loan groups.[5] Most of these debts were converted into special loans, with the same characteristics as the FDES loans. A new financing

TABLE 14.   The 1978 Giraud Plan: Financial Restructuring

Loans from the State = FFr 10.2 billion debt	
FDES: FFr 9 billion:	Converted to special participatory loans at
Crédit Nationale: FFr 1.2 billion:	0.1% annual interest
Credit from Private Banks = FFr 9.4 billion debt	
FFr 600 million:	Converted to equity held by banks
Interest charges:	Waived
Credit Lines:	Maintained as revolving credits
Other private sector debts = FFr 17.9 billion	
GIS: FFr 11.2 billion:	Converted to special participatory loans at
Other Special Loan Groups: FFr 700 million:	0.1% annual interest
Direct Bond Issues:	Status unchanged: Remain responsibility
Overseas Borrowings:	of the steel companies

Source: Adapted from Masson 1986.

institution was created, the Caisse d'Amortissement pour l'Aciér (CAPA), managed by the Caisse des Dépôts et Consignations. CAPA paid off the debts owed to small investors by these intermediary loan groups. As the Senate's finance committee noted, the government had rejected nationalization, but CAPA was in effect the first step in that direction (Masson 1986). CAPA also took over the payment of interest on the loan groups' 0.1 percent loans (NEDC 1981). The steel firms' other liabilities included direct bond issues and borrowings from abroad, which the firms agreed to honor directly, given the extent to which their financial charges had now been alleviated.

The other side of the Giraud Plan involved the reconstruction of the steel groups' equity. The value of their shares was written down, reducing Usinor's capital from nearly FFr1.5 billion to FFr476 million, and Sacilor's from FFr432 million to FFr216 million. Two new holding companies were created. La Société financière Usinor-Chatillôn controlled the merged group Usinor-Chatillôn-Neuves-Maison, and La Société financière Sacilor controlled Sacilor. These new financial holding companies controlled the steel-industry groups by both direct participation in their capital, and indirect participation through a number of intermediary holding companies that represented the old shareholders in these firms. The capitalization of the two new holding companies thus represented the interests of the old creditors, to the detriment of the old shareholders (see table 15).[6] These measures also entailed the establishment of new boards of directors at the two steel groups, and the naming of new managers (Claude Etchegaray at Usinor and Jacques Mayoux at Sacilor).

These measures were nationalization in all but name. The state did not directly take over the firms' debts to the public and private banks, but ensured that these creditors were given a significant stake in the new financial holding companies. The state did, however, take over responsibility for the firms' debts to private investors, and the loans from FDES and other state funds were rendered so soft that they were practically shares with the dividends waived

TABLE 15.   The 1978 Giraud Plan:
Holding Company Capitalization

Caisse des Dépôts et Consignations:	FFr 600 million
Creditor Banks:	FFr 600 million
FDES:	FFr 300 million
GIS:	FFr 300 million
Crédit Nationale:	FFr 200 million
Total:	2 billion
Usinor's holding company =	FFr 1.28 billion
Sacilor's holding company =	FFr 720 million

Source: Adapted from Masson 1986.

for the foreseeable future. The Ministry for Industry argued that these convoluted financial interventions were a one-off governmental intervention in a *"secteur en mutation"* that, in the face of market loss to new producers, needed assistance for strategic adaptation. Since the sector could not adapt alone, it must necessarily call upon public aid; the economy's development and ultimately the well-being of the general population was at stake (Ministère de l'Industrie 1979).[7] The "virtual conversion of loan into share capital"—very similar to the debt-to-equity conversion that subsequently took place at BSC—saved Usinor some FFr865 million on its profit/loss account in 1978 and reduced Sacilor's 1978 net loss by FFr1.3 billion (NEDC 1981, 22). In contrast with BSC, however, the French steel groups' debts were widely held. Although most of the loans and financing, both in 1978 and in subsequent years, were ultimately state subsidized and administered, they were mediated through many institutions, public and private. No one creditor, not even the state itself, acted as the primary source of capital or as dominant stakeholder.

Despite the Giraud Plan, the steel groups' financial problems had not been solved in the long-term. Their debts continued to rise. In 1979, a series of financial protocols between the principal creditors, the government, and the steel groups, reconstituted the groups' working capital yet again, to try to alleviate the worsening financial charges and to enable the steel companies to meet their commitments to those few creditors not covered by CAPA. Meanwhile, CAPA's outlays increased more rapidly than initially envisaged and by 1980 its own debts to the state totaled FFr3.3 billion. See table 16 for a listing of Usinor's debts.

During the 1981 financial year, a total of FFr4.8 billion in long-term, low-interest FDES loans was released to the two groups. The loans came in installments, beginning in March and continuing through the May and June election periods, until September.[8] Although funding from the FDES was in theory meant to finance new investments, the 1981 steel loans were an attempt to support the steel groups' accounts, so that they could continue to meet their

TABLE 16.   Usinor's Debts at Year-End (FFr million)

	Convertible Bonds	Long-Term Bonds	Collective Loans[a]	Other	Total Long-Term Debt
1979	547	385	47	5,603	6,582
1980		1,103	34	5,596	6,733
1982		1,513	454	6,068	8,036

Source: From *Moody's International*, various issues.
[a]Usinor's share of the industry's long-term collective loans.

financial commitments. In addition, the government, the steel companies, and the creditors agreed in May 1981 that whatever the outcome of the presidential election, a new rescue plan for the industry would have to be drafted before year's end. In the event, a Socialist president and Assembly nationalized the two steel groups in November 1981.

Financing the Nationalized Firms

By 1986, nationalization appeared to have been more a means than an end in itself. . . . For the Socialists the ultimate goal of nationalization seems to be to make firms compete in an international market economy. (Machin 1988, 208)

When you are facing a crisis, there are only three solutions. . . . The American solution is typically capitalist: the owner pays. The Japanese system is typically Japanese: the customer pays. And the European is typically European: the state pays. We are now trying to reach something between the American solution and the Japanese solution. (Francis Mer, chairman of Usinor Sacilor, *Financial Times*, April 26, 1989)

The formal nationalization of Usinor and Sacilor changed little in their relationship with the state. The finance law of November 27, 1981, was amended to authorize the state to convert the loans previously agreed to by the FDES into shares (FFr7.02 billion for Usinor and FFr6.78 billion for Sacilor). Turning the state-as-lender into the state-as-shareholder in this manner didn't cost the government anything, as no compensation was involved. A small number of private investors continued to hold stakes in the companies as minority shareholders. (At the end of 1981, the government held 74 percent of Usinor's shares directly and a further 16 percent indirectly, the remaining 10 percent being privately held.)

Nationalization of the steel firms predated the rest of the Socialists' nationalization program, and was quite distinct in that all parties agreed that state ownership was both necessary and inevitable. The Assembly debates on the proposals dealt with the technical and industrial aspects involved and some right-wing politicians even argued that the 1981 law didn't go far enough: "Your project, Mr. Industry Minister, doesn't respond at all to the steel industry's big problems. The industry has need above all of an industrial plan of modernization and investment. You are only proposing a mini financial plan" (Deputé Masson, RPR; quoted in Masson 1986, 76; my translation). The lack of opposition to nationalization marked a significant turnaround. In 1977, senior officials at the Ministries of Finance, Industry, and

Labor had produced a report that argued against partial or total nationalization: "It hardly seems worthwhile for the State to own firms whose financial situation is so bad and whose balance sheet is negative" (Hayward 1986b).

The November 1981 nationalization was based heavily on a Socialist proposal made to the Assembly in December 1980.[9] This had also been a purely financial and juridical proposal, envisaging the creation of a new state holding company that would take over the shares of Usinor, Sacilor, Creusôt-Loire and Ugine-Acier, and all their subsidiaries. The only differences between this proposal and the final government solution a year later were that Creusôt-Loire was left out of the nationalization law, and the unitary state holding company was not created.

The final aspect of the nationalization was a FFr5 billion block grant. The only organizational change involved the two managing directors. R. Lévy, a polytechnicien and former vice-president of Elf-Acquitaine was named head of Usinor, and C. Dollé, a private-sector businessman and long-time Socialist Party supporter, was named head of Sacilor. Both men had previously been involved in steel industry management.

Although state ownership was now formalized, it took the government a long time to tackle the industry's problems. In all of the new government's documents and reports on nationalization and planning, there was a heavy emphasis on financial issues: the financial system was to be more closely linked with the practice of planning; financing would be a special instrument in the realization of industrial plans; decentralization would involve the promotion of new financial instruments. Over and over, the concern was to find ways of getting low-cost financing to both public and private industries. There seems to have been an underlying assumption that if the government could just ensure that industries had access to enough of the right kinds of money, industrial restructuring and a national industrial renaissance would inevitably follow. This emphasis on the firms' financial health was perhaps more than a little influenced, in the case of the steel industry, by the need to sort out the complex tangle of debts involved, and by the large numbers of people and institutions with financial interests at stake. The more basic issue of restructuring the industry, and solving the intense rivalries between Usinor and Sacilor over how the industry should be restructured, was never really tackled.

In contrast with the Thatcher governments in Britain, the new Socialist government put a great deal of emphasis on industrial policy. Where the British Conservatives spoke in terms of "letting managers manage" and "getting the state out of industry," the French Socialists spoke overtly of restructuring and refinancing the big manufacturers, and using the nationalized industries to promote investment and job creation. By 1983, the notion of job creation had been quietly dropped from ministerial speeches, replaced with an emphasis on making industries competitive again. The most important development in this last regard was the development of *contrats*, a contractual relationship between the state and the nationalized enterprises, including steel.

Minister for Industry Laurent Fabius's policy was that the nationalized enterprises were strictly equal with private-sector enterprises. The contract plans outlined management criteria such as productivity, competitiveness, and profitability. The multiyear contracts guaranteed agreed levels of state investment funding, on the condition that the enterprises meet set target figures for profits or for loss reductions (Commission de Reforme de la Planification 1982). State managers supposedly had complete autonomy within the terms of the *contrats de plan*.[10] Sacilor and Usinor signed their contracts with the Ministry of Research and Industry in February 1983. The agreements were primarily aimed at reducing the two groups' financial charges to 5 percent of sales by 1986. In return, the government promised to contribute FFr3.5 billion in shares and other financial aid to Sacilor (Ministère de l'Industrie et de la Recherche 1983, Février 23, Contrat de Plan, Sacilor). The state's financial contribution to Usinor was FFr3.65 billion, FFr300 million in *prêts participatifs* (participatory loans) (Ministère de l'Industrie et de la Recherche 1983, Février 16, Contrat de Plan, Usinor).[11]

The contracts involved more negotiation than did the British EFLs. On the other hand, BSC's management was freer to make decisions within the financial constraints, whereas managers at Usinor and Sacilor had to make some fairly detailed commitments about research and development spending levels, investment programs, and reorganization. Despite these differences, the two governments were doing essentially the same thing—managing the affairs of industries in trouble primarily by setting borrowing limits on the funds made available, either directly from the state or through its intermediaries.

Meanwhile, as in the United Kingdom, there were still a number of small, independent steel producers, struggling to survive the retrenchment of the early 1980s. Unlike in the United Kingdom, however, the government in France had no qualms about using the state-owned companies to bail out the private sector. After nationalization, the French steel firms simply bought out private companies in trouble. Until the end of the decade, the Socialist administration continued to be overt in justifying financing for the nationalized industries in terms of the national economy. Industry Minister Fauroux told *Le Monde* (June 6, 1989) that "il serait désastreux pour la France de laisser les grandes entreprises nationales, qui portent une grande partie de l'avenir industriel français, se marginaliser faute de capitaux propres."[12]

Despite the injection of new capital endowments after nationalization, the financial problems of Usinor and Sacilor continued unabated. The Socialist government had planned to spend some FFr26 billion to eradicate the steel groups' losses by 1986, but their accumulated losses rose, even with the price and production controls imposed by the EC, and the two steel groups quickly absorbed over a third of the new cash set aside for all of the nationalized industries in 1982. Finding alternative forms of financing became crucial—the nationalized industries needed access to the private capital markets. Where the British opted for privatization, the French created new mixtures of public/private finance. The government established yet another financial agency, the Fonds d'Intervention Sidérurgique (FIS), to raise funds toward the FFr8–9 billion that Usinor and Sacilor each needed to invest for restructuring and recovery (see table 17). The FIS's role was to ease the financial burden on the Treasury by borrowing on the domestic market and making loans to Usinor and Sacilor. The two steel groups issued convertible bonds to the FIS in exchange for the loans, which the government subsidized by keeping interest payments below 4.6 percent.

The other problem in financing the state-owned steel companies came from the EC, which had decreed that all state subsidies to steel firms should cease by the end of 1985. In December 1984, the Socialist government wrote off Usinor and Sacilor's accumulated debts. In 1985 the EC approved new injections of state aid, spread out over 1985, 1986, and 1987. As the final stages of merging and restructuring Usinor and Sacilor had only just got under way, however, they still needed massive injections of capital, most of which would have to come from the state and not all of which would be going to strictly restructuring purposes, either. So in late 1985, Usinor and Sacilor began issuing convertible bonds, with subscription reserved for the state or the public sector. This was widely reported in France as a means of raising capital that would circumvent the EC's requirement to end subsidies.

Meanwhile, the new Center-Right government under Prime Minister Chirac was faced with enormous losses at Usinor and Sacilor. The government that had campaigned on a platform of privatization and ending the state's

TABLE 17.   Usinor and Sacilor: Net Operating Losses and Long-Term Debt

	1982	1983	1984	1985	1986	1987
Net Losses (FFr million)						
Usinor	4,990	5,460	7,400	3,490		
Sacilor	3,740	5,610	8,140	5,260		
U/S Combined Long-Term						
Debt (FFr million)					12,500	5,600
Usinor	8,040	13,180	15,700	17,690		
Sacilor	8,610	10,130	10,170	7,600		
U/S Combined					34,000	30,000

Source: Data from Reichert and Sedar 1987; *Financial Times*, various issues.

involvement in financing industry took two quite remarkable steps. Usinor and Sacilor still had between them some 50,000 private shareholders. Late in 1985 M. Mer, the new managing director of the two steel groups, wrote these shares down to zero, rather than waste more money buying out the private shareholders (*Economist*, December 6, 1986), a step usually taken only in a case of outright bankruptcy. In addition, shortly after the 1985 National Assembly elections, with Usinor's cumulative losses at FFr21 billion, the new government simply wrote off the government's shareholdings in the group. Chirac had admitted that all those previous equity injections were outright grants.

The financing of the nationalized steel firm has now taken a new twist. Early in 1991, President Mitterrand relaxed his policy of neither nationalization nor privatization ("ni . . . ni . . . "), with a decree allowing domestic or foreign private groups to take minority stakes of up to 49.9 percent in state companies, on certain conditions.[13] Usinor Sacilor, with around 12 percent private share ownership at that point, welcomed the decree as opening the way for it to find financial partners and to improve its image with the European Commission's competition directorate (*Financial Times*, April 11, 1991). It also hoped for a way to reduce its FFr28.9 billion net debt, built up in large part to fund its international acquisitions. By 1990, Usinor's net debt equaled its equity, as valued by the state, a ratio that was high in comparison with its European competitors (*Economist*, September 14, 1991). Yet the chairman made no moves to sell any of the company's shares to private investors. Instead, Usinor announced in July 1991 that it would sell 10 percent of its shares to the state-owned bank Crédit Lyonnais, for FFr2.5 billion, in December. This more than offset the FFr1.7 billion of dividends that Usinor had paid to the government in the previous two years. After paying for the Usinor shares, Crédit Lyonnais then launched a rights issue— to which the government subscribed by giving the bank an extra 10 percent of Usinor's shares. Crédit Lyonnais has been state-owned since 1945, but by 1991 the state held only 50.9 percent of its equity directly. The bank is listed on the bourse, with a further 30 percent of its shares held by other state-owned companies.

Francis Mer claimed Usinor sold its shares to the bank simply because Crédit Lyonnais is one of the firm's two principal bankers. The bank claimed that it was acting like a German bank, taking a substantial stake in the company in order to help develop a relationship that is profitable in the long term. However, even before the 1993 return to power of a Center-Right government in France, the burgeoning state budget deficit and the gradual injection of more private capital into the state-owned industries suggested that privatization would eventually be in the cards for Usinor. In May 1993, the new RPR-UDF government under Prime Minister Edouard Balladur released a list of twenty-one state-owned financial institutions and industrial concerns that it intends, eventually, to privatize. Usinor is on the list. Francis Mer is said to support privatization, once the steel market picks up again. The Crédit Lyonnais purchase may be a way to access as much state capital as possible, without violating EC aid rules, while the firm is still owned by a supportive deep pocket. The deal had to be approved by the European Commission under its rules governing state aid to industry. The Commission decided that Crédit Lyonnais had, indeed, acted as a private investor might have done if the firm had been a publicly quoted company, and that it had taken the decision independently of the French government.

It is interesting to note the comparisons between these recent developments and the history of financing the French steel industry over the longer term. Are we again seeing the steel industry, now represented almost solely by the giant Usinor, turning to long-term loans to finance its expansion plans, and with a growing number of stakeholders providing debt and equity financing to the firm?

The Case of Creusôt-Loire

An interesting counterexample to the gradual state takeover at Usinor and Sacilor is the case of Creusôt-Loire. Although the 1981 nationalization affected only the two biggest steel groups, by early 1985 95 percent of the industry was nationalized. The industrial and financial groups that were nationalized in 1982 had included a number of specialty-steel subsidiaries, such as those of the PUK and Saint-Gobain-Pont-à-Mousson groups. (PUK had already arranged to give up its steel activities to Sacilor, before the 1981 elections [Cheval 1987].) The special-steels sector, which had mostly been left out of the nationalization and 1982 *plan d'acier*, was also in financial difficulty. Most of these firms agreed either to be taken over outright by one of the two state-owned giants, or to sell their steel subsidiaries to them. The case of Creusôt-Loire is a prime example. Others included S.A. Imphy, la Société des Forges de Gueugnon, and la Société Metallurgique de Normandie. The terms of these takeovers varied according to the circumstances, but often involved complex financial and juridical structures (Masson 1986). Public resources were thus used to remove the threat of bankruptcy from the steel groups, exactly as in the British Phoenix cases. The difference was that in France there were no ideological or political problems with doing this via outright nationalization.

The initial rescue of Creusôt-Loire was quite straightforward. In 1981, the private sector engineering conglomerate Creusôt-Loire got into financial difficulties, mainly because of its loss-making steel activities. Creusôt-Loire was a major special-steels producer, and the biggest steelmaker not included in the various public steel interventions of 1978. A rescue package negotiated with the banks wasn't able to solve the root problems and by 1983, with losses approaching FFr2 billion, it was clear that a more radical rescue plan was needed to save the company from bankruptcy (see table 18).

This time the state, shareholders, and banks were involved in a FFr6 billion financial restructuring of the group that included transferring its steel activities to Usinor and Sacilor. In 1981, Usinor had already taken over 75 percent of the capital in one of Creusôt's umbrella steel companies. Creusôt-Loire now sold most of its steel activities to the two nationalized steel companies, for some FFr1.2 billion (*Financial Times*, October 8, 1983). Seven thousand employees also were transferred to the public sector. The chairman was reported to be eager to hive off Creusôt's remaining steel assets to the state, too. In addition, Creusôt sold part of its stake in the nuclear plant construction company, Framatome, to the state Atomic Energy Agency. The banks provided FFr2 billion in financing and there was also a share capital increase and a convertible bond issue.

In May 1984 the chairman of Creusôt-Loire said the group would need a further FFr2.3 billion cash injection to stave off bankruptcy, but the government would not approve this move unless additional equity funds were provided by the parent group, Schneider. Schneider refused. The creditor banks (BNP, Crédit Lyonnais, and Société Générale—all state owned) offered to reschedule the outstanding Creusôt-Loire debt in return for a stake in one of the financial holding companies of the Schneider group. The chairman again refused, arguing that this amounted to an attempt to nationalize the group. In December 1984, Creusôt-Loire was placed into official receivership, the largest bankruptcy in French industrial history.

The collapse of Creusôt-Loire "sparked off one of the most vitriolic and public battles between the state and the chairman of a private sector group ever witnessed in France" (Green 1986, 99). The battle between the chairman and the government illustrated that there were definite limits to the terms on which the government was prepared to bail out a private-sector company, and

TABLE 18.   Creusôt-Loire Year-End (FFr million)

	Net Profit/(Loss)	Long-Term Debt
1979	(254)	2,208
1980	(106)	2,090
1981	12	2,501
1982	(578)	
1983	(1,807)	3,532

Source: Data adapted from *Moody's International*, various issues.

limits to the concessions that could be extracted in return. The problem was exacerbated by the timing of the 1984 crisis, for under the politics of austerity the Socialist government could not afford any "backdoor nationalizations," either politically or economically.

Creusôt-Loire could perhaps have been saved but, given the massive financial problems and amount of financing needed, only with more involvement by the state and state-owned banks. Creusôt-Loire agreed to off-load its steel-making activities in 1981–83, but strongly resisted giving the public sector an equity stake in the firm, as this would have given the provider of financing closer involvement in the firm's affairs. Sheerness Steel left the British Independent Steel Producers Association, protesting that the closer involvement with the state was too high a price to pay for being bailed out. Creusôt-Loire went bankrupt rather than pay the price.

3. The Blurred Public-Private Boundary

From the entire prenationalization period of price controls and subsidized credit, to the state sponsored restructuring of 1978, and on to the financing of the nationalized Usinor-Sacilor, the blurring of the boundary between the public and private sectors is far more obvious in this case than in each of the other three analyzed here. It is clear that the boundaries of government-industry relations were not determined by notions of state versus private ownership. It is also clear that the French state was overtly and intimately involved in financing the survival and adaptation of practically an entire industrial sector. This blurring of the public-private boundary, along with an active state industrial policy, is usually seen as a defining characteristic of French political economy, and in marked contrast with Britain. The government involvement also extended to other aspects of industrial affairs. For example, a regional-aid component was added to each of the steel plans from 1978 to 1984, designed to soften the impact of steel plant closures in the north and east. The FFr3 billion Special Industrial Adjustment Fund (FSAI) provided loans and subsidies to firms wishing to establish themselves in the designated areas. Most of the aid in fact went to Peugeot and Renault, for projects in Nord-Pas-de-Calais and Lorraine (Ministère de l'Industrie 1979; see chap. 4). This ostensibly "environmental" policy involved the state very closely in the affairs and investment decisions of both the restructuring steel firms and those being encouraged to invest in the conversion areas (Gendarme 1985). Yet, as the previous chapter showed, the same characteristics of a blurred public-private boundary and active state involvement also applied in the case of the British government's involvement in the restructuring of BSC. There were, indeed, marked differences between the two cases—and the case of PSA in the next chapter shows still more variations—but these differences were the result of firm-level financial structures.

In the 1990s, however, the rules of the game in France have changed considerably. The reforms and deregulation of the French financial system described in chapter 1 amounted to a systematic withdrawal of the state from close regulation and direction of the credit markets during the 1980s. If privatized, Usinor Sacilor would not have to depend upon a latter-day version of the GIS to access a tightly controlled bond market, and the prices of both its raw materials and its products would not be determined, after lengthy negotiations, by the Ministry for Industry. However, as shown by the case of BSC, even a pro–free market government is liable to get intimately involved in the financing of major manufacturers during an economic downturn. The French state has withdrawn from overt control over the credit markets, and is no longer as intimately and overtly entwined in every aspect of the national financial system. The methods and markets used to finance a major manufacturer are now quite different. Yet the public-private boundary is still indistinct—witness the cross-shareholdings being built up between publicly-owned industrial and finance companies, and the sizable private equity holdings being built up in some of the state-owned companies. If the Center-Right government manages to make more progress with privatization than its predecessor did in 1986–88, what will happen to this growing network of ownership stakes? If history is any guide, it is likely to be transferred into the private sector, giving firms such as Usinor access to a combination of public and private sources of financing, and giving a large number of stakeholders an interest in the firm.

4. Assessment

French Steel and the National Financial System

The story of the French steel industry illustrates the extent to which the postwar state subsidized and administered the credit market, as well as the limitations on the abilities of this *dirigiste* state. It also shows how that system has changed, with the state's withdrawal from the financial system, and the increasing reliance of major manufacturers on equity financing. The story also illustrates the very French use of financial holding companies, and their propensity to mix public and private investment capital.

During the period of postwar concentration, the smaller French steel firms joined together under the umbrella of holding companies that were primarily vehicles for financing the firms. The restructuring of the 1978 Giraud Plan continued the pattern, giving the holders of the near-bankrupt firms' debts a stake in the new holding companies. The linkup between Crédit Lyonnais and Usinor Sacilor may be part of a similar pattern, the development of cross-shareholdings between firms wholly or partially owned by the state. In each case—holding company or cross-shareholding—the risks involved are spread out across a number of interests, and, hence, so are the stakes. Unlike BSC in 1981–88, Usinor can no longer be said to have a clearly identifiable dominant stakeholder in the form of the government. True, it is still almost wholly owned by the state, and its new 20 percent owner is in turn a state-owned company, but the link has been weakened.

The propensity to mix public and private investment capital is also a distinctive feature of the French financial system that marks it off from the British. While the British Treasury looks askance at such things, the French Trésor is quite happy to encourage the development of new financing instruments that lead to public-private hybrids. As the equity market develops in France, it is apparent that this encouragement also extends to new forms of shareholding.

Finally, we can see that the liberalization of the French financial system, and the development of new markets over the course of the last decade, have enormous implications for a major, capital-intensive firm such as Usinor. It may now be able to weather cyclical downturns without falling into the debt-trap that ensnared the steel firms in the late 1970s. It has more options, more sources of financing, both domestic and international.

Similarities between France and Britain

The previous chapter outlined four aspects of the British Steel case that also show up in that of French steel. To reiterate, these are: the conversion of debt into equity prompted by the initial crisis (in Britain through the use of New Capital, in France with the complex financial restructuring of the Giraud Plan); the use of the major state-owned firm to bail out smaller, private producers (privatization via the Phoenix schemes in Britain, straight nationalization in France); the imposition by the state of borrowing limits to try to enforce rationalization of the dominant firm (EFLs in one case, contracts in the other); and finally, by the late 1980s, the search for alternatives to direct state financing of the industry that led to privatization in Britain and new forms of financing in France. Again, these similarities are striking precisely because so many other aspects of the two cases, particularly the national financial systems involved, are so different.

Firm-Level Financial Issues

This brings us, finally, to the firm-level financial issues involved in this case. The availability of financing was clearly a major issue for the pre-1979 steel firms. The financial system was oriented around the state-administered and often state-subsidized credit market. The equity market was not well developed. In a very real sense, the firms had no choice but to finance their operations, both short- and long-term, with debt. The consequences, as we saw, were crippling debt-servicing burdens during a time of crisis in the late 1970s, and multiple stakeholders that were an obstacle in the subsequent period of restructuring. The cost of the firms' debt financing was clearly also a major issue. Even when much of the debt was directly or indirectly subsidized by the state, it became impossible to maintain it in a time of crisis. As in the previous case of BSC, although debt may be a preferable form of financing in good times, servicing it is problematic for a highly cyclical capital-intensive industry once the cycle turns downward again.

The attitudes of the providers of financing to the French steel industry from the late 1970s to the present are less obvious but no less crucial. The various state, parastatal, and private providers of the firms' debts seem to have been willing to finance the firms over the long haul, even as the industry as a whole spiraled down into crisis. They were probably reassured by the role of the state in approving and administering most of the firms' credits, and there is evidence that the role of the CSSF and GIS in channeling investment to the firms may have disguised the extent of their financial difficulties until it was too late. (Private investors in the car firm British Leyland also seem to have been similarly reassured by the role of the state in providing the bulk of BL's financing. See chap.5.)

Of more significance is the fact that there were multiple interests involved in financing the French steel firms. Even after formal nationalization in 1981, the complexity of the firms' debts and the number of institutions and interests represented on their holding companies meant that the government did not begin to act like a dominant stakeholder until the 1984 Steel Plan. Only then did it start to make long-term, strategic decisions for the industry, and play a more active, hands-on role in directing the two firms' restructuring strategies. In addition, as in the case of BSC, the state was ultimately the only actor willing and able to bail out the industry when it was in crisis, and to finance it over the long term. However, with the development of new forms of financing since the mid-1980s, and with the equity in the firm now held by an additional (although still state-owned) institution, the role of the state, and its ability to act as dominant stakeholder, may be diluted once again.

For the French steel industry, as for BSC, the cost of financing clearly had a crucial impact on the firms during a period of crisis and restructuring. The burden of servicing their debts ultimately forced the large and small companies to the brink of bankruptcy when the industry began to founder in the mid-1970s. Equally important is the fact that debt financing was really the only available option for the industry in the postwar era, as the equity market was still small and illiquid, and the state relied almost entirely on the credit markets to channel investment funds to the industry. However, it was not just the fact of their debts and lack of alternate options that had such a major impact on the firms when the crisis came, but rather the lack of a dominant stakeholder willing to support the firms through the enormous financial costs of restructuring. The state did eventually play this role, but not until some years after formal nationalization, thanks to the complexity of the old debt-issuing holding company structures. And, since the late 1980s, that role is again being diminished as the state tries to find other sources of financing for the nationalized industries.

The next case, however, illustrates that a private-sector firm in postwar France could survive the restructuring turmoil of the 1980s without national-ization, and without overreliance on the credit markets. Unlike the steel firms of the mid-1970s, Peugeot SA did not become enmeshed in a web of debt-laden holding companies, but did still get access to enormous sums of financ-ing, with only limited recourse to assistance from the state.

CHAPTER 4

Peugeot SA

Peugeot is not often studied in French government-industry relations, despite the fact that it is France's largest private-sector company, the nation's biggest exporter in terms of turnover, and a dominant force on the French stock market. Some have seen the firm as dependent on the goodwill of the government of the day (for export assistance, protection of the home market, and aid for takeovers), and others have emphasized government interference in the firm's labor disputes in the early 1980s. Mostly, however, it seems to be left out of studies of France because it is seen as an uninteresting aberration, a major family-owned firm that has remained aloof from the kinds of intimate government-industry relations found in, say, the steel sector. Analysis tends to focus instead on Renault, nationalized at the end of the Second World War. What is interesting about Peugeot SA, however, is not just that it has remained firmly in the private sector, but how it has done so, and how it found the financing to undergo a long, slow process of restructuring over the course of the past decade, when other major manufacturers in Britain and France had to rely primarily on the state. Analyzed from this financial perspective, it is clear that PSA is not an aberration, but is, rather, very much a product of the French system of industrial financing and corporate governance. It is also clear that the fact of its private ownership is not the most important part of the story.

By 1979, auto production in France had become concentrated into two dominant firms, the privately owned Peugeot (PSA)[1] and the state-owned Renault. PSA's auto division, which accounts for 95 percent of its business, is split into three *Sociétés*—Peugeot, Citroën, and Talbot—each of which has a network of subsidiaries and plants, including subsidiaries in Britain and Spain.[2] In 1979 the company had a total of 277,000 employees, produced some 1.8 million vehicles, and had 43.3 percent of the French auto market and close to 15 percent of the European. It also made an after-tax profit of FFr1.8 billion (FFr1,800 million). By 1989, employment was down to 158,000 while production was over 2 million units; net financial indebtedness was negligible; and the company made a net profit of FFr10.3 billion. Its share of both the French and the European markets, however, was down sharply. By 1992, PSA was Europe's third-largest producer, but had only a

12.2 percent market share. As in the other cases analyzed here, the 1980s were a tumultuous decade for the company, involving heavy investment in new technologies, closure of old plants, and fierce labor disputes. By the second half of the decade, the firm had moved away from its old strategy of functioning as an integrated auto manufacturer, and instead saw itself as primarily a designer and assembler of cars, attempting to emulate Japanese production methods.

Of the four cases analyzed here, PSA is the only one to have remained continuously in the private sector. This has naturally had an impact on its relationship with successive governments. Far more interesting than its formal ownership, however, is the financial structure that has underpinned the firm, and the question of whether it can continue to sustain PSA through what promises to be the equally turbulent decade of the 1990s. In addition, Renault's postwar status as the nation's "national champion" is slowly being fundamentally altered, raising questions not only about the role and financing of nationalized industries in 1990s Europe, but also about the potential impact on PSA, and that firm's future access to capital.

This chapter follows the format of the previous two case studies. The financing of Peugeot is examined in part 2. Part 1 gives a background discussion of the restructuring of the firm in the 1970s and 1980s, its relationship with the government, and the implications of changes in the status of its domestic rival, Renault.

1. Peugeot in the Postwar Period

The large-scale construction and sale of automobiles first happened in France, involving firms with such names as Berliet, De Dion, Panhard et Lavassor, Renault, and Peugeot. In 1913, Peugeot produced 5,000 vehicles, making it the largest automaker in France, and the second-largest in Europe after Ford UK (Laux 1976).[3] The name Peugeot has a long and venerable reputation in French business, beginning as a small smelting works in the Montbéliard region near the Swiss border early in the nineteenth century, and expanding into bicycle manufacture in the 1880s, and then into automobiles. By the end of the 1880s there were two major Peugeot metalworking concerns. One made hand tools; the larger firm, Société Peugeot Frères (later Les Fils de Peugeot Frères) began making bicycles in 1886 and produced four steam-powered tricycles—the first Peugeot "cars"—in 1889. In 1896 Armand Peugeot incorporated the Société Anonyme des Automobiles Peugeot to begin full-time car manufacturing. By 1913, the two most successful car companies outside the Paris region were Berliet in Lyons and Peugeot in Montbéliard. Berliet subsequently became a leading European truck and heavy machinery maker, and sold out to Citroën in 1967. By 1929, Renault, Peugeot, and Citroën were the

Big Three French automakers, integrated producers that between them had 63 percent of auto sales in France. The remainder were much smaller firms, assembling parts from outside suppliers.

Expansion and Restructuring of a Conservative Family Firm

By 1950 the depression and Second World War had further reduced the many French auto manufacturers down to the three major firms—Renault, Citroën, and Peugeot. Peugeot had a reputation for caution and until the mid-1960s had only one basic model, periodically updated. In 1968 it branched into a new market segment for the first time with its 504 model. In 1974, the family brought in the first outsider, Jean-Paul Parayre, and charged him with transforming their "somewhat stodgy and provincial industrial empire" (*Financial Times*, September 6, 1984) into a major-volume car producer. A product of the grandes écoles (the Polytechnique and the École Nationale des Ponts et Chaussées), Parayre had been a member of the elite circles of the civil service, at one point working for then-Prime Minister Jacques Chirac.

Peugeot began its expansion by taking over Citroën. Michelin owned most of that firm's stock in 1974, and was not pleased when Citroën lost money that year. Citroën took out a FFr1 billion loan from the government, off-loaded its truck-making Berliet subsidiary to Renault, and began to pass control of the car-making operations to Peugeot. PSA initially took 38 percent of Citroën's stock from Michelin, and when the firm made a profit in 1976 purchased the rest of its stock and formed a new company, Peugeot-Citroën. The new firm made a profit in 1977, and repaid the FFr1 billion government loan early and in full. Parayre was then one of the main architects of Peugeot's acquisition of Chrysler's European operations, in 1978, for $230 million in cash and some $200 million worth of stock. In 1979 PSA launched a massive investment program to rationalize car-component production, and another to develop new car models. By 1980, its plant at Sochaux in the Franche-Comté region was the biggest industrial site in France, employing some 41,000 workers.

However, absorbing and integrating its three constituent parts—Peugeot, Citroën, and Talbot—posed a considerable problem for the group (Jones 1983). The integration of the Chrysler purchase caused Peugeot the most headaches. Renamed Talbot, the firm represented the single biggest financial drain on PSA after 1978. There were difficulties in merging the Talbot and Peugeot dealer networks in Europe, and productivity at Talbot's huge Paris plants was low. In 1980, PSA slipped into the red.

Parayre launched a three-year restructuring program that reduced the group's worldwide work force by almost 70,000. As losses and debts accumulated, in 1982 the family called in a second outsider, Jacques Calvet, to help sort out the group's finances. Another top civil servant, Calvet was a graduate of the École Nationale d'Administration, had worked for Giscard d'Estaing when he was finance minister, and had just been fired from his job as chairman of the state-owned Banque Nationale de Paris by the new Socialist administration. Calvet replaced Parayre as chairman of PSA in 1984, and went on to oversee a dramatic turnaround in the firm's organization and financial health, gaining in the process the reputation of a forceful and outspoken miracle worker.

As in Britain, auto production facilities are concentrated in a few geographic regions in France. Part of Peugeot's restructuring involved shifting car production away from Paris to large integrated assembly centers in the provinces. The region around Paris, once the heart of the French auto industry, has experienced major employment losses in recent years, while in the regions of Nord and Lorraine auto employment has increased. The other historic regions of Franche-Comté and Rhône-Alpes continue to have around 20 percent of the industry's employment (Documentation Français 1980, 4583). Citroën's renovation cycle, begun in 1983 when the firm was on the verge of bankruptcy, ended in March 1988 with the final closure of the old 2CV plant at Levallois, Paris.

When Calvet joined the firm in 1982, his main tasks were to return the firm to profit, to maintain the confidence of the banking community in the troubled group, and to reduce the work force of the French divisions by a further 12,000. Between mid-1983 and late 1984, in a series of dramatic clashes with the government and the unions, he succeeded in cutting the size of PSA's work force by over 20,000. Over the next few years, Calvet oversaw the introduction of a Just-In-Time supply system and highly automated plants, and began ambitious plans to invest ten percent of turnover in continued recovery (*Economist*, May 20, 1990). Part of the restructuring meant reducing the number of the firm's suppliers from 2,000 in 1981 to just 950 by the end of 1988. The United Kingdom also proved to be a major market for the group. Introducing stable labor relations has been another matter, however. In 1988, Peugeot cut a further 3,000 from its work force, half from the huge Sochaux plant with its large immigrant work force, and labor unrest increased. Nor is the restructuring over. In the highly competitive European market of the 1990s, Peugeot continues to introduce new technology and reduce costs. After a warning from Calvet that "It is not a very easy 1993 in front of us" (*New York Times*, December 17, 1992), the firm announced in the new year that Automobiles Peugeot would cut 2,597 jobs over the course of 1993, its largest work force reduction since 1988. A month later, Citroën announced it would axe some 5 percent of its labor force. Unions reacted angrily, calling the cuts "unacceptable" (*Financial Times*, January 6, 1993). See table 19 for an overview of the restructuring of Peugeot SA.

The Political Context

> I never negotiate with the state. I explain very clearly what I want to do, why I want to do it and what the consequences of not doing it will be. Then I wait for the government to agree. (M. Calvet; quoted in *Wards Auto World* (24) April 1988, 29)

Two factors have dominated the political context of Peugeot's restructuring—intense labor disputes that also involved the government, and a basic agreement between firm and government over industrial and trade policies. As with the French steel closures a few years before, the retrenchment at Peugeot triggered bitter strikes and riots. By the late 1970s, immigrants, largely from North Africa, comprised 34 percent of the auto industry's labor force, and accounted for as many as 75 percent of the assembly workers in the Parisian car plants. Citroën in particular was infamous for subjecting its immigrant workers to very poor pay and working conditions.[4] Until the strikes at the Citroën and Talbot plants in 1982, the major unions made little effort to represent the immigrants (Benoit 1982). After the government exercised a rarely invoked option to call in formal mediation in the strikes, press attention to the immigrants' plight increased and the labor confederations finally began to take their demands seriously (Zukin 1985). The mediator's recommendations largely supported the immigrants' demands and Citroën agreed to a set of revised employment practices for semiskilled workers.

TABLE 19. Restructuring of Peugeot SA

	1979	1980	1982	1984	1986	1988	1991
Employment (thousands)	277	245	208	187	165	158	
Production (millions)	1.81	1.44	1.28		1.70	2.08	2.05
Market share							
France %	43.3	36.6	30.2	33.1	32.1	34.2	
Europe %		14.6			11.6	12.9	12.1
Profit/(loss) (FFr millions)							
Trading[a]	2,850	(2,590)	(3,900)	(950)	3,840	14,870	8,490
Net	1,800	(1,500)	(2,150)	(340)	3,590	8,850	5,530

Source: Data from Peugeot Annual Report, various issues; *Moody's International*, various issues.
[a]Trading profit = before tax and interest.

Then came the showdown. In the summer of 1983, Calvet announced that Peugeot and Talbot must cut a combined 10 percent of their work force—a record at that time for a French company. Included were nearly 3,000 redundancies at the Talbot plant at Poissy on the outskirts of Paris. The government and unions accepted job reductions through early retirement, but balked at outright redundancies. Calvet was adamant, linking the job cuts with a FFr1.2 billion two-year investment program to modernize the Poissy plant. Meanwhile, the CGT was agitating for Peugeot-Citroën to be nationalized. The government appointed an expert to "evaluate" the proposed job cuts. The CGT saw this as forcing Peugeot to be less secretive of its plans, but Peugeot management dismissed the expert as "parallel to, not supplanting, their usual procedures" (L'Usine Nouvelle, September 1, 1983; my translation). The expert's position was cast in so ambiguous a light that it is hard to see his appointment as an instance of increased government intervention toward Peugeot. His appointment was in any case rapidly overtaken by events at the Poissy plant itself.

In October, the government refused PSA permission to lay off the 2,900 employees at Poissy unless management significantly improved the retraining and redundancy terms. Calvet threatened to close the plant altogether. In late 1983, the government finally got Calvet to compromise on 1,900 redundancies at Poissy instead of 2,900—a compromise reportedly reached without consulting the unions (Financial Times, January 9, 1984). The workers' reaction was explosive. In the new year of 1984, Peugeot closed the Poissy plant after three days of rioting. More than half of Poissy's 17,000 workers were immigrants, and racial tensions exacerbated the conflicts. The labor confederations could not control their rank and file, and local leaders of the CFDT, the most militant of the labor groups at Poissy, asked Peugeot management to call in the Compagnies Républicaines de Sécurité (CRS) riot police to evacuate the plant. The conflict was a major problem for the Socialist government, widely seen as a test of its ability to maintain a dialogue with its social partners. One of Calvet's counselors subsequently complained that "Every time Peugeot requests such authority, the ministry [of labor] asks the company to reduce the number to be laid off, to delay the layoffs, and to compensate more generously those about to depart" (Perrin-Pelletier 1986). In fact, Calvet's stubborn, confrontational stance resulted in his winning almost all of the cuts he wanted.

Labor relations at the firm continue to be antagonistic. Unrest erupted in late 1989, with a seven-week strike centered at the main assembly plants at Mulhouse and Sochaux in the northeast. Only 2,000 out of 35,000 workers went out on strike, but the two sites were effectively closed down. After five years of restructuring, during which Peugeot workers accepted lower wage awards than those given at Renault, the strikers wanted a higher share of the recovery than the 2.7 percent pay increase on offer. The most militant group from the CGT wanted increases up to 30 percent. Calvet refused to negotiate. After five weeks of deadlock the government called in a negotiator. Even then, Calvet made it clear that he was prepared to sit out the strike indefinitely if necessary. The strike petered out until its official end on October 24, when the workers accepted a 9 percent pay increase for the lowest-paid, and increased profit incentives.

Calvet's penchant for taking on the authorities and winning extended to other areas. In July 1988, the new Socialist government overruled its own environment minister, who had supported EC proposals to reduce the exhaust emissions of small cars.[5] This was reported in the press as "a victory for Peugeot, and its chairman Jacques Calvet," who had fiercely attacked the emission proposals (*Financial Times*, July 22, 1988).

Even as PSA was challenging the government's ability to prevent job losses and plant closures, the two sides had long been in agreement over most other issues concerning the industry—in contrast with the case of BL (chap. 5)—particularly concerning protection of the domestic market. In the immediate postwar period of reconstruction the auto industry was not, unlike the steel industry, a high priority for the French planners (Perrin-Pelletier 1986). Eventually, however, successive governments saw the preservation of a wholly domestically owned auto industry as a major policy goal. This benefited both Peugeot and Renault. High protective tariffs ended once the EC was established, but the government retained its power to control foreign investment, keeping out the American producers in the 1960s and the Japanese since the late 1970s. Severe restrictions on Japanese imports also began in 1977, with a 3-percent market-share limit that was judged to be just below the level at which the Japanese producers would find it worthwhile to develop a strong French distribution system (Altshuler et al. 1984). This contrasts with Britain, where there has been a clear and increasing strategy of forging links with the Japanese producers. Right up to the late 1980s, successive French governments accepted the argument that even slight reductions in trade restrictions would flood the market with Japanese cars. French car imports did, indeed, rise by 40 percent in 1981–82, when redistributive measures increased real disposable income faster than production (Hall 1986).

Until early 1989, control of the market remained tight, with new Japanese cars representing barely 2.9 percent of the market. When Nissan began fully to operate its plant in Britain in 1988, France declared that it would not treat the cars produced as of British origin, since their local content was less than 80 percent, and instead counted them against its import quota on Japanese cars. Then came the EC's single-market proposal, and with it a shift in the attitude of the French government. When an end to some of the more restrictive anti-Japanese trade practices was first proposed in 1988, Raymond

Lévy, then-chairman of Renault, protested that "We need time and we need shelter" to prepare for the coming "economic war" with Japan, adding "we are competing with people who are not of our way of life" (*Economist*, March 26, 1988). On the whole, however, Lévy's reaction to the policy shift was basically supportive, and he soon clashed with his opposite number at Peugeot. Calvet railed against the dangers of free trade, the creation of a single European market, the 1991 Maastricht Treaty on European Monetary Union, and the Japanese producers' penetration of the European market. On May 31, 1992, Calvet announced he may run for the French presidency in 1995.

However, the French government's enthusiasm for the single European market is bringing some dramatic changes to auto industry policies. In April 1989, Industry Minister Fauroux announced that the British-made Nissan cars would no longer be treated as Japanese imports. The ostensible reason was Nissan's assurances that local content would reach 80 percent by year's end. More importantly, the government was symbolically softening its stand against the Japanese producers, recognizing that it risked having Japanese goods in France after 1992, without the benefits of Japanese investment and employment.[6] The day before, Toyota had announced that it was following Nissan in building a plant in Britain. Fauroux and then-Finance Minister Bérégovoy began to tout for foreign investment. *Le Monde* editorialized that "Tel est le prix à payer au mécanisme européen" (April 20, 1989). After decades of agreement on the industry's policy agenda, PSA, and especially its chairman, find themselves increasingly at odds with the government. Peugeot's relationship with the state may shift in other areas, too, given the changes that are being proposed for the state-owned Renault, and the possibility of that firm's return to private ownership in the near future.

Peugeot, Renault, and the European Community

Renault was nationalized at the end of the Second World War (ostensibly to punish its collaborationist owner), and given the status of *régie*, an institution that, under French law, was obliged to make cars "for France" rather than for a profit. Unlike other French nationalized industries, it could not raise capital publicly and wasn't quoted on the Bourse. On the other hand, Renault was also explicitly protected as a *régie* from bankruptcy, and the state did not require dividends on its equity. The government injected considerable amounts of capital into the firm over the years, allowed it favorable tax treatment, and gave strong support both for the strategy to develop smaller cars and for the push to expand exports in the 1970s (Jones 1983). The chairman was government-appointed, and various ministerial representatives sat on the management council. Renault expanded over the years through a series of minority-holdings and technology-sharing agreements with private companies, rather than through takeover bids (Green 1981).[7] See table 20.

In 1981, Renault was being hailed by pronationalization advocates as the model of good state management. The firm suffered a great deal during the 1980s, however, seeing its share of the European market fall from 14.6 percent and first place in 1982 to 10.7 percent and sixth place by 1987. Between 1981 and 1985 it lost a total of FFr33 billion. In 1984 it began to restructure, shedding some 25 percent of its work force over the next four years. In return, the company was plagued with industrial-relations problems, a strike by just 230 workers at a single strategic plant cutting car production by 80 percent in October 1988. However, Renault has also managed a recovery in the last few years, staying in the black since 1988. Still, the firm had cumulative debts of FFr23.8 billion in 1989, even after a government write-off of FFr12 billion of its debt in late 1987.

The Chirac government's 1987 debt write-off for Renault is reminiscent of its moves at Usinor, taking Renault's debts from FFr54 billion to FFr42 billion. However, the government declined to inject further state funds into the company and Industry Minister Madelin announced plans to convert Renault into an ordinary state-owned company, removing its *régie* status. Madelin proposed letting Renault raise up to 50 percent of its capital from the public, although the firm would first have to achieve a positive net worth and pay off its debts. Hence the 1987 write-off. All of this was actually the next step in a process begun by the Socialists in 1985, when George Besse was made PDG with the explicit goal of staunching the firm's losses. After his murder in 1986, the mantle passed to Raymond Lévy. In November 1989 Renault restructured its balance sheet, to make its published capital figures look more like those of a private company,[8] and the French government told the EC that Renault was now a company like any other (although it still paid no taxes).

TABLE 20.   Restructuring of Renault

	1979	1980	1982	1984	1987	1989	1991
Employment (thousands)				215	190	170	147
Market share							
France %	35.0	40.5	39.2	31.0	32.8	29.0	
Europe %		14.7	14.6	12.6	10.7	10.2	10.0
Net profit/(loss) (FFr million)	1,800	(1,500)	(2,000)	(12,700)	3,500	9,300	3,080

Source: Data from *Financial Times*, various issues; Documentation Français 1987; Quinn 1988.

Then, early in 1990, the EC took on the French government over a FFr20 billion subsidy it had made to Renault. The EC had allowed the Chirac government to write off some of Renault's debts on the condition that the state remove its guarantee against Renault going bankrupt and that the company cut its car-production capacity by 15 percent and its truck capacity by 30 percent. The EC also overlooked FFr20 billion in past subsidies and existing government-guaranteed debts. By the end of 1989, however, the capacity cuts were only 11.5 percent and 9 percent, respectively, while the law to formally change Renault's status was still wending its way through the Assembly following the change in government. The EC's competition commissioner, Sir Leon Brittan, demanded that FFr8.4 billion of the written-off loans be repaid, and threatened to take Renault and the government to the European Court. A settlement was eventually negotiated by Prime Minister Rocard and the EC's industrial commissioner, whereby Renault repaid FFr3.5 billion of the write-off and reinstated another FFr2.5 billion of long-term debt to its balance sheet. Renault also, finally, changed its status to that of a joint stock company.

Meanwhile, another major change was taking place at Renault. The firm had maintained production deals with the private-sector Swedish carmaker, Volvo, since the early 1980s. In 1990, the two firms announced a share exchange, giving Volvo a 20 percent stake in Renault with an option on a further 5 percent, in return for a 25 percent Renault share in Volvo's carmaking subsidiary.[9] This was the first significant injection of private and overseas capital into a French nationalized firm. The two firms were keen to strengthen the tie between them. In the summer of 1992 they announced two joint ventures, in component buying and quality control, to pool their resources and "to act as if the two groups were one company" (*Financial Times*, June 24, 1992). Raymond Lévy didn't rule out a formal takeover, and his successor to Renault's chairmanship, Louis Schweitzer (previously managing director at Renault and before that chief of staff to Laurent Fabius for a number of years), was also supportive of privatization. Interestingly, in light of subsequent events, Schweitzer argued that his company must remain majority-French-controlled if privatized (*Financial Times*, March 16, 1993). Renault emerged in 1992 as the fastest growing volume carmaker in Europe, increasing its sales volume by 5 percent in the first eight months of the year, and seeing pretax profits in January–June jump fivefold over the previous year. Such numbers made the firm look even more attractive as an early privatization candidate, and it was no surprise that Renault was on the privatization list announced by Prime Minister Balladur in May 1993.

With the Center-Right back in power in Paris, it therefore came as no surprise when the two firms announced their merger in September 1993, involving the entire Renault group and Volvo's automotive operations. The

French government was to hold 47 percent of the shares in the new company, and Volvo 18 percent. The remaining 35 percent would be held by a newly created holding company, itself 51 percent-owned by the French state and 49 percent-owned by Volvo. The holding company was intended to "secure the fundamental interests" of Renault-Volvo shareholders by approving "major issues" such as capital increases (*Economist*, September 11, 1993). In the event, the merger collapsed under an onslaught of protest from Volvo's small shareholders in Sweden, some union members, and much of the Swedish press. The Volvo shareholders rejected the plan, and by December the merger was off. At year end 1993, the Balladur government was reiterating its intention to privatize Renault in the near future.

Although the story of Renault and its transition from *régie* to company may seem a side issue in this analysis of Peugeot, the changes in Renault's status and its future in the private sector could have a profound impact on Peugeot SA. The following section describes PSA's financial structure, its position on the Paris Bourse, and the protection offered by its corporate-governance structure of family-owned holding companies. If Renault ends up a private, quoted company, Peugeot will no longer enjoy favored status as the only auto SA and the nation's biggest private firm. It will have a competitor in its access to private capital, and if the shift in government policy toward acceptance of Japanese imports holds, Peugeot will find itself not only competing for capital, but also in a fierce battle for domestic market share. The 1980s may come to be seen as the final glory days of the venerable Peugeot name.

2. The Financing of Peugeot SA

> Our company is relatively safe from such attempts [to destabilize the stockholder base] because it is fortunate enough to have an important stockholder base which has shown time and again its loyalty in the past and which is very much attached to the pursuit of development with serenity. Moreover, the significant stock market capitalization amount contributes to steer aside the threat of intrusion in its capital by parties which would only impose themselves, playing a negative role. (The Management Committee, PSA Annual Report 1986, 54; English-language edition)

Unlike the private steel companies described in chapter 3, Peugeot has relied primarily on equity financing, rather than debt, throughout its history. However, the crucial point about the firm's financing is not just that it turned to the Bourse for funds, but rather that the firm's corporate governance structure—and the national financial system in which it operates—has had profound implications for the availability and cost of that equity financing and, even more important, for the attitudes of the investors themselves. This becomes apparent once we analyze PSA's relationship with the French equity market, and the workings of the firm's family holding companies, in the 1980s. Yet we still find some interesting similarities with the other cases analyzed here, not least the fact that the state was involved in providing the firm with access to significant sources of financing at key junctures. Finally, government-legislated changes in the French financial markets have had a considerable impact on PSA in recent years, and will continue to do so in the 1990s.

The most important point to bear in mind, however, is that the case of PSA is not an outlier, presented in juxtaposition to the other three cases where the firm involved was nationalized for much of the 1980s. Rather, the Peugeot case illustrates the same issues about firm-level financial analysis, the blurring of the public-private boundary, and the similarities—as well as the differences—between government-industry relations in Britain and those in France. One of the arguments developed in chapter 6 (summarizing the case studies) is that the case of Peugeot SA in the 1980s has more in common with that of the nationalized British Steel Corporation than with either the case of the French steel industry, or that of fellow car manufacturer British Leyland.

Peugeot and the Bourse

From the time of its founding in 1896, the Peugeot firm has been financed primarily with equity capital. The original Société Anonyme was constituted with FFr800,000 in capital and 800 shares—350 going to founder Armand Peugeot and the rest to family and friends. In its early years, the firm turned frequently to equity and bond issues to finance expansion. FFr1.6 million in new shares were issued in 1898—the same year that the company turned a FFr117,433 net profit and paid its first dividend of 5 percent (Laux 1976). Share capital increased rapidly in subsequent years—by FFr2.6 million in 1900, by FFr1.25 million in 1906, and by a further FFr5 million in 1911. Three series of 4.5 percent bonds were also sold in 1908, 1909, and 1911, respectively. In 1913, 20,000 FFr500 shares were issued, raising Peugeot's capital to FFr30 million. Of these shares, the family bought 8,000 and the Montbéliard branch of the bank Société Générale took another 6,000 (ibid.). Although Peugeot did receive some financial assistance from banks in the Nancy region, its reliance on equity financing and capital from family and friends was typical of firms in the fledgling auto industry in France. As we shall see in the next chapter, the U.K. auto industry also relied heavily on equity capital in the first half of the twentieth century, although the financial consequences in the 1960s and 1970s were far more negative for those firms than for Peugeot.

Another aspect of PSA's early years that stands out is that the firm was held in high regard by the financial community. The low rates of interest charged on the bond issues in 1908–11 "indicates the high financial reputation of the firm and the family" (Laux 1976, 118).[10] Similarly, in 1978 Peugeot-Citroën raised a medium-term loan on the markets that, as the *Financial Times* noted (February 8, 1978), had terms almost as good as the big state-guaranteed borrowers.[11] This reputation continued into the 1980s and, along with the "friends" who were early and constant investors in the firm, goes a long way toward explaining why Peugeot was able to weather the first half of the 1980s. As described in chapter 2, when British Steel announced a lower dividend in 1991–92 and waived its interim dividend for 1992–93, investor reaction was immediately and sharply negative, sending the firm's share-price plunging and prompting gloomy prognoses from equity analysts and brokers. In strong contrast, Peugeot SA paid no dividends whatsoever from 1981 to 1985. Stockholders' equity over the same period plummeted from FFr10.18 billion in 1981 to a low of FFr5.29 billion in 1985, long-term debts rose, and there was plenty of talk in the press about PSA's "financial difficulties" (see table 21). Investor reaction was not as sharply negative as in the U.K. a few years later, however. Different firms in different industries do, of course, have different prospects as far as investors and analysts are concerned, but one major reason for the different reactions to the two firms' suspension of

TABLE 21. PSA's Share Structure

	Shares Outstanding (millions)	Dividend (FFr)	Stockholders' Equity (FFr miln)	Long-Term Debt (FFr miln)	Net Financial Indebtedness (FFr miln)
1977	9.55	11.5	7,470	5,560	
1978	12.31	13.5	11,580	6,780	
1979	12.50	15.5	13,600	9,190	
1980	12.52	8.0		9,770	
1981	12.52	0.0	10,180	11,590	
1982	12.52	0.0	8,150	13,810	
1983	12.52	0.0	5,710	15,420	
1984	12.52	0.0	5,290	17,050	33,060
1985	15.06	0.0	6,680	21,500	32,060
1986	16.21	10.0	10,540	22,130	29,870
1987	20.21	17.0	20,530	15,720	18,640
1988	24.95	28.0	29,260	14,220	5,960
1989	49.93	16.0	38,530	6,560	1,910
1990		19.5			8,270
1991		13.0			9,390

Source: Data from Peugeot Annual Reports, various issues; *Moody's International*, various issues.

dividends was the different financial systems involved—both in terms of the workings of the national stock market, and in terms of the individual firms' systems of corporate governance.

A number of Peugeot-family investment groups hold a sizable proportion of PSA stock between them. In addition, there are investors in the equity of both PSA and of at least one of the family holding companies that are often referred to, in the company's annual reports and in the press, as "friendly institutional investors." Their identity is not publicly known, and French regulations require disclosure of the identity of only those shareholders holding more than 5 percent of the capital of any company. However, Société Générale reportedly has 2 percent of Peugeot SA's capital, and PSA has in turn acquired 2 percent of the Société (*Le Monde*, April 19, 1989). A 1978 newspaper article on the takeover of Chrysler's European operations mentions the parapublic financial institution Caisse des Dépôts et Consignations as one of PSA's minor shareholders (*Financial Times*, August 12, 1978).[12] Aside from the Chrysler Corporation between 1981 and 1985, the only other known major shareholder in PSA is the tire manufacturer Michelin, a stake leftover from the takeover of Citroën in 1974–76. The attitude of these investors stands in marked contrast to that of the institutional investors that dominate the London Stock Exchange. Not only did the French investors not sell their Peugeot shares when the firm's financial problems mounted, they actually subscribed to new equity when, after years of zero dividends and "financial difficulties," Peugeot SA launched a series of major and successful share issues in the mid-1980s.

In July 1985 PSA issued 2.5 million shares in its first new issue since 1963, raising FFr925 million in fresh capital "with the largest new share issue to hit the Bourse for many years" (*Financial Times*, July 15, 1985). Then, in 1986, the Chrysler Corporation decided to sell off its 12.5-percent share in PSA. Since 1978, when PSA had taken over Chrysler's European operations, the American company had one representative on the Peugeot board, but had reportedly treated its equity stake as a portfolio investment. Chrysler sold the stake in order to help fund its own ambitious capital-spending program. According to press reports, French commercial and industrial groups "friendly" to Peugeot agreed to buy around a quarter of Chrysler's stake, mostly through warrants issued to Chrysler with a bond issue in 1983. The bulk of the remaining shares were sold through an international placing, in order not to hold back the group's performance on the Paris Bourse. Some fifty-nine U.K. financial institutions reportedly bought shares (*Financial Times*, July 11, 1986). Peugeot increased its capital stock still further in the summer of 1987 with the issue of 1.69 million new shares, a 20 percent stock dividend, and the redemption of warrants. The stock issue raised FFr2.7

billion to help finance a three-year investment program and to reduce the firm's long-term debt. At year-end 1987, the number of shares outstanding had gone up to 20.21 million, and stockholders' equity was at FFr20.53 billion. In mid-1989, the firm conducted a two-for-one stock split, doubling the number of shares outstanding to 49.93 million.

The other side of the PSA financing story in the mid-1980s was a sharp increase in long-term debt—from FFr9.7 billion in 1980 to FFr15.42 billion in 1983 and a peak of FFr22.13 billion in 1986. Net financial indebtedness hit FFr33.06 billion in 1984 and FFr32.06 billion in 1985. In the second half of the decade, however, debt levels came down sharply. By 1989, long-term debt was just FFr6.56 billion and net financial indebtedness had fallen to just FFr1.91 billion. Since then, debt levels have been edging upward again. A key aspect of Peugeot's ability to reduce its debt levels so dramatically in 1986–89 was the government's program of liberalization of the French financial markets and the new financing options this created, which will be discussed in a later section of this chapter.

The Family Holding Company

Unlike Renault or Honda, Peugeot has remained aloof from international ties. It has no equity stakes in other auto manufacturers, and no others have a stake in PSA. They have undertaken a joint venture with Fiat in commercial vehicles, and a number of joint ventures with Renault,[13] but these do not involve any form of share swaps or equity stakes in the parent companies (*Economist*, February 24, 1990). Peugeot remains largely under family control by that most French of institutions, the financial holding company.

There are three private family-associated holding companies through which the Peugeot family maintains a large and unified stake in PSA. The holding company Société Foncière, Financière et de Participation (SFFP) is closely held by the family and not publicly quoted. Through the Société the family holds shares in the Peugeot parent company. A second holding company is Les Fils de Peugeot Frères. To recall the early history of PSA, there were two major Peugeot metalworking firms by the late 1880s, the larger of which, Société Peugeot Frères, subsequently became Les Fils de Peugeot Frères. Les Fils had gone into tricycle manufacturing and also made a few early cars separately from Armand Peugeot's car-making firm. In 1910, the auto, bicycle, and sewing-machine branches of Les Fils merged with Armand's company. In return, the owners of Les Fils received some FFr8.75 million in new shares in Automobiles Peugeot (Laux 1976). The third holding company is called La Français de Participations Financières. The family also continues to play a direct role in the management of the firm (see table 22).

TABLE 22.   PSA's Major Shareholders and Voting Rights

	Frères, LFPF & SFFPa		Groupe Michelin		Chrysler Corp.
	% shares	% votes	% shares	% votes	% shares
1977	49.00	-- —	9.00	——	
1978	41.00	——	7.00	——	
1979	37.28	——	7.00	——	15.50
1982	36.65	——	9.20	——	14.00
1983	34.62	——	9.20	——	14.38
1984	34.62	——	9.20	——	14.38
1985	34.50	——	9.00	——	14.20
1986	26.31	——	7.10	——	——
1987	22.72	34.19	5.83	9.02	
1988	22.72	34.36	5.82	9.06	
1989	22.78	34.58	5.82	9.04	

Source: Data from Peugeot Annual Report, various issues; *Moody's International*, various issues.

aLes Fils de Peugeot Frères; La Français de Participations Financières; and Société Foncière, Financières et de Participations.

Through the 1980s, Pierre Peugeot was one of two general managers on the Board of Directors. Antoine Peugeot was reelected to a statutory six-year term as a member of the Supervisory Board in 1990.

Family-dominated firms are far from a rarity among French corporations, although the proportion declined more rapidly in the decade up to 1990.[14] According to a survey by 3i of over 2,000 family-owned businesses with turnover of at least FFr20 million in 1980, 58 percent of the businesses were still in family hands ten years later, but 25 percent were no longer family controlled and the remainder had ceased trading. The loss of family control was most marked among companies involved in manufacturing and construction (cited in *Financial Times*, March 3, 1992). Nevertheless, the following observation about firms still controlled by their founding families still largely holds true:

> The web of control is more complex than it appears. Since many of the manufacturing companies are controlled through holding companies or investment banks, there exists a plethora of unofficial allegiances, sometimes supported by cross-holdings of equity stakes and by reciprocal board memberships. This structure makes the largest French companies almost invulnerable to hostile bids. (*Economist* 1988)

Part of that web for Peugeot SA are the aforementioned unidentified "friendly investors." In a 1986 interview, Calvet noted that the Peugeot group felt well protected from potential predators because of the large family and Michelin shareholdings, "and other friends have a few percent here and there" (*Financial Times*, July 11, 1986, 25).

Despite their holding companies, the family's combined holding in Peugeot fell sharply after the mid-1970s, from 49 percent in 1977 to 36.65 percent by 1982. Part of the reason for this fall was the Chrysler purchase, which involved both a cash payment of around FFr1 billion, and a share of Peugeot stock. The cash part was straightforward; the cash-rich Peugeot company "simply took a billion francs out of the till" (*Fortune*, December 4, 1978). Giving Chrysler 1.8 million new shares of Peugeot-Citroën amounted to 15.5 percent of PSA stock, making Chrysler the second-largest shareholder after Michelin.

However, share percentages alone are not the whole story for a French company like Peugeot. As table 22 shows, long-term holders of shares in a Société Anonyme enjoy a higher percentage of voting rights than just their shareholding percentage might imply. In the case of PSA, this means the family interests and Michelin, among the publicly identified shareholders. In 1989, for example, the family groups held 22.78 percent of the shares outstanding and 34.58 percent of the voting rights, while Michelin had a 5.82 percent shareholding and 9.04 percent of the voting rights.

The stakes of Peugeot's major shareholders were further diluted in 1985, when neither the family, nor Michelin, nor Chrysler took part in the 2.5 million share-issue that year. Calvet subsequently said they had stayed out of the issue because they had decided that small shareholders "should be given a chance instead" (*Financial Times*, July 11, 1986). However, part of the reason was that the firm had specifically asked the family to waive their rights in the new equity (as will be discussed later in this chapter). Also, Michelin had its own recovery and balance-sheet restructuring to worry about and Chrysler was similarly preoccupied with internal problems. Perhaps the Socialist government's post-1981 austerity measures were also being felt and the family felt strapped for cash. Whatever the reason for their staying out of the new capital, by the end of 1986 the family's share of Peugeot stock had fallen to 26.31 percent. Meanwhile, the firm was beginning to realize the benefits of its earlier investments and in 1986 Peugeot SA distributed dividends to its shareholders for the first time since 1980 (Documentation Française 1987, 4831).

With this change in fortune, there seems to have been increased concern within the firm that it was becoming more vulnerable to a possible takeover. In the summer of 1987, along with the above-mentioned FFr2.7 billion share-issue, the family moved to ward off any such attempts. The Société Foncière opened its capital to "friendly institutional investors." In addition, the third family holding company, La Français de Participations Financières, opened up to French institutional investors (again, unidentified) who reportedly may have acquired some 15 to 20 percent of the company's capital. With the additional funds these moves brought in, the family invested in the new shares and so prevented its percentage of PSA stock from declining much further (*Economist*, September 12, 1987). Under the share and warrant issue, existing holders of Peugeot shares were entitled to buy one unit for every fifteen shares they already owned. Each unit comprised one share priced at FFr1,525 and one warrant priced at FFr175 to buy another share. (The warrants expired in 1990, when they could be exercised at FFr1,700.) Although the details of exactly what SFFP got from Peugeot in the PSA share-issue are not clear, it seems likely that the family holding company got warrants along with its shares. This would be a further block to anyone attempting an unfriendly takeover of Peugeot stock.[15]

It is clear that certain key aspects of Peugeot's corporate governance structure—a unified family stake via the holding companies, a number of friendly investors, additional voting rights for long-term shareholders— enabled the firm to raise much-needed new capital in the mid-1980s, and to protect itself from potential hostile takeover. In addition, the long-standing financial reputation of the Peugeot family, the firm's dominant position on the relatively underdeveloped Bourse, and the supportive attitude of its investors, helped PSA to survive the financial difficulties of the early 1980s. Also, French company law tends to confer considerable power on a single person, the PDG, the Président-Directeur-Général. Calvet (and before him, Parayre) was, in effect, a chairman of the board and chief executive rolled into one, and then some. PDG's are typically not answerable to anyone. "Votes are rare; if a proposal is put to vote, it is tantamount to a vote of no confidence in the PDG" (Barsoux and Lawrence 1991).

Yet despite all of the above, even the fiercely independent, solidly private-sector Peugeot SA, with its PDG who hated entanglements with the state in general and with the Socialists in particular, had to have recourse to government-subsidized financing in the mid-1980s.

Recourse to Government Financing

> Peugeot has traditionally avoided seeking direct state support because of fears that it could undermine the private character of the car group. However, recourse to the FIM is seen differently, and was encouraged in a recent French Government sponsored report of the car industry. (*Financial Times*, November 15, 1984)

The state had already helped to finance Peugeot SA, providing loans to support the firm's expansion in the mid-1970s. When PSA took over Citroën,

Socialist government finally ended price controls on cars in 1985. In June 1989 then-Finance Minister Pierre Bérégovoy tried to convince Calvet and Renault's Lévy of the inflationary dangers of increasing car prices on July 1 (*Le Monde*, June 13, 1989). He could only attempt to convince the two men, however, not impose his will. The control of car prices and of the credit markets in general likely had more impact on the car firms than did the production levels and goals stipulated in the national economic plans:

> Either the firms did not abide by the production levels and goals set by planning, or, because of the power of the companies, these production figures simply reflected the car makers' targets. This was even true of Renault. . . . (Fridenson 1981, 142)

Until the mid-1980s, government controls over the purchase of foreign currencies also limited the degree to which companies could obtain financing abroad. Perrin-Pelletier, one-time counselor to the president of PSA, cited this in 1986 as a further constraint on the financial affairs of big firms like Peugeot (Perrin-Pelletier 1986), although PSA did build up considerable foreign currency indebtedness. Today, however, Peugeot's options are quite different.

At the time of the huge new equity issue in 1985, Calvet was working on a strategy to progressively lighten the Peugeot group's debts. This meant using new financial instruments to reduce interest expenses and to refinance the debt. As part of the issue of the 2.5 million shares, Peugeot took advantage for the first time of new legislation allowing the firm to ask shareholders to abandon their preferential rights for a new equity issue. This allowed PSA to place the issue more quickly on the then-bullish Bourse. Then it set about negotiating new and more flexible financing vehicles with the banking system to restructure its debt portfolio and reduce its overall financing costs. Two aspects in particular are worth noting here—the switch to local currency debt and refinancing of foreign currency term borrowings, and the issue of domestic commercial paper. In addition, in 1987 Peugeot took advantage of defeasance to remove a FFr1 billion debenture borrowing from its balance sheet (PSA Annual Report 1987 and 1989; defeasance is a debt-reduction tool that involves establishing an irrevocable trust that will generate sufficient cash flows to service the decreased debt).

At the end of 1982, some 40 percent of PSA's medium- to long-term debt was foreign-currency denominated (*Business International Money Report*, June 29, 1987). The relaxation of *encadrement*, or credit controls, over the next few years allowed PSA to instead turn to French franc financings and so reduce its foreign currency indebtedness. In 1985, FFr5.438 billion of the firm's FFr21.524 billion long-term debt was repayable in foreign currencies (the bulk in Ecus and pounds sterling). By the end of 1986, the proportion had fallen still further, to FFr3.898 billion out of a total FFr22.131 billion (PSA Annual Report 1986), and by year-end 1989 only FFr893 million of that year's FFr6.555 billion long-term debt was repayable in foreign currencies (mostly Spanish pesetas; PSA Annual Report 1989). Those foreign currency borrowings that were retained were all refinanced through the underwriting of several multiple-option financing facilities or MOFFs. Peugeot negotiated its first French franc MOFF in 1987—a five-year FFr2 billion facility with a group of thirty-four French and international banks that could be used for Automobiles Peugeot, the Citroën division, or both, or retained on standby (*Financial Times*, June 24, 1987).

Peugeot first issued commercial paper in the Euromarket in the autumn of 1985, and when legislative changes allowed the creation of a domestic commercial paper market, PSA "was more than eager" to get involved (*Business International Money Report*, June 29, 1987). In the market's first two years of operation, Peugeot SA was the largest issuer, responsible for about 10 percent of the total outstanding (ibid.). In addition, as France's largest exporter, PSA was keen to take advantage of the development of new means to reduce foreign exchange and interest-rate risk, including the Paris market's development of futures and options. Thus Peugeot has not only taken advantage of the new atmosphere of liberalization and deregulation in the French markets, it has been at the forefront of the development of those markets.

3. The Blurred Public-Private Boundary

Between the role of the Peugeot family and the determined opposition of PDG Calvet to state intervention, PSA is clearly the most overtly private-sector of the firms analyzed here. The state's control over car prices and the availability of credit in the postwar period certainly did have an impact on the firm, and government intervention in the conduct of the labor disputes in the early 1980s did amount to a degree of intervention in the firm's affairs. Overall, however, Peugeot SA was indisputably a private-sector company. Yet even PSA had recourse to government aid when things got tough in the mid-1980s. Admittedly, the sums involved were nowhere near the levels of public assistance that went to the French and British steel firms over the course of a decade, or to the British carmaker BL; and they could be called part of a national industrial upgrade program, rather than a state bailout of a particular, struggling manufacturer. It's probable that Peugeot SA would have survived even without the added cash. Nevertheless, this most private of firms undoubtedly benefited from access to the deep pockets of the state at a crucial juncture—both directly, in that it received funds, and indirectly, in that the aid helped to improve its balance sheet and credit rating and so provide it with access to new sources of financing.

In addition, the role of the French administrative elite must be considered. It is still common to find graduates from the top schools entering the civil service, sometimes as advisors to top politicians, then using this career as a springboard into the top echelons of private industry. Parayre and Calvet are cases in point. As one news report dryly observed of M. Parayre's move to the private sector: "In Peugeot, his arrival and that of a £115 million state loan to help cement the marriage with Citroën are not considered a total coincidence" (*Financial Times*, August 12, 1978). Although Peugeot repaid its 1976 loan from the government in full and ahead of schedule, without the aid at this earlier critical juncture, the firm would have found it far harder to begin its program of expansion, and perhaps would have been in a less healthy financial position at the time of the Chrysler deal a few years later.

All of this amounts to a blurring of the boundary between the public and the private sectors. Ultimately, the state is always involved in providing major manufacturers with access to capital. However, there is an additional aspect of Peugeot-government relations that is even more interesting in this regard— the firm's role in successive government regional investment schemes, and specifically those under the auspices of the FSAI. Even before the advent of a Socialist administration in 1981, the government saw the labor-intensive auto industry as a means "to carry out its regional development objectives" (Green 1981, 45). Some high politicking was involved, in determining who got access to the fund, and under what circumstances.

The FFr3 billion FSAI, established in 1978, provided a package of loans and subsidies to firms wishing to establish themselves in economically depressed areas. The amount of aid was based on the size of the proposed investment and included exemption from the tax on industry for new investors. From September 1978 to March 1981, the FSAI assisted 143 projects involving 21,553 jobs at a total investment of FFr7.8 billion. Most of this aid went to Peugeot and Renault for projects in Nord-Pas-de-Calais and Lorraine (Ministère de l'Industrie 1979).

Early in 1979, the Barre government announced a bid to get Ford to construct its new European assembly plant in the depressed steel region of the Lorraine. Renault and Peugeot objected strenuously, citing rumors that Ford would get preferential treatment up to three times the going rate of government assistance for factory development. The two French companies won rights to grants from the new FSAI for their counterproposals, which were accepted by the government when Ford backed out of negotiations. Green (1981, 46) sums up the general conclusions drawn about the episode:

. . . the government used Ford's apparent interest in a site in France to engineer a "French solution" to the need to create alternative employment for the men released from the restructuring of the steel industry. This was both preferable to further foreign investment which might be damaging to the domestic industry as well as being more satisfactory in terms of its regional policy and employment impact.

FSAI funds were also used to encourage both Peugeot and Renault to locate facilities in the coal-mining and textile communities of the Nord (Documentation Française 1980, 4583).

Meanwhile, Chrysler France had proposed establishing a gear-box plant alongside its factory at La Rochelle. Peugeot decided after its takeover to consider other locations, partly for production reasons but also partly because it was "interested in going where the subsidies were more attractive" (Hayward 1986b, 135). The plant, with its 2,700 jobs, was established at Valenciennes, where all job creation was entitled to full FSAI assistance.[16] The regional planning agency, DATAR, had apparently done much to steer Peugeot toward the Valenciennes area, where Usinor had just announced 5,900 redundancies (ibid.). According to Hayward, the Valenciennes development "involved intense negotiations between Peugeot and the heads of FSAI, of DATAR and the member of the Treasury Division who was secretary of Crédit National" (ibid., 136). The negotiations lasted ten months, all told, with Peugeot pushing hard to get the maximum regulatory, physical, and financial concessions for its chosen site. It won some very favorable terms. The local land-use planning committee agreed to reclassify thirty-five hectares of agricultural land as suitable for industry, special arrangements were made for road and rail access to the site, and gas and oxygen pipelines were shifted (ibid.). Under the final agreement, 50 percent of Peugeot's investment cost was met by the central government through the FSAI, one-third of the subsidy being received at the outset. Even the Communist-controlled municipality involved cooperated in easing any difficulties to the development. All the details were settled by June of 1979—the public inquiry of September to November merely ratified a fait accompli.[17]

4. Assessment

PSA and the National Financial System

The tale of Peugeot SA is illustrative of a number of aspects of the French national financial system—the workings of the Bourse in the 1980s; the uses of holding companies and networks of friendly investors; the role of top civil servants in private industry; and, finally, the changes in the markets in recent years. PSA waived its dividend for five years in a row, without reproof from the Bourse, in strong contrast with the case of British Steel. The corporate governance structure whereby the family retains a unified interest in the firm via holding companies is also very French, as is the role of those unidentified friends. This amounts to a network of ownership interests and risks, as in the case of French steel, but with the crucial difference of one dominant voice in the form of the family. Between them, the friendly investors and the role of the family help to explain PSA's autonomy from state financing and its clout on the Bourse. In addition, since the early history of the firm, the family's reputation and the structure of holding companies that own its shares explain why PSA was able to rely for so long on equity as the primary source of its long-term capital, when many other French manufacturers had to turn to the state-subsidized and controlled credit markets. Because the state-administered debt market was the dominant source of industrial finance after 1945, however, most analysis of French government-industry relations has tended to focus on firms such as the steel companies that were heavily reliant on this debt financing, and on the institutions that controlled and channeled the funds. Although PSA was unusual in its reliance on equity financing, it was by no means an aberration—other, predominantly family-owned firms also survived the postwar period by relying primarily on the Bourse, and benefited from similar structures of friendly investors and unified holding companies.

Jacques Calvet's own career path has also been typically French— graduating from the ENA; taking up various posts in the administration, including head of the personal staff of Giscard d'Estaing when he was finance minister; being appointed deputy managing director of the Banque Nationale de Paris in 1974 and rising to the position of chairman; and finally moving to a top position at Peugeot SA. In the summer of 1992, he even said he was considering running in the 1995 presidential election. "In France, Calvet's is considered a model career" (Barsoux and Lawrence 1991, 67). He is a top industrialist who has been credited with using his intimate knowledge of the upper reaches of the French financial system and civil service "to obtain some aid, generous tax deductions, and recognition that his publicly quoted company is as important as Renault" (*Sunday Times*, April 23, 1989). The same is true of his predecessor at PSA. Jean-Paul Parayre graduated from the École Polytechnique and joined Chirac's staff as a highway engineer. He moved to the Ministry for Industrial and Science Development in 1969, where he dealt with the auto industry until the Peugeots asked him to join the firm in 1974.

The recent changes in the financial markets have given Peugeot access to new sources of financing and new financial instruments to improve its balance sheet. However, the development of the French Bourse, the advent of a single European market in 1992 (albeit still an uneven one), and the liberalization of European equity markets in general, also pose a considerable challenge to the firm going into the 1990s. Add to this the probable privatization, full or partial, of Renault in the near future, and PSA may find that it will no longer be able to access equity capital as easily in the future. Would investors be as tolerant of a firm that waives its dividend for five years straight if it were not the largest company on a relatively small Bourse, or if it were not the only publicly quoted auto firm in which they could invest?

Furthermore, the gradual removal of import restraints on the Japanese auto manufacturers will significantly increase the competitive pressures on Peugeot through the remainder of the 1990s. Without protective trade barriers, and with state aid closely scrutinized by the EC (as Renault has already discovered), how will the government ensure the survival of this important manufacturer? One answer might be a further blurring of the public-private divide, with partially government-owned and parastatal institutions such as Caisse des Dépôts and Crédit National becoming more actively involved in financing PSA, just as they are already involved in Usinor Sacilor.

Similarities between Britain and France

As in the previous two cases—and as in the next case, that of British Leyland—the state was involved in providing this major manufacturer with access to significant sources of financing at key junctures, even though the firm was never nationalized. Also, as in the other three cases, PSA was not always as clearly on one side of the public-private divide as its ownership status might suggest. The firm also played a major role in the government's regional assistance programs, becoming intimately concerned with industrial policy for the sector as a whole, and for particular regions. (Interestingly, the British automaker BL was similarly closely involved in regional development programs.) Finally, Peugeot was also anxious to reduce its debt burdens in the 1980s. The context was different from that of BSC and the French steel firms, who had their finances restructured and a considerable portion of their debts converted into publicly or privately held equity by the state. Peugeot initiated its own restructuring that involved the use of new markets and new financing instruments to reduce its debts. But the impetus was very similar.

Firm-Level Financial Issues

Because Peugeot SA has always been an influential privately owned firm, the importance of the availability and costs of its financing and the attitudes of the providers of that financing are obvious. Nevertheless, the analysis of these issues in Peugeot's case is comparable with the cases of firms that spent some of the past fifteen years under state ownership.

Capital was available to Peugeot from the banking system and, more especially, from equity investors. It enjoyed an influential position on the Bourse and could call on family and friendly institutional investors for fresh funds. It also, ultimately, had recourse to government loans in a crunch. This, in turn, had an impact on the costs of the firm's financing. Its ability to access equity capital meant that, although it was anxious to reduce its growing debt burdens in the mid-1980s, PSA was not as burdened by high debt-servicing costs as the other cases analyzed here. It certainly did not face the kind of burden that threatened to bury the French steel firms in the late 1970s.

More striking than the issues of the costs and availability of its financing, however, is the attitude of Peugeot's providers of capital. This was crucial. Friendly investors supported the firm through its period of financial difficulties in the early 1980s, and subscribed to new equity capital in 1985 and 1987, even though Peugeot had paid no dividend for five years. The same has not been true for British Steel in recent years or, as we shall see in the next chapter, for Jaguar in the mid-1980s. In addition, the Peugeot family is a dominant stakeholder in the firm. They hold a significant portion of the company's capital, and have a long and distinguished reputation in French financial and industrial circles. More importantly, they have played a key role in managing the firm's expansion and restructuring from 1974 onward, drafting a talented outsider to direct the acquisitions of Citroën and Talbot; supporting another outsider in his standoff with labor over plant closures and job layoffs; and maintaining their financial interest in the company through a tumultuous and expensive period of reorganization and new investment. All in all, their attitude has been reminiscent of the British government's stance with regard to BSC and its outspoken chairman, Ian MacGregor, in the early 1980s, and is in contrast to the French government's role where the fragmented and debt-laden steel firms were concerned.

For Peugeot, the costs of financing were less of a consideration at a time of crisis than was the case at BSC or the French steel firms. The availability of financing was important in that PSA had access to more financing options than did Usinor or Sacilor—its history, reputation, and particularly its corporate governance structure, allowed it to make use of the fledgling equity market at a time when others could not or would not. In addition, its rival, Renault, was nationalized, leaving PSA to enjoy its preeminent position on the private market. The most interesting aspects of the Peugeot case, however, are that its corporate governance structure gave it a number of long-term investors that stuck by its restructuring efforts, with one dominant stakeholder particularly supportive of management's plans; and that ultimately even Peugeot had to have recourse to government financing during its struggle to restructure. The state is thus implicated even in this case, indirectly in that its regulations and liberalization measures shaped and then reshaped the national financial system in which PSA operates; and directly in that it helped to finance the firm in a crunch.

The next chapter, and the final case, takes us back to a firm that crossed to and fro from private to state and back to private ownership again, in the space of fifteen years. As with Peugeot, the tale of British Leyland and its offspring, Jaguar plc, and successor, the Rover Group, illustrates both the role of government in providing firms with access to financing, and the importance of firm-level financial structures and the workings of the national financial system for a major manufacturer's ability to survive and adapt in a highly competitive and rapidly changing world.

CHAPTER 5

British Leyland: From BL to Jaguar and the Rover Group

In 1979 British Leyland was seen in Britain as a prime example of the worst excesses of nationalization—an unwieldy giant, losing millions of pounds of public money weekly and turning out inferior products. It did, however, have over 23 percent of the British car market. In 1989, after its purchase by British Aerospace (BAe), the newly named Rover Group promoted itself as "not a giant carmaker by any means but quicker, leaner, fitter" and claimed to produce two-thirds of all British-made car exports (Personal Interview, Cowley, May 1989). Its home market share, however, had fallen to barely 15 percent. Although the Society of Motor Manufacturers and Traders (SMMT) claimed the industry "creates more employment, generates more income, and ships more exports than any other manufacturing industry" (Trade and Industry Committee, 1986–87, HC 407, memorandum), the industry's net trade deficit of nearly £7 billion (£7,000 million) was a huge percentage of the nation's annual visible trade deficit in 1989 (*Financial Times*, October 12, 1989). Then again, by 1991 the trade situation had improved—the industry even managed a £121-million trade surplus in the final three months of the year, according to the SMMT (*Financial Times*, February 12, 1992). The sharp devaluation of sterling after September 1992 suddenly put the Rover Group in a much better position. As a firm that manufactures only in the United Kingdom and that therefore has a high percentage of U.K.-manufactured components, Rover's production costs were now much lower than those of competitors (whose imported components had become much more expensive), and the price of its exports to continental Europe were far lower. Nevertheless, the very factors that allowed Rover to benefit from the rapid depreciation of sterling also make the firm vulnerable— a mid-sized manufacturer that is primarily oriented to only its domestic market, a market about to become even more fiercely competitive as the new Japanese production plants come on-line.

British Leyland, or BL, like the British Steel Corporation, has generated much debate within the United Kingdom about economic nationalism, industrial competitiveness, and the need to maintain a viable domestic producer. Like BSC, BL was also a nationalized company, privatized by the Conservative government after a decade of restructuring and retrenchment. However, the debates surrounding the fate of Britain's sole domestically owned mass-market carmaker have been the most politicized and contentious of the four cases analyzed here. Unlike Peugeot, BL has not been sheltered from overseas competitors producing within its home market, and it has not remained aloof from the international linkages developing in the industry. Unlike BSC, BL is not the only major firm involved in its industry in the country—it must compete with Ford, General Motors, Peugeot, Nissan, and now Honda and Toyota, all of whom have also received financial assistance in one form or another from successive British governments. And the apparently straightforward privatization of BL has emerged as the most scandal-ridden and complex sale of them all.

With the often-vitriolic debates surrounding the only remaining British-owned mass-market carmaker—nationalization versus private ownership; market protection versus competition from inward investors; the financial shenanigans of the Rover sale to BAe—it is easy to lose sight of some of the more interesting facts concerning the financing of BL and its offspring, Jaguar. This chapter discusses the original nationalization of the British Leyland Motor Corporation, the firm's postnationalization financing, the case of Jaguar, and the privatization of the Rover Group. The analysis bears out the conclusions drawn from the previous three cases. First, that financial issues, and particularly the attitude of "investors," are as important for a nationalized company as a privatized one. Second, that beginning our analysis at the level of the firm reveals aspects of the workings of the national financial system not as discernible in a top-down approach that focuses on institutions and national structures. Third, that there are some surprising similarities between this case and one of its counterparts in France. Finally, that there is no clear divide between the public and the private sectors, and the role of the state is pervasive.

Once again, the chapter starts with some background description before moving on to the details of the financing of BL in part 2. Part 1 outlines the crisis and the restructuring at BL and subsequent privatization, and describes the firm's political context—in particular, the presence of foreign-car manufacturers in the United Kingdom, which has had a profound impact on the firm's relationship with successive governments.

1. The Restructuring of British Leyland

As in France, the British auto industry developed out of the bicycle industry. The first major firm, the Daimler Motor Company, began production around 1896. The early firms manufactured entire vehicles, rather than relying on outside component suppliers like the Americans, in part because of the ease of raising large amounts of capital (Lewchuk 1986). However, the relative avail-ability of financing led numerous small producers to set up shop, and no British firm came close to establishing the kind of market share that Ford achieved in the United States. The number of firms producing for the British mass market slowly fell, but they did not begin to take advantage of econ-omies of scale until the 1950s, when a series of mergers altered the structure of the domestic industry. Austin and Morris merged to form the British Motor Corporation (BMC), then took over the smaller companies of Jaguar and MG. The commercial-vehicle producer Leyland took over Standard- Triumph and bought up the smaller companies of Rover, Albion Motors, and AVC. These strategies seemed successful in the buoyant market of the 1950s and 1960s, and neither concern moved seriously to restructure or rationalize its acquisi-tions.

When the Labour Party returned to office in 1964, it actively promoted the idea of industrial restructuring. A common assumption in the government and the auto industry at that time was that production units were too small to compete internationally. Leyland and BMC began discussing merger possi-bilities in 1964, but vacillated over the details. In 1968, Leyland won govern-ment support for its proposal to take over the failing BMC. Through the Industrial Reorganisation Corporation (IRC) the government made an initial loan of £25 million, followed by a further £10 million, to assist in the merger (Hague and Wilkinson 1983). The new British Leyland Motor Corporation (BLMC) that resulted had over 40 percent of the British car market (Cowling et al. 1980).

Crisis, Nationalization, and Restructuring

Once again, the merger strategy seemed successful, as BLMC proved profit-able in the early 1970s. In 1974 the British auto industry as a whole earned £1.3 billion of export exchange. As with the mergers among French steel producers, however, the large, diverse BLMC continued to have conflicting subsidiaries, unintegrated plant, and chronic underinvestment in new technol-ogies and models. The Jaguar and Rover businesses had not been self-sufficient in cash generation for many years (Edwardes 1983). All of this left the company in a vulnerable position to face the ensuing crisis period of the mid- to late-1970s. BLMC was nationalized in 1975 (see part 2) and renamed British Leyland.

The now majority-state-owned British Leyland's share of the domestic market continued to fall (see table 23). Michael Edwardes took over as chief executive in 1977, renamed the company BL, and oversaw a retrenchment strategy of plant closures, work-force reductions, and concentration on the domestic market. Solving the company's poor labor relations was defined as the key strategic problem. Between 1978 and 1982, the size of BL's U.K. work force fell by 50 percent (although some of these losses resulted from the sale of peripheral businesses). Redundancy payments alone cost the company £98 million in 1981 and £30 million in 1982. Production of the historic Triumph and MG sports cars ended.

Edwardes argued that vast investment was needed to make an impact on the "Dickensian facilities" at the BL factories (Edwardes 1983). Most of this came from the government in a series of equity investments, designed to support Edwardes's so-called Survival Plan. The company was also restructured internally, replacing the old divisions by function and geography with just two major divisions, Cars and Land-Rover-Leyland. The Cars division comprised the Austin Rover Group, Jaguar Cars, and the component manufacturer Unipart. Land-Rover-Leyland comprised the bus- and truck-maker Leyland Vehicles, Land Rover, and a number of overseas truck and Land Rover operations. Each subdivision was given its own board and authority over operations was greatly decentralized (Edwardes 1983).

In 1983, BL made its first pretax profit since 1978, but its output of cars was still falling and import penetration of the domestic market was up to over 57 percent (Trade and Industry Committee, 1982–83, HC 353, HC 407). Its debt-servicing requirement was around £75 million a year (Trade and Industry Committee, 1983–84, HC 490). BL was now thirteenth in the world-league table of car producers, "slightly smaller than Daimler-Benz, slightly larger than BMW and with the product and financial strength of neither" (Wilks

TABLE 23.   British Leyland: Market Share, Production, and Employment

	% of U.K. Car Market[a]	Production (thousands)	Year-End Employment
1975	30.8	605	
1977	24.3	651	176,000
1979	19.6	503	146,000
1980	18.2	395	143,300
1981	19.2	413	117,000
1983	18.6	445	101,400
1985	17.9	383	77,000
1987	15.0	465	44,800
1989			49,000
1991[b]			35,000
1992[b]			33,000

Source: Data from Jones 1983; Williams 1987; *Moody's International*, various issues.
[a]Cars = Austin Rover, Jaguar, Range Rover; minus Jaguar after 1983.
[b]Rover Group only.

1984a, 229). An official at the Department of Trade and Industry estimated that because of the cuts at BL, some 300,000 jobs were eliminated from the components industry between 1980 and 1985 (HC 407, qu.40). Such figures led a TUC study to conclude that: "the U.K., European and world motor industries have been living through a period of intense restructuring. In the U.K. this restructuring of production has been particularly savage. But it has not left the U.K. industry in a stronger position" (Trades Union Congress 1984).

As in the cases of BSC and the French steel and auto industries, car manufacturing in Britain is highly geographically concentrated. Retrenchment by BL, other auto manufacturers, and some components manufacturers thus had serious repercussions on the regional economies of the north west of England and the west and south Midlands. According to one study, the percentage of Coventry's workforce employed by BL fell from over 14 percent in 1978 to just 9 percent in 1985. Austin Rover is still Oxford's largest manufacturing employer, even though employment at the nearby Cowley plant plunged 40 percent between 1978 and 1981 (Walker 1987). By the end of the 1980s, however, the industry was beginning to disperse into new regions, as the government's policy of attracting inward investment led to the siting of new auto plants in the northeast and Derbyshire.

There was another side to BL's restructuring—its burgeoning relationship with the Japanese auto manufacturer, Honda. In 1980 BL needed new models but lacked both the time and the financial resources for major research and development. Management and unions alike recognized that collaboration with an outside firm was needed (Transport and General Workers Union 1980). In 1981 BL signed an agreement with Honda for the joint development of a new car model for the U.K. and Japanese markets. The BL board had actually approved the agreement in October 1979, but signing had to wait until the government had agreed to finance BL's 1980 corporate plan. The relationship developed rapidly from a license for BL to build a Honda-developed car into jointly developed cars with shared technical resources. The jointly developed Maestro was launched in 1983. The Rover 800, launched later in the decade, was the result of shared technical resources, and the two went on to collaborate on a new series, the Rover 200 and Honda Concerto, for the 1990s. The relationship was cemented in 1989, when Honda took a long-expected 20 percent equity stake in the renamed Rover Group (for £116 million). Rover now owns 20 percent of Honda's British manufacturing operations.

Privatization

A large part of the restructuring of BL during the 1980s was the result of privatization. Smaller component and other manufacturing facilities were hived off from BL and sold in the early 1980s. The first major sale came in 1984, when Jaguar was hived off and floated on the stock exchange as a fully independent carmaker. The firm was subsequently taken over by American mass-market producer Ford in 1988. The tale of Jaguar's privatization, the hype surrounding its initial flotation, and the subsequent speed with which it ran into financial difficulties on adverse investor sentiment, is studied in more depth in part 2 of this chapter.

A further round of sales came in 1987. Early in the year, with the European truck market on the upturn, Leyland Truck was hived off from BL and sold to the Dutch firm DAF, with Rover taking a 40 percent stake in DAF in return. The government wrote off most of Leyland Trucks' debt to facilitate the purchase (*Financial Times*, May 3, 1989).[1] Then the Leyland Bus subsidiary was sold to a management consortium for £4 million, and the Unipart spare-parts business was bought out by its employees and City institutions (*Guardian*, January 14, 1987).

The final sale was that of the renamed Rover Group itself. In late 1987 the chairman of British Aerospace (BAe) said that he was interested in the Rover Group's Land-Rover subsidiary and its stake in DAF, and might be willing to buy the whole group. By the following April, BAe had reached a conditional agreement with the government. In July 1988, following modifications of the terms of the sale that were mandated by the European Commission, BAe formally agreed to buy Rover, paying the government £150 million for the state's shareholding in the group.

The retrenchment and restructuring of British Leyland/BL/Rover over the past fifteen years makes it hard to classify the firm. In 1978, British Leyland was clearly a medium-sized volume manufacturer, producing for the mass market. By 1993, the Rover Group targeted too broad a market for a specialty maker, yet had too small a production run to be on a par with Peugeot or Renault. Chairman Day has said on a number of occasions that Rover is no longer a volume car producer. Nor has the consolidation ended in the fiercely competitive environment of the 1990s. The Rover Group eliminated some 2,000 jobs in 1991 (mostly through voluntary redundancy and natural wastage). In 1989 GM's British subsidiary, Vauxhall, made a record operating profit of £250 million and ousted Rover from second place in the U.K. market (*Financial Times*, December 27, 1989). The group is now intent on what management calls a plan of "Roverisation." Spurred in part by what it has learned from the relationship with Honda, and in part by the increased competitive pressure from other Japanese manufacturers now producing within the United Kingdom, Rover is attempting to meet Japanese standards of productivity, and to incorporate "lean manufacturing" and the latest technologies into its production processes. As in the 1980s, this means massive sums of investment—in the summer of 1992, BAe announced that investment programs at Rover would involve spending some £200 million in each of the next two years (*Financial Times*, July 24, 1992).

The Political Context

The political context of BL's restructuring has been very different from that of Peugeot SA in France, and different also from that of the British Steel Corporation. Unlike PSA, British Leyland has not seen eye-to-eye with successive governments over auto-industry policy. A major bone of contention has been the Special Car Tax. This 10 percent additional tax added on to the wholesale price of cars (in addition to VAT) was first introduced in 1971, as a temporary measure, on the grounds that "wage leapfrogging and overheating of the economy originated in the motor industry" (Trade and Industry Committee, 1982–83, HC 407, qu.1836). Although the tax was supposed to be removed when conditions were "right," it was still around in the 1980s, with DTI officials claiming that its retention was in keeping with Treasury policy on indirect taxation (ibid.). In fiscal year 1986–87, the tax yielded £980 million in revenue (DTI figure, Trade and Industry Committee, 1987–88, HC 316). The tax is unique in the EC and has been a constant source of complaint from all auto and auto-component manufacturers. House of Commons committees also regularly condemn the tax. Component manufacturer GKN has called it "an outstanding example of discriminatory treatment of the automotive industry" and BL said it was "a special penal tax on [the] industry." Component manufacturer Turnell and Newall plc said the tax is "anomalous and arbitrarily limits the size of the U.K. car market" (Trade and Industry Committee, 1982–83, HC 407).

BL and other auto manufacturers have also repeatedly complained about the adverse effects of exchange-rate fluctuations and government policies on sterling over the years. In 1981 BL argued that the main reason why it was not able to achieve its goals was that government policy meant very high levels of sterling on foreign exchanges. Edwardes stated that if the exchange rate and inflation had stayed at the levels assumed in 1978, "our profits would have been £1.7 billion higher and we wouldn't need an additional £990 million from the government . . . . Exchange rates are by far the biggest factor in our failure to deliver the internal generation of funds" (Trade and Industry Committee, 1980–81, HC 294).[2] Unlike others, BL did not benefit from a reduction in raw materials costs, as most of its raw materials are purchased domestically.

As in France, the British auto market has been protected in recent years with bilaterally negotiated Voluntary Restraint Agreements. After 1977, these shielded the home market by limiting the Japanese producers to an 11-percent market share. Nevertheless, the British market has been more open than the French. Edwardes told a 1982 inquiry that he had "always felt, personally, that there should be selective import control where individual cases warrant it" (Trade and Industry Committee, 1981–82, HC 194). Not only was the limit itself less stringent than in France, however, but its impact was considerably less due to one of the key aspects of auto-industry policy in the United Kingdom—the long-term presence of foreign manufacturers in the domestic market, and the post-1979 Conservative government's active encouragement of inward investment by new producers from overseas. The presence of foreign manufacturers, and the resolution of labor disputes in the industry, have been the two main factors dominating the political context of BL's restructuring.

The closures and cuts at BL triggered industrial unrest, although not on a scale comparable with Peugeot in the 1980s or BL itself in the 1970s. More interesting was the attitude toward labor disputes that predated the period of restructuring. By 1978, British Leyland was popularly seen as a hotbed of radical unionism, with militant shop stewards such as Derek "Red Robbo" Robinson, the Longbridge union convenor, defying union authority. Sixteen unions, organized along distinct craft lines, competed with each other as fiercely as with management. As far as management was concerned, the issue of labor relations, and how to subdue the militants, was the dominant concern after 1975. Edwardes put considerable time and energy into his strategy of circumventing local union organizers and balloting the employees directly on his proposals for restructuring the firm. For the 1980 plan, for example, Edwardes announced that if 75 percent of the workers voted approval, he would seek additional financing from the government; if the ratio was 70 to 75 percent, BL would debate its options; if approval was below 70 percent, he couldn't make the recovery work and would recommend the government dismantle BL. Eighty percent of the employees voted on the plan ballot, of whom 87.2 percent voted in favor. Such tactics, combined with recession and layoffs, greatly decreased strike activity at BL in the 1980s. Labor relations at Rover are now very different, after a New Deal agreed between management and unions in April 1991. Workers were given greater job security and improved conditions in return for their commitment to more Japanese-style job flexibility and work teams (see "Old Rover Learns new Japanese Tricks," *Financial Times*, October 10, 1992, sec. 2, p.1).

The presence of overseas manufacturers in the U.K. car market has had a profound impact on BL's (and its predecessors') fortunes over the years, and on the attitudes of successive governments toward the domestically owned firm. After the nationalization of British Leyland in 1975, both the Labour and subsequent Conservative governments had an uneasy relationship with the firm. On the one hand, although BL has never been a favored national champion in the sense of Renault, "the great unspoken justification for BL is that it is British" (Wilks 1984a, 96). On the other hand, the presence of multinationals that produce more cars and more jobs than BL has tempered enthusiasm for the British producer, as well as giving it a great deal of competition in its home market. This has led to some apparently paradoxical policy decisions, with the government both financing BL's restructuring, and vigorously attracting foreign producers. In the 1970s the government even bailed out one foreign producer facing bankruptcy—Chrysler U.K. (see part 3).

This long-term domination of the national market by both home-based producers and multinationals and importers makes Britain unique among major car-producing countries. All but one of the big assemblers in Britain today are foreign-owned, by Ford and GM of the United States, Peugeot of France, and now Nissan, Toyota, and Honda of Japan.[3] Ford has consistently led the pack in terms of market share, with a 30 percent share in 1989 compared to Rover's 15 percent. (Ford opened its Dagenham plant in 1931. Despite cutbacks in recent years, it is still one of the country's top employers, with some 39,500 employees in late 1991, compared with a peak of 80,000 in early 1980.) Peugeot Talbot's market share has rapidly increased, from just 4 percent in the mid-1980s to 7.3 percent in 1991. An increasingly large percentage of the market is attributable to the captive imports of these multinationals—up from 16 percent in 1987 to 20 percent in 1988 (Society of Motor Manufacturers and Traders 1988). In addition, many of the cars produced by GM and Talbot tend to have a British-based content of barely 50 percent by ex-works price (Trade and Industry Committee, 1982–83, HC 407). Ford also dominates in the arena of industrial relations, with its annual pay negotiations one of the most influential in the industrial-relations calendar.

After 1979, the new Conservative government actively encouraged inward investment by foreign firms, particularly in less-developed regions of the country. The first major agreement was reached with Nissan. Its plant in Sunderland began production in 1985, quickly increasing its output and announcing a target of 200,000 cars a year. By the spring of 1993, the target had been raised to 300,000, with some 80 percent of the cars meant for export to continental Europe. Although the government cannot directly demand domestic content levels, as this would contravene the Treaty of Rome,[4] it has, in effect, been able to do so as part of the conditions for investors such as Nissan to receive industrial development assistance. Nissan got back around 20 percent of the Sunderland plant's costs, through a combination of tax breaks, £35 million in selective industrial development assistance, and £70 million in regional development grants (HC 407). The secretary of state for trade and industry justified this aid on the grounds that Nissan will invest some £200 million in the region and employ over a thousand people (Trade and

Industry Committee, 1987–88, HC 343). The next big auto investment came from Toyota, which announced in April 1989 that it would develop a greenfield site in Derbyshire. Unlike Nissan, Toyota did not receive direct state aid as this is not a designated assisted region. After the subsidies granted Nissan, the Rover Group had apparently lobbied the DTI heavily "not to give such an advantage to a second Japanese carmaker" (*Financial Times*, April 19, 1989). The Burnaston plant opened in December 1992, and at the time of writing Toyota was planning on producing 100,000 cars a year at the new site, expandable to 200,000 a year. Toyota has also opened an engine plant at Deeside in north Wales. The third Japanese manufacturer, Honda, started making its own engines in Swindon in 1989, and opened a car plant there in October 1992 with planned annual production of 100,000 cars by 1994.

By the mid-1990s, these Japanese plants will have the capacity to produce at least 600,000 cars a year, with over 70 percent destined for export to the rest of Europe. Some analysts speculate that production could reach a million or more cars annually by 1999. The presence of the new Japanese competitors has galvanized at least one of the American multinationals to respond—in November 1992 GM opened its biggest investment in the United Kingdom to date, a £190-million engine factory in Cheshire (*Economist*, November 28, 1992). In addition to the new investments, overseas-based producers have also been taking over the smaller U.K. luxury-car makers. Ford now owns Jaguar and Aston Martin; GM has Lotus. When Vickers considered selling Rolls-Royce Motor Cars to BMW of Germany early in 1992, there was a flurry of press coverage bemoaning the fact that, with Honda owning 20 percent of Rover, the contemplated sale would leave only one carmaker in wholly British hands, a small sports-car company called TVR.

It is this ambivalent attitude toward a domestically owned car industry that is at the heart of the political context of BL's restructuring. On the one hand, government, politicians, and trade unionists are delighted at the employment and investment levels represented by the likes of Nissan and Toyota, and by the technological and financial benefits to Rover of its relationship with Honda. On the other hand, there is economic nationalism—the feeling that some significant level of domestically owned car-making capacity is crucial for the economic well-being of the nation. Cries of economic nationalism were heard most loudly late in 1985, over proposals to hive off parts of BL and sell them to the American manufacturers General Motors and Ford. The DTI had sounded out the possibility of Ford taking over BL's Cars division, Austin Rover. BL management resisted the deal (Trade and Industry Committee, 1985–86, HC 291). Meanwhile, discussions were under way with GM to take over Leyland Vehicles, the truck-making division that included Land Rover. The BL board felt that this deal would be a good one, but it died in early 1986: "It was clearly not politically acceptable to the Government" (BL Chairman Day, Trade and Industry Committee, 1985–86, HC 423).

The political unacceptability came from the storm of patriotic fervor that greeted the news in the House of Commons that the great name of Land Rover might be sold to the Americans. The government was already in trouble over the Westland affair, and back-bench economic nationalism and anti-Americanism was running high.[5] Also, three by-elections loomed. Just how the pullout from the GM deal was engineered isn't clear. Some report that the government said the Land Rover bid was too low and GM pulled out (HC 423). Others claim the government offered GM the Trucks division and 49 percent of Land Rover, with conditions about U.K. content and manufacturing that GM rejected (*Guardian Weekly*, March 30, 1986). The *Economist* claimed the DTI left only the debt-laden Trucks division in the deal. Either way, a few days after discussions with GM ended, news of the Ford-BL talks leaked out and another storm erupted in the Commons. The Cabinet swiftly pulled out of the talks with Ford.

This, then, is the basic history and background to the case of British Leyland through the 1980s. BL is, in many ways, the most politicized of these four cases and, as a result, the firm's fate is usually seen in terms of larger debates about economic nationalism, industrial competitiveness, labor relations, and the necessity or wisdom of trying to maintain a viable domestic auto manufacturer in an increasingly competitive world. In all of these debates, however, the financial structure of the firm tends to be overlooked, and in particular, the fact that the government never really took on the role of dominant stakeholder as it had done at BSC.

2. The Financing of BL

Much of the academic and political analysis of BL and Jaguar is cast in terms of what was, or would have been, "better" for the firm in the short or long term, state or private ownership. As in the previous three cases, however, a look at firm-level financial issues shows that the true picture is more complicated than a simple contrast of state and private ownership. The public-private boundary was often blurred in unexpected ways. Also, most importantly, analyzing the financing of a firm such as BL reveals a great deal about the national financial system in which it operates. The story of the financing of BL is divided into four sections—the nationalization of BLMC in 1975, the postnationalization financing of British Leyland, the case of Jaguar, and the 1988 sale of the Rover Group to British Aerospace.

Nationalization

By 1914, the twenty-three publicly quoted auto firms in Britain found 65 percent of their capital on the public markets and only 10 percent from retained earnings (Lewchuk 1986). The original source of most of the financing in the industry had major long-term repercussions. The profitable firms continued to distribute a "significant proportion" of their profits as dividends during the interwar years, rather than reinvesting in new capacity or new technology. "Between 1922 and 1939, Austin paid out nearly 70 percent of profits on ordinary and preferred dividends and on interest on long-term bonds" (Lewchuk 1986). Then came the defensive mergers of the 1950s, which were largely the result of insufficient productive capacity to meet the new mass-market demand. Neither of the two major producers was in a very strong financial position when the market began to deteriorate in the late 1960s.

The Industrial Reorganisation Corporation had assumed that creating large organizations under one ownership would stimulate reorganization without the need for further state involvement. This was not the case. In 1975 BLMC had a pretax loss of £76 million, and had rapidly increased short-term borrowing to finance operations and investment (Wilks 1984a). The company continued to pay dividends into the early 1970s, distributing over 94 percent of reported profits to its shareholders (Lewchuk 1986). In late 1974 the banks became "seriously concerned" about BLMC's losses and met with the company and the Department of Industry. The outcome was a government-guaranteed bank loan of £50 million for working capital for BLMC, and the appointment of a team headed by Lord Ryder to investigate the company (Wilks 1984a). In April 1975 the government announced that it accepted the Ryder Report as the basis for future policy toward the company. In July the British Leyland Bill was passed, nationalizing the company's assets.

> The Ryder Report was produced from scratch in under four months, and accepted almost immediately. In addition to Lord Ryder the team included a merchant banker, a practising accountant, a trade unionist and a former Ford executive, none of whom could be expected to have a detailed knowledge of the company. The time scale is only reasonable if the team had some clear idea of the shape of their final report. (Wilks 1984a, 99)

After accepting Ryder, the Department of Industry purchased 78 percent of BLMC's equity from private shareholders for £46.5 million, and subscribed £200 million for new shares in the reconstituted British Leyland

Limited. The National Enterprise Board (NEB) assumed responsibility for the government shareholding in February 1976.

As in the case of the French steel companies, British Leyland was nationalized at a time of acute financial crisis. It seems that the government intended to maintain the company in its existing form, but with substantial aid and public ownership. British Leyland's own concept study was accepted wholesale. According to then-Managing Director Barber: "What they did was to ask some of our management and particularly our finance director . . . to prepare a plan on completely ideal assumptions—what would you do if you had all the money you wanted" (Adeney 1988, 280). Meanwhile, British Leyland's management was primarily concerned with industrial relations rather than the need for any radical restructuring within the company. The two major unions at British Leyland were the TGWU and the AUEW. The deputy general secretary of the TGWU was a member of the Ryder team and subsequently of the National Enterprise Board (NEB). The leadership of the two unions was also involved in the formulation and promotion of Labour's Social Contract. The unions' influence was felt by the Ryder team, British Leyland management, and the government itself. The unions were better at exercising influence at this level than at controlling their membership. There were a series of wildcat disputes in the industry in the 1970s. Industrial-relations problems were aggravated at British Leyland by a multiplicity of pay-bargaining units and settlement dates, and confusion over the measured-day-work system recently introduced (Wilks 1984a).

The Ryder Report justified the government financing the company out of its crisis. Edwardes called it "a public 'prospectus' for government funding of the company"—but it was bizarrely based on a study that itself assumed a free availability of cash. The Ryder Report was seriously overoptimistic, projecting an increasing and stable market, and called for an injection of substantial funds to meet this increased demand. Overall, Ryder assumed a government commitment of £1.2 billion until 1981. In the event, the sums involved were far higher.

Postnationalization Financing

The nationalized British Leyland was initially owned and financed through the NEB. After the first £200 million share-issue, additional funding was advanced over the next few years, some as equity, the remainder as NEB loans that were converted to equity in 1980.

British Leyland's nationalization was fundamentally different from that of British Steel in three respects. The firm's equity was held by the National Enterprise Board, not the Department of Industry; a few private shareholders remained; and, crucially, it continued to draw funds from the private banks. Under an agreement negotiated by Secretary of State Varley, the NEB approved the firm's corporate plan and the firm then went to the banks for additional financing. See table 24 for an overview of the funding of BL.

Securing government funding became an integral part of each corporate plan from BL. The 1978 plan depended on winning £450 million from the government, to see BL through the year. The plan had first to be approved by the NEB, then the Department of Industry. The strategy of the new chief executive, Michael Edwardes, was to present each financing request as an ultimatum: if it wasn't approved, they would either have to sack him or close BL. The plans were always accepted. Meanwhile, BL continued to do business with its private bankers. According to Edwardes (1983), BL was about to run out of money when he took over as chief executive in late 1977. The Labour government had its own problems with a hung Parliament. Edwardes says that the clearing banks came to BL's rescue, with loan facilities of £80 million to keep it going and existing government assurances as their only security.

Early in 1979 the British banks, "impressed by [BL's] progress," agreed to advance a loan of £115 million, in conjunction with a group of overseas

TABLE 24.   Provision of State Funds to British Leyland, 1975–76 to 1983–84

1975–76	£46 m	Purchase of shares from private shareholders.
	£200 m	Initial equity funding under British Leyland Act 1975.
1976–77	£70 m	Loan from NEB
	£30 m	Loan from government under Section 8, Industry Act 1972.
1977–78	£50 m	Loan from NEB
1978–79	£300 m	Equity from NEB
	£150 m	Equity from government under Section 8, Industry Act 1972.
	£25 m	Equity committed to NEB for their stake in Wholesale Vehicle Finance Ltd., set up as NEB subsidiary to finance BL dealers' stocks.
1979–80	£150 m	Equity from NEB
1980–81	£300 m	Equity from NEB
March 1980		Total of £150 m in NEB and Section 8 loans converted to equity
Total 1975–80	£1,321 m	
1981–82	£620 m	Additional equity from state
1982–83	£370 m	Additional equity from state
1983–84	£100 m	Additional equity from state
	£25 m	Equity for finance of BL's dealer stocks

Source: Adapted from Trade and Industry Committee, session 1980–81, HC 294; session 1983–84, HC 490.

banks (Edwardes 1983, 90). Later that same year, the government agreed to a further equity injection of £150 million. By the end of 1980, some £450 million had been secured from the private sector, most as bank loans (Trade and Industry Committee, 1980–81, HC 294). It is clear that private capital only flowed into BL because of the involvement of the state as loan guarantor. On the other hand, the willingness of the private sector to continue to advance funding to the financially precarious firm seems to have encouraged the government to do the same.

BL was controlled and monitored separately from the other nationalized industries. After the transfer of BL's shares from the NEB to the Department of Industry in 1981, the DTI drew up a Memorandum of Understanding laying out its relationship with the firm. BL was to act as far as possible as an independent commercial company, and to seek a commercial return that would be defined "from time to time" after consultation with the government. BL also had to advise the department of proposals involving spending of over £25 million or any "strategic or political significance." In 1981 BL's long-term strategic objectives were defined as returning all constituent businesses to the private sector, either together or separately; disposing of peripheral businesses; and achieving a rate of return that would attract external funds without government support (Comptroller and Auditor General 1983). Thus the 1983 plan aimed to borrow funds on normal commercial terms and obtain private investment over the next two years. Edwardes's successor, Sir Bide, acknowledged that "We do not want another penny piece from the taxpayer if we can possibly avoid it. The right way to get money for a viable business is through the market" (Trade and Industry Committee, 1982–83, HC 353).

The firm had in fact continued to receive at least a minority of its funding from the private sector (see table 25). Edwardes confirmed in January 1982 that BL had just completed a series of negotiations with British and overseas banks for eight- and ten-year loans totaling £277 million, "a very big loan project" (Trade and Industry Committee, 1981–82, HC 194). Such borrowings did not need the approval of Parliament.

This relationship with the banks gave BL a bargaining chip in 1982 when the Cabinet pushed BL to hive off and sell the Land Rover operations. The privatization of parts of BL was already underway. The earliest sales were relatively uncontentious, as plants and businesses were sold outright to other purchasers. Sales in 1981 surpassed the planned target, raising £53 million (Trade and Industry Committee, 1981–82, HC 194), while 1982's sales raised £25 million (Trade and Industry Committee, 1982–83, HC 353). As with BSC, it was up to the firm to decide how much Parliament should be informed of a sale. The DTI did not stipulate sale procedures and did not give detailed consideration to proposals that appeared in the corporate plan. It maintained that the sales did not raise national-policy issues, and that the

TABLE 25. BL Long-Term Debt (£ million)

	Secured Loans[a]	Unsecured Loans[a]	Term Bank Loans[a]	Other[b]	Total Debt Outstanding
1980	16.1	41.2	120.0	16.0	193.3
1981	17.4	33.2	112.5	24.5	187.6
1982	40.4	33.2	314.6	40.3	428.5
1983	26.4	33.2	364.4	18.9	442.9
1984	3.4	33.2	235.6	159.3	431.5
1985	2.1	33.2	354.0	153.1	542.4
1987	0.6	135.0			135.6

Source: Data adapted from *Moody's International*, various issues.

[a]Loans have varying due dates and interest rates.

[b]Includes unsecured Industry Act loans, unsecured Swiss Franc loan, unsecured French Franc bonds, and other debts not separately identified.

company itself was the best judge of the merits of its actions (Committee of Public Accounts, 1983–84, HC 103). BL's board supported these peripheral sales but was not willing to risk the greater company by selling off major parts such as Jaguar, or by selling prematurely at too low a price. The board could argue that such sales would not be in the best interests of BL's 80,000 private shareholders. Nevertheless, Edwardes claimed that Prime Minister Thatcher "made extensive changes" to the draft public statements on BL's 1981 funding plan, to emphasize privatization over recovery (Edwardes 1983, 239).

In 1981 the Cabinet called in outside consultants to study BL's planned split into two companies, Cars and Land Rover. BL's board and the Department of Industry had already approved the plan, but the consultants all opposed on the grounds that it would inhibit privatization. However, the Cabinet seized on one report that Land Rover was already salable, and pushed BL to study the implications. The Cabinet apparently wanted the sale to obviate the need for £100 million in government funding in 1983 and 1984 (ibid.). "It took three months of hard argument in a very tense atmosphere to show that this was not in any sense a realistic plan" (ibid., 248). With the backing of two merchant banks, BL finally convinced the government that the short-term proceeds of Land Rover's sale would not relieve the government's funding obligations, due to the loss of cash flow from Land Rover. Most important, BL could also point to the understanding it had with its bankers that the business would be run commercially, and that BL would not dispose of any assets that provided security for the loans. The fact that a minority of BL's financing was in the form of private debt gave the firm some leverage over a determined Cabinet.

Just why the state's equity was initially held by the National Enterprise Board isn't clear. Edwardes speculates that the ministers felt ill-equipped to tackle the firm's problems and assumed that the industrialists who staffed the NEB had more expertise, especially as Ryder himself was appointed NEB chairman in 1975. However, after the 1979 election the NEB's powers and responsibilities were cut drastically. When a dispute between the NEB and Rolls-Royce came to a head, the entire board resigned. The new chairman said he wanted nothing to do with BL or Rolls Royce, and the NEB withdrew de facto from supervision. In March 1981 the shareholdings were formally transferred to the Secretary of State for Industry.

Meanwhile, as in the cases of the French and British steel industries, the state's financial rescue of the firm included a debt-to-equity restructuring, with the bulk of the equity closely held by the state. In 1980 the new government, despite the monetarist Secretary of State Keith Joseph's strong instincts to the contrary, approved BL's request for £300 million as a "last chance lifeline." Although "[t]he theory said you shouldn't pay . . . they paid the cheque. They looked at the employment consequences and the balance of payments and they were absolutely horrified" (Peter Walker, quoted in Young 1989, 201). At Edwardes's request, the government also converted existing loans of £150 million into equity, thus saving interest payments and strengthening the company's balance sheet. In response to the 1981 and 1982 plans, again over Joseph's initial objections, the government approved a total of £990 million in state funds, with a further £100 million in 1983. By 1987, the government held 99.8 percent of BL's shares (*Moody's International*).

Edwardes told the government that without the £990 million BL would be unable to borrow any more from outside sources and would have to go into liquidation (Trade and Industry Committee, 1980–81, HC 294). This alarmed M.P.s with constituencies around the West Midlands, but the prime minister's advisor, Alan Walters, and some Conservative M.P.s, reportedly thought that closure might be a good idea (Edwardes 1983). The majority in government simply wanted BL back in the private sector as soon as possible. As with the earlier Chrysler rescue (see part 3), the ultimate argument in favor of funding was that it would be cheaper than allowing the company to close. Most estimates of the cost of liquidation ranged from £1.2 billion to £3 billion: "large enough to persuade the Treasury that a gamble on rescue would be cheaper" (Wilks 1984a, 217). The Transport and General Workers Union thought that it would take five years to totally wind down BL, at a cost of £10.2 billion (Transport and General Workers Union 1980).

In September 1981, Patrick Jenkin became secretary of state for industry. He had no ideological abhorrence of government intervention in industry and, according to Edwardes, intervention "grew substantially on a variety of issues" (1983, 245). There were increasing battles over Edwardes's refusal to fragment the company for privatization. When his contract expired in late 1982, neither Edwardes nor the government sought to renew it.

Direct state funding of BL ended in 1984. The following year management confirmed that BL didn't intend to ask the government for any more. From now on, "we are going to raise such money as we need from the market in the normal way and from the privatisation programme that we have" (Trade and Industry Committee, 1984–85, HC 569). Still, BL was not in the best of financial health. By 1987 the car division, Austin Rover, had an accumulated debt of £1.5 billion. In late 1988, Secretary of State Lord Young said that if it were not for the involvement of the government, the Rover Group would be in liquidation in five minutes. His conclusion was blunt: "it is only the Government support in terms of the Varley Marshall assurances which enables the banks and others to provide the sorts of money that they are providing today" (Trade and Industry Committee, 1987–88, HC 487).

As at BSC, there were attempts to make the state effectively the dominant stakeholder at BL, with the transfer of the company to direct ministerial control in 1981, the stipulation of monitoring guidelines, and the debt-to-equity conversion. However, the case of BL differs from that of BSC in one crucial respect—the firm continued to draw upon other sources for a significant proportion of its financing. In addition, successive governments were not as single-minded in their support of the firm. Where BSC was the only major steel producer in the United Kingdom, BL was one of a number of mass-market car manufacturers. In contrast to Peugeot SA, it had to compete for attention not with one other domestically owned producer, but with two long-established American multinationals and, after the mid-1980s, with new Japanese investors. See table 26 for an overview of BL's financial status from 1978 to 1992.

The Case of Jaguar

> Jaguar . . . is a company at risk and the main danger to the company in many ways and perhaps paradoxically is not the competition, it's not your BMWs, your Porsches and Mercedes Benz, it's the attitude of the City and the financial institutions to Jaguar. (Prof. G. Rhys to *World in Action*, June 5, 1989)

Private bankers may have been "willing and supportive" where the state-backed BL was concerned, but the stock market turned out to be less than kind to its offspring, Jaguar. The 1980s were an eventful decade for Jaguar. Its 1984 flotation was hailed as another successful example of Thatcher's privatization program. Then, as sterling appreciated against the dollar and severely hurt profits, the firm's share price tumbled and investors swiftly withdrew. Jaguar finished the decade caught in a hostile bid and ultimately successful

TABLE 26. BL Financials 1978–79 to 1991–92
(£ million, April–March Financial Year)

	Operating Profit/(Loss)	Extraordinary Items	Net Profit/(Loss)
1978		(38)	(38.0)
1979	(46.2)	(23)	(144.0)
1980	(293.9)	(139)	(535.5)
1981	(244.6)	(152)	(497.0)
1982	(125.8)	(59)	(292.9)
1983	4.1	(64)	(151.5)
1984	(11.7)	163[a]	80.6
1985	(39.5)		(138.0)
1986	(246.4)		(892.1)
1987	16.8		26.8
1988	50[b]		
1989	64		
1990	55		
1991	(52)		
1992	(49)		

Source: Data adapted from Trade and Industry Committee, various issues; Williams et al. 1987; *Moody's International*, various issues.

Note: From 1984, BL minus Jaguar. From 1986, Rover Group (Austin Rover and Land Rover).

[a]1984 Jaguar sale = extraordinary profit of £186.1m.

[b]From 1988, the Rover Group subsidiary of BAe

Operating Profit = after accumulated depreciation and amortization, before tax, interest, and extraordinary items. Extraordinary Items = costs of closures and rationalization.

buyout. The secretary of state for industry had a profound effect on Jaguar's buyout, while arguing that he sought to be as little involved as possible.

Jaguar started life in 1922 as the Swallow Sidecar Company in Blackpool. It was floated and renamed as SS Jaguar in 1935, then taken over by the British Motor Company in 1966 and so became part of BL cars. Edwardes had fought for BL to hold onto Jaguar, but once he left the company the picture changed. The BL board recommended the secretary of state sell Jaguar, as this was "in the best interests of BL plc and the best interests of Jaguar" (Trade and Industry Committee, 1983–84, HC 490). In 1984, 100 percent of Jaguar's shares were offered and the government netted £297 million on the sale (see table 27).[6]

The City was very enthusiastic about the flotation. In 1980, Jaguar had lost over £50 million: "I'm sure that absolutely nobody in the City would have given us much chance of our survival in 1980" (Chairman Egan, to *World in Action*, June 5, 1989). Had Jaguar tried to go to the Stock Exchange then, "it

TABLE 27. Jaguar: Year-End Financials (£ million) and Employment

	Employment	Net Current Assets	Net Profit	Long-Term Liabilities
1980	9,725		(52.2)	
1981	8,286		(36.3)	
1982	7,832	24.2	6.5	17.6
1983	8,659	(2.8)	49.5	43.9
1984	9,662	35.1	42.6	44.6
1985	10,441	57.4	97.6	46.4
1986	11,324	73.3	83.4	58.0
1987	12,273	6.9	61.3	46.0
1988	12,835	(38.1)	28.4	

Source: Data from *Moody's International*, various issues.

would just be greeted by laughter" (Rhys, op cit.). But the American market picked up and with a favorable exchange rate the Jaguar of 1984 was in profit. The investment rush made Jaguar management nervous: "we drew up a table which demonstrated that at something like $1.90 to the pound or $2 to the pound, we'd actually be losing money" (Egan, op cit.). The City—whose analysts had little against which to compare Jaguar, as they were no longer used to investing in quoted car companies—scrambled to buy shares, ignoring Jaguar's warnings that the profits could easily disappear.

At first, all seemed well. But Jaguar needed major investment and the weakening of the dollar in 1985 crippled its financial performance in the United States, its most important market. In 1987 the company hit even bigger difficulties with the stock market crash and exchange-rate changes. Advisors told their clients to sell and Jaguar's share-price plummeted. Egan called the swift City criticism "savage." By 1989, critics of Britain's equity markets pointed to Jaguar as an example of City fickleness at its worst (see table 28).

In early 1989, Jaguar was again suffering financially from a cheapening dollar and weaker American retail market. Pretax profits in 1988 fell from £97 million to £47.5 million. Speculation grew in the City that a major predator would emerge when the government's Special Share expired at the end of 1990. Analysts predicted that Jaguar's shares were in for "a bumpy ride" (*Independent*, March 17, 1989). Meanwhile Ford, like its competitors, was keen to take over a luxury marque, and Jaguar was a prime purchase target.[7] By September 1989, speculation was rife about Peugeot, Volkswagen, or Volvo as potential partners for Jaguar. Then, on September 19, Ford announced its intention to take a 15 percent interest in the firm. Jaguar management was not pleased. In two days of frenetic trading, Jaguar shares jumped from 405p to 510p, only to fall again in October on news that Ford

TABLE 28.   Jaguar Share Prices
and Dividends Paid

	Price High	Price Low	Dividends Paid
1984	225	168	4.75p
1985	365	236	8.60p
1986	585	333	9.50p
1987	630	257	10.50p
1988	353	236	11.00p

Source: Data adpated from *Moody's International*, various issues.
Note: At the end of 1988, 42,038 shareholders held the 182.9
million Jaguar shares outstanding. As of March 1988, the Bank of
New York held 24 percent.

might be seeking to acquire Saab-Scania's car division instead. Three weeks later, with Jaguar's shares still rising, GM announced that with Jaguar management's backing it planned to take a minority stake in the firm. Plans for cooperation with GM would be presented to Jaguar shareholders within a month. There were hints of GM taking a 30 percent stake and injecting £500 million of new capital (*Economist*, November 4, 1989). On October 28, the United States antitrust authorities cleared GM's request to take an equity stake in Jaguar.

Then, on October 31, with Ford's stake standing at 13.2 percent, Secretary of State Ridley announced in the House that the government would not invoke its Special Share and block a takeover of Jaguar, if the shareholders voted to overturn the 15 percent ceiling. The announcement was made without consulting Jaguar even though Egan reportedly made a "last minute plea" to Ridley not to waive the Special Share (*Financial Times*, November 9, 1989). With the announcement Jaguar's share price jumped by another 122p. The next day, Ford made a full bid of £1.6 billion, at 850p per share (*Financial Times*, November 4, 1989). Egan met with Ford executives, pronounced himself satisfied that Jaguar would be allowed to operate as an independent company under Ford, and recommended the shareholders accept Ford's offer. The vote to accept passed in early December and the government promptly renounced its Special Share a year before it was due to expire.

Ridley justified his October 31 announcement by arguing that the Special Share restrictions were "clearly causing uncertainties about the company's future by prompting speculation over how my powers may be exercised, so distorting the basis on which all parties involved have to reach their decisions" (*Financial Times*, November 1, 1989). But the timing of the announcement, and the very fact of its being made, did, of course, fundamentally affect the decisions of those involved. Ford was given a green light to attempt a takeover. GM was told that the government would make no effort to secure its proposals for a joint venture. Jaguar management were clearly told that they would no longer be protected. The stock market was given the signal that a takeover was expected and Jaguar's share price jumped accordingly.

When Jaguar was privatized in 1984, it initially benefited from access to more private capital, but in the long run it was more vulnerable, and had less access to predictable financing, without the state-loan guarantees it had enjoyed as part of BL. Jaguar's nervousness at the City's hype was justified when the City turned on the firm in 1987. Jaguar's chairman concluded that the City "should shoulder the burden of starting the big dialogue between themselves and companies like ours and the government to . . . make it much more difficult for companies to be easily bought and sold" (*World in Action*, June 5, 1989).

Jaguar's fortunes continue to seesaw dramatically. It had pretax losses of £58.3 million in 1989, £66.2 million in 1990 and £226 million in 1991. By 1990, the firm had a debt-to-equity ratio of 3.5:1. Its sales in the United States and Britain plummeted in 1991, causing production to be cut to only 23,018 vehicles, the lowest level since 1982, from 41,833 in 1990. In February 1992, Jaguar announced a further 650 job cuts, on top of the 4,000 cut in 1991, reducing its total U.K. work force to around 7,400. In November 1991, ownership of Jaguar was transferred from Ford of U.K. to its American parent, in order to transfer Jaguar's losses to the parent at a time when Ford of Britain had exceptionally heavy losses of its own. In 1991–92, Ford injected £135 million in new equity capital into Jaguar as part of a financial restructuring of the subsidiary. Ford also made substantial loans to Jaguar, including £125.8 million in long-term debt (Jaguar, 1992 annual report). With these loans Ford began the process of replacing commercial banks as Jaguar's banker, and also provided additional working capital.

Jaguar faces the same challenge as any other car company—finding the financing to keep up with the competition. In January 1993, the firm announced that it plans to invest about £700 million during the next five years in the development of new models and the modernization of its production facilities (*Financial Times*, January 23, 1993). The firm has the benefit, however, of being able to turn to a parent company for new materials and technological innovations, rather than having to develop such advances itself. According to Nicholas Scheele, who took over as chairman of Jaguar Cars Ltd. in April 1992, this means that the firm is now "in an environment where we can look at the long term. . . . Before, Jaguar had to be very short-term" (quoted in the *Wall Street Journal*, July 22, 1992).

Privatization of the Rover Group

> [Sir Humphrey] insisted that this was not a cover-up, it was responsible discretion exercised in the national interest to prevent unnecessary dis-

closure of eminently justifiable procedures in which untimely revelation would severely impair public confidence. (Lynn and Jay 1984, 152)

The secretary of state's impact on Jaguar's financial market was profound but subtle. In the case of Rover's sale to British Aerospace, changes in the financial package involved were instrumental in the sale. The aid package was not at all subtle and, at first, was wholly secret. Initially, the deal seemed very straightforward. BAe paid the government £150 million, the EC permitted an injection of state aid to ensure that Rover's five-year plan would be implemented, and most of Rover's debts were written off. The purchase was widely supported at the time. As one union officer put it: "at least it's a British proposal" (Trade and Industry Committee, 1987–88, HC 487). Over the ensuing months, however, it became clear that far more had in fact been involved. The secretary of state for trade and industry had used secret financial incentives to ensure that the deal went through, and the support for BAe as purchaser was based on political rather than economic considerations.

At the time of the purchase, BAe was Europe's largest aerospace company and Britain's largest manufacturer and first-rank exporter (*British Aerospace Business Review*, April 1989).[8] In December 1987 the BAe chairman said he might buy the whole Rover Group in order to get the Land-Rover subsidiary and Rover's stake in DAF. In March 1988 BAe declared a serious interest, and by April had reached a conditional agreement with the government. The EC ordered the state to reduce its aid to Rover from £800 to £547 million. BAe would also have to confirm that the aid was being applied to Rover's five-year corporate development plan. BAe formally agreed to these terms on July 14. It paid the government £150 million for its shareholding in the group, and agreed to make no substantial car-making disposals for five years. Rover's chairman claimed in 1988 that "a considerable proportion of our surplus cash . . . has gone to service debt" and that accumulated debt was Rover's "biggest problem" (Trade and Industry Committee, 1987–88, HC 487). The EC did not allow the government to write off all of Rover's debt, but left it with £100 million. However, in addition to the £547 million of direct aid, the government allowed BAe to operate as any other company under tax law as regards Rover. BAe was allowed to set £500 million of Rover's past losses against future profits for tax purposes, and to transfer £17 million to £25 million of capital losses to set against any capital gains that BAe might incur (*Economist*, July 16, 1989).

The first protests about the purchase involved accusations of asset stripping. BAe Chairman Professor Roland Smith had stated that "We are buying the business in order to develop it [not] to rationalise and asset strip" (Trade and Industry Committee, 1987–88, HC 487), but only days after the final agreement Rover announced that two works would be closed in 1990, with 4,000 job losses. Rover said that the closures had long been planned and could no longer be delayed as EC approval of the £547 million in aid depended on capacity cuts, but the charge of asset stripping stuck, especially as BAe was already suspected of making some £450 million from asset stripping of Royal Ordinance, a previous purchase from the government.[9] "We fear that if the going gets rough, Rover Group may be sacrificed to ensure continuity within BAe" (union officer, to HC 487). Investigations were begun by the National Audit Office, the Committee of Public Accounts, and the Trade and Industry Committee.

Meanwhile, the opposition Labour Party was questioning the tax benefits BAe gained from the Rover deal. Then came a round of revelations. The new secretary of state, Nicholas Ridley, admitted in November 1989 that BAe was allowed access to Rover's capital losses and unclaimed capital allowances for tax calculations, to offset the EC's mandated reduction in state aid to Rover. The EC had estimated that these tax benefits would yield £25 million to BAe. Ridley admitted that BAe had secretly calculated a benefit of £35 million. These revelations came from confidential letters from the DTI, published by Ridley to regain the upper hand as allegations and suspicions about the deal snowballed (*Financial Times*, December 13, 1989).

Secretary of State Lord Young had described the £547 million in aid as £469 million in recognition of historic debt and £78 million to support Rover's investment program in the assisted areas. In December, it came out that an additional £38 million in secret inducements had been given to BAe. Along with the unrevealed tax benefits, the real cost of the Rover Group purchase was thus less than £100 million. In addition, Young had agreed to allow BAe to delay paying the £150-million purchase price by twenty months, to March 1990—a deal that, according to the subsequent European Commission case in the European Court of Justice, benefited BAe to the tune of £33.4 million. The DTI also agreed to pay up to £20 million in regional grants to BAe as a lump sum, instead of spreading the payments out over four years as usual (*Economist*, June 23, 1990). (With interest rates around 15 percent, this amounted to another £35-million bonus for BAe over four years.) Finally, Young gave BAe a subsidy of £11 million toward the cost of buying out the few remaining private Rover shareholders, and the costs of external advice linked to the sale. Details about this £11 million "were scattered throughout obscure parliamentary documents" (ibid.). As these inducements were revealed, Young said he had not told the EC about them because he did not consider them to be state aid. BAe had reportedly come close to backing out when the EC reduced the aid payable to Rover, and these extra "concessions" tipped the balance (*Financial Times*, December 7, 1989).

There were also charges of undervaluation in the sale. The National Audit Office concluded that Young had undervalued Rover by at least £56.6 million. A study by the University of East Anglia had valued Rover at

£450 to £600 million (*Economist*, June 23, 1990). The EC had apparently decided not to question the original valuation too closely, lest it be responsible for the collapse of the deal. It thus felt unable to inflict much of a penalty on BAe when the full facts were revealed. Nevertheless, in June 1990 the Commission announced that BAe must repay £44.4 million in "sweeteners" that it had received from the government as part of the purchase, as these broke Community rules on state aid. So BAe was somewhat castigated by the EC but on the whole got a good deal, especially when other factors are added in. In July 1989, the price of Honda's 20 percent equity stake in Rover was £116 million. Rover/BAe also received £90 million from the 1989 sale of a 24 percent holding in DAF, and £36 million from the sale of Rover's software house (*Financial Times*, December 7, 1989).[10]

The EC's case against the government's 1988 payments to Rover took some time to wend its way through the courts. In February 1992, the European Court of Justice threw out, on procedural grounds, the European Commission's order to force BAe to repay the £44.4 million (*Financial Times*, February 5, 1992). The competition commissioner asked the Commission to reopen the case by commencing formal proceedings on the state aid. In March 1993, the Commission again ordered British Aerospace to repay £44.4 million, on the recommendation of the new competition commissioner, and further ordered the firm to repay the interest that had accrued since Brussels first ruled in 1990 that the "sweeteners" constituted illegal state aid. At the time of writing, BAe had agreed to pay the government £57.6 million, made up of £11 million for the actual aid received and £46.6 million in interest payments. However, BAe also said that it expected to recover £15.4 million in tax relief (which would have been available on the interest payments), making a net repayment of £42.2 million, and a total acquisition cost of £192.2 million (*Financial Times*, May 27, 1993).

In many respects, BAe was in a position to force the best deal for itself from a government anxious to sell Rover but acutely aware that a foreign purchaser would kick up another political storm. On the other hand, purchase by a competitor might have jeopardized the agreement with Honda. Allowing the company to be broken up just when it was turning profitable, and after pumping in millions in state aid, was also politically unacceptable. Flotation was too risky, given Rover's slim profits. The government had to find a purchaser who was British, noncompetitive with Honda, and willing to keep most of Rover's factories going. BAe was the ideal purchaser, and was itself once state-owned, having been privatized in two stages, in 1981 and 1985.[11] Political considerations thus played a heavy part in Rover's sale. When political expediency dictates, the most free-market of governments is not above a little *dirigiste* interventionism, not to mention deceit of Parliament.

By the autumn of 1991, BAe itself was in a perilous financial position.

Chairman Sir Roland Smith was forced to resign after a botched £432 million rights issue that halved BAe's share price, followed by his announcement that the firm's 1991 profits would be half the £300 million the City was expecting. The City reportedly attempted to assemble a European consortium to break up BAe, but gave up when Thomson-CSF and Aerospatial of France, and Daimler Benz of Germany, said they were not interested (*Financial Times*, October 4, 1991). In addition, it was widely believed that the government, through the Ministry of Defense, would block any move by a consortium of foreign defense companies to take a controlling stake in BAe, by exercising its rights under its Special Share. Similar to the Special Shares in Jaguar and British Steel, this limits foreign shareholdings in BAe to 29.5 percent. Rumors also abounded for a while that Britain's General Electric Company might buy a 30 percent stake in BAe, and it was generally understood that the government would not stand in the way of a GEC stake or even full takeover.

In February 1992, BAe announced a 1991–92 pretax loss of £112 million, compared with a pretax profit of £376 million the previous year, and there were still sporadic rumors of GEC's possible interest in parts of the company. A year later, the aerospace firm announced losses for 1992–93 of £1.2 billion, including an exceptional provision of £1 billion for restructuring. The industrial and financial restructuring included reducing the company's capital. The new chairman, John Cahill, described 1992 as "the most testing year in the group's history." The stock market has tended to blame BAe's recent poor performance on the "distractions" of its acquisitions in the 1980s, including a Dutch construction business, a property developer, and Rover (*Financial Times*, September 26, 1992). These were acquired as potential sources of revenue when the firm's military contracts became less lucrative, but the purchases turned out to be ill-timed and Rover, for one, has not been contributing to the parent company's financial health of late—it had a £52 million operating loss in 1991, and a £49 million loss in 1992 (compared with a £55 million profit in 1990). In July 1992, Rover opened a £200 million manufacturing center at its Cowley complex in Oxfordshire. The company's largest single investment since 1988, Rover claims the center is one of Europe's most advanced and flexible car plants.

British Aerospace suffers from a "chronic inability to generate cash" (*Financial Times*, August 3, 1992). Throughout 1992 and into 1993, there were periodic speculations in the press that the firm would eventually have to sell one or more of its acquisitions made in the 1980s to raise some much-needed cash and reduce its overhead. When BAe bought Rover in 1988, its agreement with the government included not selling the carmaker for five years. That pledge expires in August 1993. BAe could find itself in the same position as the British government in 1988—anxious to off-load Rover, but unable to find a suitable domestic purchaser. Unlike the government, however, BAe will not be under political pressure to keep the firm British. A merger with a European carmaker is possible, but at the time of writing the most likely outcome seems to be a full linkup with Honda. By early 1993, the Honda-Rover relationship had produced a number of jointly developed vehicles, including the new generation Honda Accord and Rover 600 series. Rover is now dependent on Honda technology for three of its four main car ranges, and would face sharply increased research and development costs without its partner. It has also benefited enormously from the chance to learn Japanese manufacturing practices such as lean production and distribution and the creation of a flexible work force. John Cahill says that the date of August 1993 is "increasingly a red herring" because BAe has no intention of selling Rover (*Financial Times*, April 7, 1993). A Honda spokesman reportedly said that "If BAe wished to sell Rover Group . . . [i]t would be difficult to continue the sharing of technology and designs if it was sold to another manufacturer" (ibid.).

3. The Blurred Public-Private Boundary

As in the other cases analyzed here, the boundary between the public and private spheres of action and decision making around BL, Rover, and Jaguar, was not as clear-cut as the division of the industry into a state-owned BL and its privately owned competitors seems to imply. The most obvious example is that the nationalized British Leyland continued to draw on the private credit markets—principally domestic and overseas banks—for a significant proportion of its short- and long-term financing. Furthermore, the government gave assurances to those private creditors that their loans would be made good in the event that the firm collapsed. Although the initial Varley-Marshall assurances were made by a supposedly more intervention-oriented Labour government, its free-market Conservative successor allowed the continued flow of private capital into a state-owned company, and maintained the spirit of the assurances. It also allowed a close research and production relationship to be developed with the privately owned Honda.

Then there was the public aid to privately owned firms. In the case of British Steel, the state used BSC to channel funds to the smaller, private-sector firms, to protect them from the worst of the early 1980s' steel slump, and to ensure the financial viability of the new Phoenix ventures. In the case of the British auto industry, aid to the private sector has been overt, direct, and plentiful, for decades. The 1968 takeover of BMC by Leyland, for example, was facilitated by loans from the Industrial Reorganisation Corporation. Since 1976, the auto industry has received more assistance under the guise of regional policy than any other industry (Moore, Rhodes, and Tyler 1986). As in France, there has long been a connection between auto manufacturing and regional development programs. In 1960, the Conservative government denied the industrial development certificates necessary for expansion to a number of auto manufacturers, unless the investments went to designated underdeveloped regions (Quinn 1988). In the 1980s, most aid to the industry came via regional-development aid. The 1984 designation of most of the West Midlands as an Assisted Area allowed industry in the region to take advantage of various development grants and subsidies.[12] There have also been numerous small schemes to assist the components sector on a per-project basis (Trade and Industry Committee, 1986–87, HC 407).[13] It has been said that the state support for BL has been the largest (indirect) support given to the components industry (ibid.).

Government aid to private car manufacturers has not been limited to domestically owned firms. Nissan was given considerable "industrial development assistance" for its plant in Sunderland in the early 1980s. A decade earlier, even as plans were under way to nationalize BLMC in 1975, the Labour government was also actively involved in bailing out another major carmaker—the U.K. subsidiary of American-owned Chrysler. With inflation and stagnation hitting the British economy, Chrysler had begun to talk of cutting back its overseas operations. It had taken over the British Rootes motor company in 1967 and both parent and subsidiary were now taking heavy losses. By the mid-1970s, Chrysler UK contributed £170 million a year in export earnings to the British balance of payments (Wilks 1984a). The Treasury estimated that a close-down would cost £150 million in redundancy payments, unemployment benefits, and lost tax revenue. Any rescue package that would keep Chrysler UK in operation through 1976 at less than £150 million would therefore be a savings. In addition, the Labour government feared the effects of closures in Scotland, where nationalism was becoming increasingly vocal and where plant closures would be a severe blow to its policy of devolution.

The Department of Industry and the Treasury rejected the long-term aid represented by nationalization, and British Leyland declared that it would be too great a commercial burden for the newly nationalized firm to take over the Chrysler operations itself. So a short-term rescue plan was devised, to buy time for both company and government. Chrysler signed an agreement, covering the years 1976 to 1979, under which the government guaranteed loans necessary for capital expenditure if Chrysler UK made progress on various agreed objectives (see Wilks 1984a). The final cost to the government has been estimated at between £64 million and £72.5 million (Wilks 1984a; Jones 1983). Secretary of State for Industry Eric Varley had reportedly wanted to let Chrysler UK "go to the wall" but was overruled by Prime Minister Harold Wilson (Edwardes 1983). Chrysler UK struggled on until 1978, when Peugeot SA acquired Chrysler's European operations. Employment in the U.K. operation (renamed Talbot) subsequently plummeted from 25,000 in

and does not appear to have been hampered by institutional limitations to such mixes. This is where limiting the study of Britain to two primary cases causes a problem—which is the aberrant example on this issue? We've seen that the public-private boundary was breached with apparent unconcern, and even downright ingenuity, on a number of occasions and in a variety of ways, where the financing of major manufacturers was concerned. However, it is also true that where public and private capital ended up in the same venture, the British government felt compelled to justify such mixes in terminology very different from that used by the governments of France. Extending the analysis of firm-level financing to other British manufacturers would show whether the aversion to mixing public and private capital has, indeed, been the rule of thumb; or whether, as in the Phoenix and BL cases, such mixing is far more common than studies of British government-industry relations have hitherto assumed.

British Leyland was different from the other nationalized firms in the United Kingdom in a number of respects. Not only did the government not object to its continued relationship with the private credit markets, but the state's relationship with the firm was always more ambivalent than in other cases, thanks to the presence of foreign-owned manufacturers in the home market, and to the fact that a U.K. government had already bailed out one of them. One can also speculate that abrogation of its responsibilities under the Varley Marshall assurances not only would have involved the new Conservative government in an even closer relationship with BL, but also would have caused some serious friction with the banks concerned. Perhaps the prime minister pushed for early privatization of as many of BL's constituent parts as possible, because she was unhappy at the government's involvement in a partially privately financed firm? With both the Labour governments of the 1970s and the Conservative governments of the 1980s, there is a strong air of "muddling through" in their dealings with the industry as a whole and with BL in particular. Perhaps it is this atmosphere that led to the uncharacteristically overt mixing of public and private capital in the financing of BL.

Similarities between Britain and France

Despite all of the differences emphasized between the case of British Leyland and that of the other firms studied here, there are also some distinct and striking similarities that cut across industrial and national boundaries. The most obvious is, of course, the inevitable role of the state in providing an important manufacturing concern with access to significant sources of financing at critical junctures—in this case, state loans followed by nationalization. As in France, the auto industry has been closely involved in regional economic development schemes, and has benefited significantly from the indirect aid provided under the auspices of regional assistance. As in the case of Peugeot and its takeovers of Citroën and Chrysler Europe in the 1970s, the government also provided the loans to facilitate the Leyland takeover of BMC in 1968.

Another striking similarity was the conversion of some of BL's debts into equity at a time of financial crisis—just as at BSC and Usinor, and at Peugeot. As in the other cases of nationalized firms, the government also sought alternatives to direct state-provision of financing for BL—although, in the case of BL, this happened earlier in the decade, and was more due to unease at the whole concept of the firm being nationalized, than to the kinds of financial constraints that affected the French government's relationship with Usinor in the late 1980s. Finally, we find that in both the case of Rover and that of Renault, the government used some "creative accounting" to circumvent EC-mandated limits on state aid to the firms.

Firm-Level Financial Issues

The two sources of financing that were most readily available to the auto industry in Britain were the stock market and the state. BLMC and the nationalized BL did also turn to the banks for financing—indeed, it was the concern of the banks at the state of BLMC's finances in 1974 that led to a government-guaranteed bank loan followed by nationalization. Nevertheless, the early firms had turned to the stock market for the bulk of their funds. At privatization in 1984, a capital-intensive firm the size of Jaguar had no realistic alternative but a listing on the London market; there was no private indigenous carmaker to purchase the firm, and there were no financial holding companies with interests in industrial investment to take it over. The Rover group was eventually taken over by an even larger, publicly traded company. Unlike the French steel firms, the primary source of funds for British firms was not debt, but equity. This has often been seen by manufacturers themselves as a drawback. The chairman of ERF Holdings, a heavy commercial vehicle manufacturer, said of his EC competitors:

> . . . they have the ability to borrow money more easily than we do . . . at lower rates of interest, or have the ability to borrow money . . . without having such commercial risks to bear. A lot of our competitors are owned by banks, for example. In Sweden we know that Volvo-Scania are very much controlled by the Swedish banks and they are obviously successful companies but they do have perhaps financial resources more available than we have. (Trade and Industry Committee, 1986–87, HC 407, qu. 769/770)

Once crisis hit, however, the only other source of financing was the state. It should be noted that between 1984 and 1988 the debt levels of the still-nationalized BL jumped markedly. During these four years, the firm was caught in an unusual situation: by mutual consent, aid was no longer available from the state, but neither was private equity capital, the two sources usually most available to auto firms in Britain. The mid-size Jaguar now relies on the deeper pockets of its American-owned parent, Ford, while Rover is under the wing of British Aerospace. In 1975, however, the mass-market British Leyland Motor Corporation, under pressure from its creditors and facing possible bankruptcy, had no choice but to turn to the state.

The nationalized BL sought to reduce the cost of its debt financing in the crisis period of the early 1980s, with a debt-to-equity restructuring, although the continued access to debt financing from the private banks meant that this was not as complete as the British Steel Corporation's financial restructuring. BL subsequently complained that the retention of debt on its books was a hindrance to the firm's financial health. More notable from this case, however, is the fact that equity financing can also be costly. As mentioned in part 2, the profitable U.K. auto firms had continued to distribute a "significant proportion" of their profits as dividends, even in the lean years of the 1920s and 1930s. BLMC paid dividends into the 1970s, distributing over 94 percent of its reported profits to its shareholders (Lewchuk 1986). As at British Steel in 1992, the need to maintain a dividend and the confidence of the stock market investors during a downturn was costly for Jaguar in the mid-1980s, for BAe more recently, and perhaps for the prenationalization BLMC. This cost was not borne by Peugeot, however, operating in a national financial system where the investors who dominate the equity market have a different relationship with, and a different set of attitudes toward, the firms whose equity they hold.

Ultimately, the crucial aspect of firm-level financial issues at BL, Jaguar, the Rover Group, and even BAe, was the attitudes of the financial providers involved. Two specific points stand out—the ambivalent attitude of the government toward the nationalized BL, and the attitudes of the stock market investors toward the privately quoted firms. In the case of BL, although the government was its dominant stakeholder from 1975 to 1989, it never exercised that dominance to the extent that it did at BSC. Other interests also had a stake in the firm—namely, its private creditors—while the government was also concerned with the fate of other auto manufacturers. The political battles over the firm's restructuring, such as management's resistance to some of the privatization proposals in the early 1980s, were one outcome of this ambivalence. Another was the extent to which management's own concerns, especially their focus on labor relations and their misjudgment of the market in the late 1970s, went unchallenged by the new owner. In this respect, the case is reminiscent of the nationalized steel firms in France, where the government also struggled to dominate the agenda.

As to the stock market, it is clear that the volatile attitude of its investors toward a firm in a highly cyclical industry had a negative impact on the ability of Jaguar to survive a market downturn, and made serious long-term industrial restructuring impossible, until the firm was taken over by Ford. Unlike Peugeot SA, Jaguar did not have the benefit of a dominant stakeholder, or of friendly institutional investors, willing to back the firm over the long haul. This raises the question: if BAe was broken up, voluntarily or not, how long could the Rover Group survive as an independent entity on the London International Stock Exchange?

For British Leyland, Jaguar, and the Rover Group, the cost of debt financing was a consideration at critical times when each firm was faced with staggeringly expensive restructuring along with increasing competition and declining market share. Equally important to the process of crisis management was the availability of financing: BL's access to private-sector bank loans gave it leverage over the government when ministers wanted to break the company up for sale in the early 1980s; there were few options for privatizing Jaguar, aside from a fully public stock market flotation; and the availability of financing from the deep pockets of the state kept BL afloat from 1975 to 1984, while implicit state guarantees kept the Rover Group viable until its sale to BAe. Ultimately, however, the attitudes of the providers of the various forms of financing were the crucial factor. The state never fully played the role of dominant stakeholder as it had done at BSC, since the presence of other providers lessened the government's sense of responsibility for the firm, and other car manufacturers played an equally important role in the domestic market. The attitude of the stock market clearly had a tremendous impact on Jaguar's fortunes, in strong contrast with the attitude that PSA encountered across the Channel.

In chapter 6, the four case studies are brought together to illustrate how these different firm-level financial structures and forms of corporate governance may help or hinder a major manufacturing firm at a time of crisis and restructuring. The summary offers some conclusions arising from these cases about the importance of the availability and costs of various forms of capital, and about the attitudes of the providers of financing. The chapter then considers some examples from steel and auto firms in Germany, Japan, and the United States, to show how the analysis developed from these case studies could be extended and applied in a wider comparative framework.

CHAPTER 6

Extending the Argument: Government, Industry, and Finance in the 1990s

1. Summarizing the Case Studies

The four case studies illustrated how different firm-level financial structures and forms of corporate governance may help or hinder a major manufacturing firm at a time of crisis. From the mid-1970s to the present, the financial resources required for restructuring these steel and auto firms, and for developing and applying new technologies, were phenomenal. They needed enormous sums of capital, both to survive in the short term and to adapt over the longer term. The availability and cost of various forms of financing had an important impact on the processes of crisis management, but the attitudes of the providers of that capital were the most crucial factor.

The case-study chapters also told the stories of four major manufacturers whose survival had a high national political profile. However, these are cases with very different organizational and political histories in two different countries. The period of crisis and restructuring that each manufacturer went through, starting in the late 1970s, took place in different political contexts. These differences had an impact on industrial strategies and adaptation. In addition to the politics of adjustment, the cases also revealed some surprising similarities across nations and industries, not least of which is the blurring of the public-private divide.

The Politics of Industrial Adaptation

The political contexts of the four cases are easily summarized. By 1978, the British Steel Corporation was established as the nation's dominant steel manufacturer, and had already been under state ownership for eleven years. The public face of the politics of its restructuring centered around the 1980 steel strike, and the debate over the fate of the Ravenscraig complex in Scotland. Behind the scenes, the government's relationship with BSC underwent a subtle but profound change after 1975, culminating in the 1981 Iron and Steel Act. In contrast, the postwar French steel industry remained fragmented into a number of privately owned firms who interacted with the state through a powerful trade association. After nationalization in 1981, two dominant firms emerged—rivals for state financing who were oriented around the old geographic divisions of the industry, and who had competing production strategies. Unlike the case of BSC, the labor response to retrenchment was swift and sometimes violent. The political context of restructuring in the French auto industry was different again, with two domestically owned firms the dominant producers by 1978, enjoying the support of successive governments with protection from imports. At the family-owned Peugeot SA, retrenchment triggered intense labor disputes in which the government also became actively involved. Finally, the domestically owned mass-market British auto industry was consolidated into one dominant firm after 1968, but had to compete in the home market with long-established foreign producers and, after the early 1980s, with new arrivals. During the late 1970s, the resolution of labor disputes dominated much of the political context of restructuring.

To paraphrase Katzenstein (1985), we can see these cases as four different settings for the politics of industrial retrenchment and adaptation in the 1980s. Their recent history varies in ways that help us to identify some of the enduring patterns of policy and politics. It is also clear from these cases that political ideology does matter in government-industry relations. The External Financing Limits used at BSC, and the way in which they were used, were very much the product of a British Conservative Party government headed by Margaret Thatcher. Keith Joseph was extremely reluctant to give government aid to British Leyland, and the Cabinet was anxious to off-load most if not all of the firm as soon possible. In France, the *contrats* used in the post-1981 steel firms were born of the Parti Socialist's commitment to the idea of consultation. Where the British governments under Thatcher formulated a policy of privatization to deal with financing the state-owned firms, the Socialist governments in France under President Mitterrand encouraged, and believed in, the active role of the state in industrial affairs.

Furthermore, the steel and auto industries are dominated by a very few big firms in each country, even by only one or two. The government is dependent on these firms for information, while the needs of a huge firm are very hard to ignore, or to cast in a different light. This has led much political-economy analysis to focus on government autonomy from major economic actors, or on firms' ability to "capture" state institutions. These various aspects of the politics of industrial adjustment are not irrelevant. Part of the reason that the actions and decisions of major manufacturers straddle the public-private divide is their high political profile. All governments are inherently political animals, after all. There is a side to the story of government-industry relations that has been overlooked, however, one that has a profound impact on industrial survival and adaptation—namely, the financing of industry from a firm-level perspective.

One conclusion that can be drawn from the preceding case studies is that the state is always involved in industrial adaptation and always ends up aiding manufacturing firms during a period of crisis. The aid and involvement may be called different things in different political and national contexts, or justified in different ways, but ultimately the firms all turned to the state for help in order to survive. Again, the involvement of governments is not surprising, given the high political profile of the firms we're talking about. That the state should be a kind of "lender of last resort" is also not surprising, given the enormous sums of money involved and the fact that the return on this often long-term investment is measurable in terms of such nebulous concepts as saving jobs or the national manufacturing base. Thus, in these cases, the respective states seemed to play the role of the ultimate patient banker, bailing out manufacturing concerns that no private-sector financial interests could or would support.

While this is a compelling image, the analogy is limited and does not tell the whole story. As we have seen, there were other factors that had a profound impact on the course and outcome of restructuring for these firms—the role played by labor and the unions; whether industry management was fragmented; whether the firm was perceived as a politically essential national champion; and, most important of all, the sources of the firm's financing and its form of corporate governance. That the state seems to play the role of patient banker whatever the ideology of the government in power, and whatever the political context surrounding industrial adaptation, is one of the striking similarities found between these cases. However, it does not tell the whole story. Both the processes of industrial adjustment and the outcomes varied enormously, and in ways that can't be accounted for by a straight comparison between an "arm's-length" Britain and a *dirigiste* France. How each firm was financed had a profound impact on its options, perspectives, and decision making, and had a profound impact on its relationship with the government of the day.

National Similarities and the Public-Private Boundary

The most obvious similarity between these four cases is the extent to which the state was always involved in providing the firm with access to the enormous amounts of capital needed for survival and adaptation. Even in the case of the privately owned PSA, the state stepped in and directly helped with the costs of restructuring. There were also other areas of strong resemblance between the cases that cut across national and industrial divisions. Each government behaved in remarkably similar ways when it came to dealing with the steel industry, using a dominant firm to rationalize the whole domestic steel sector and to bail out smaller privately owned firms, and using borrowing limits as a means of trying to enforce rationalization on that dominant firm. (Note, also, that the British government occasionally justified the aid being given to BL as a way of indirectly assisting the whole industry, component manufacturers in particular, and that BL was also subject to borrowing limits.) These attempts to use borrowing limits essentially meant that each government was trying to act like a dominant stakeholder, but with mixed results.

A third notable similarity is that by the late 1980s—and earlier, in the case of BL—each government was beginning to search for alternatives to the direct provision of financing for the state-owned industries. In addition, each government also began to look for ways to get around the EC-mandated limitations on state aid to industry, either in terms of an ongoing system of financing, as in the case of Usinor and Renault, or in terms of a one-off injection of assistance, as in the case of Rover. A fourth similarity is each firm's attitude toward debt financing. Long-term debts were converted into equity during the initial crisis at BSC, BL, and the French steel firms, and in all four cases the firms were anxious to minimize their debt levels wherever possible. (The implications of this are considered more fully below.) Finally, the extent to which each of these firms played a role in government regional-assistance programs is also striking, with plant closures leading to special-investment status being conferred on the old steel-manufacturing areas, and with the auto manufacturers heavily involved in taking advantage of such schemes.

Graham (1989) points out that in the years since the classical British nineteenth-century view of state and company organization was first formulated, there developed a more interventionist and activist state that impinged on company law. This has led to a blurring of the public-private divide that is not recognized in the work of classical writers such as John Stuart Mill. As we saw in the case of BSC and the Phoenix companies, even in Thatcher's proprivatization Britain "behind the rhetoric of market forces we can see the same com-penetration of public and private sectors that is such a marked feature of the modern state" (Graham 1989, 215). This com-penetration, and the consequent blurring of the public-private boundary, showed up in all four of the cases studied here. The most obvious examples came in the case of the French steel industry, from prenationalization price controls and subsidized credit, to the state-sponsored restructuring of the privately owned firms in 1978, and culminating in the postnationalization financing of Usinor Sacilor. In the British steel industry, there were the Phoenix schemes and the government Special Share held at the privatized British Steel. The privately owned

PSA had recourse to government aid in the mid-1980s, and played a major role in various government regional-investment schemes, particularly those under the auspices of the FSAI in the early 1980s. The state-owned British Leyland also had access to private credit, while the privately owned firms in the sector—both domestically owned ones and those from overseas—have been major beneficiaries of government aid, whether from the Industrial Re-organisation Corporation in the 1960s, from various regional-development schemes in the 1970s and 1980s, or, in the case of Chrysler UK in the late 1970s, in the form of a direct bailout.

These examples also show that, contrary to the assumptions of much popular and academic analysis, the issue at the heart of the survival and adaptation of major manufacturers in the 1970s and 1980s was not merely one of nationalization versus privatization. Rather, government-industry rela-tions, and the outcome of restructuring attempts at these firms, depended on a number of factors, not the least of which was the source of the firm's financing—whether it was formally owned by the state or by interests in the private sector. This perspective of micro-level analysis is even more crucial going into 1990s. The role of the state in industrial affairs is becoming less overt across Europe, thanks to a combination of the European Community's prohibition on state aid that distorts competition and national governments' budgetary constraints. At the same time, the role of the state is just as crucial as ever, with new technological challenges assailing industries such as steel and auto manufacturing; with new competition developing from Asia and Eastern Europe; with trade and financing barriers coming down across the EC even as new nations are seeking to join the Community; and finally with the increasingly rapid internationalization of capital markets (see part 3).

Both economists and political scientists are concerned with the problem of industrial adjustment. However, economists tend to underestimate or un-dervalue the role of government in creating, sustaining, or incrementally modifying markets and national financial systems. Political scientists studying industrial adjustment. on the other hand, have focused on comparisons of industrial sectors and national government policies, and ignored or skimmed over financial markets and financial policies. The exceptions tend to be where analysis focuses on financial organizations as institutions, or on financial markets as an example of a structural constraint on the actions of the state. This was the approach taken by Zysman's (1983) ground-breaking study of industrial financing. As argued in chapter 1, these national institutions and structures are far from irrelevant, and such studies reveal a great deal about the workings of modern, industrialized economies. Political scientists tend to assume that financial markets are either essentially apolitical; somehow be-yond the control of national governments in any but the crudest or most overt ways; or the realm of highly technical people and details that are divorced from the grubbiness of everyday political or industrial concerns. Yet industrial competitiveness and strategies are fundamentally affected by the kinds of capital that firms and industries have access to, and the kinds of relationships implied by the national financial system.

It is here, at the level of maintaining and altering the national financial system, that governments have the most profound effect on industrial survival and adaptation, and in a way that is rarely analyzed in the literature. It is not the role of the state as patient banker, as industrial interventionist, or as captive creature of major manufacturers, that is the most compelling aspect of contemporary government-industry relations. Rather, it is the role of the state, specifically of government, in setting the boundaries of the national financial system. The extent to which those boundaries have a fundamental impact on industry, and particularly on the kinds of capital to which a firm has access, is revealed most clearly by a comparative analysis of industrial financing and government-industry relations that starts at the level of the firm.

Analyzing Firm-Level Financing

The most important thing revealed by these four firm-level analyses—and that in turn illustrates similarities across industries and countries as well as crucial differences in national financial systems—is the role of firm-level financial structures and forms of corporate governance. Chapter 1 suggested three possible answers to the question of just what it is about a firm's corporate governance and the characteristics of its financial structure that profoundly affect the processes of crisis management—the availability of financing, the costs of various forms of financing, and the impact on the firm of the providers of the financing involved, specifically of their attitudes toward the firm's financing needs. In each of the four case studies, it turned out that all three of these factors were important, but that the attitudes of the providers of financing turned out to be the most crucial.

The Availability of Financing

What forms of financing are available to a firm is largely a function of the national financial system. Availability is important because this in turn implies varying costs and different providers. In all four of these case studies, financing was primarily available from two sources: on the one hand the state, and on the other either the equity market (British Steel, Jaguar, Rover/BAe, PSA), or the debt market (French steel and BL). The state was thus always the "lender of last resort," but how it got involved, and with what outcome, varied a great deal.

For BSC and its successor British Steel, the majority of their financing came either from the state or the stock market. Although the firms that became

BSC weren't facing imminent bankruptcy to the extent of the carmaker BLMC at the time of nationalization, they were still in some financial difficulties in 1967, which meant accepting state ownership and aid, or shrinking to the point of near-exit from the industry. From 1967 to 1988, BSC's only source of capital was the state, but it is also clear that successive governments stumped up the cash to keep BSC going to a degree that no British private-sector investor would have done at the time. When smaller, private steel companies got into trouble in the early 1980s and needed capital to restructure their operations, they too turned to the state. The firms' owners and creditors either could not put up the sums of money needed, or were unwilling to do so. Returning British Steel to private ownership in 1988 meant turning to the stock market. Although United Engineering Steels, a former Phoenix scheme, was privatized in a different manner, once the firm became completely free-standing, UES also looked to a stock-market flotation in order to raise the kinds of capital needed for a major steel manufacturer.

The story at British Leyland and Jaguar was similar, in that their sources of financing were also the stock market and the state, but with the important difference that the nationalized BL still had debt financing available from private-sector banks. This source may have been encouraged by, and perhaps in turn also have encouraged, the financing that was forthcoming from the state. Between 1984 and 1988, when funding was not available from the primary two sources, BL/Rover's debt levels jumped markedly. The state level of financing made available by the state over a long period of time, as at BSC and at Usinor, almost certainly would not have been forthcoming from the private sector. However, the early auto firms turned to the stock market for the majority of their funding, and when it came to returning a firm the size of Jaguar to the private sector—one that needed access to considerable sums of capital—no alternative was available in Britain other than the stock market. Similarly, the Rover Group was eventually taken over by an even larger, publicly traded company. Jaguar and Rover now have access to the relatively deep pockets of their parent companies. BLMC had no choice in 1975, when under pressure from its creditors and in need of financing both to survive and to adapt, but to turn to the state.

Financing for Peugeot SA was also available either in the form of equity or from the state, but as the dominant private-sector company in France, with a long-standing reputation and with a core of supportive investors, PSA was able not only to call on bank loans from its earliest history, but also to tap the stock market for massive funds in the mid-1980s. Also, the firm has been in a prime position to take advantage of the liberalization of the French financial markets in the 1980s and into the 1990s, making use of the new financial instruments being developed to improve its balance sheet and to tap into new sources of funding. In addition, PSA was able to get funding from the state when it ran into some financial difficulties in the mid-1980s. This was called general assistance to industry for modernization purposes, but there is no doubt that it helped PSA to finance some very expensive research and development and restructuring, which had to be funded one way or another. The state aid also helped to improve the look of the firm's balance sheet, and hence its credit rating, which in turn may have helped to make other financing more readily available to PSA.

The French steel firms are different from the other three cases in that, aside from the state, the only form of financing really available to them in the postwar era was debt, and primarily government-subsidized or government-controlled debt. After nationalization, as in the other cases where the government took over ownership, financing was available from the state, and probably at levels that few private sector investors would have been able or willing to make over the long haul. This capital was thus essential for the survival and restructuring of the French steel industry. From the late 1980s, the government began looking at other ways to make financing available to Usinor, primarily via a sizable equity stake taken by another state institution. The postwar French stock market was small and illiquid, and the state saw steel as crucial to industrial reconstruction and to the development of the national economy, so the firms were tied into the state-administered credit markets with both short- and long-term financing primarily in the form of debt. For the steel firms involved in the national planning system, and working through the CSSF and the GIS, financing was usually available. Indeed, it is striking that the firms managed to get funding right up to the late 1970s. However, the costs that the French steel firms faced as a result of the form of financing that was available to them were the most obviously severe of the cases analyzed here.

The Cost of Financing
The cost of capital can be a burden on a firm that limits its options and flexibility in responding to restructuring and competitive pressures. Thus, access to cheap capital was clearly a consideration for the private steel companies seeking a bailout via BSC, and for their Phoenix offspring in the early years of operation. Both debt and equity capital carry costs, of very different kinds, some of the consequences of which were illustrated in these four cases.

The cost of debt financing is most obvious in the case of the postwar French steel firms. They were burdened by debt-servicing costs to the point that they were basically bankrupt in all but name by 1977—this despite the fact that much of the debt involved was directly or indirectly subsidized and disbursed by the state. Debt financing is not at all an inherently bad idea. It can be cheaper and easier to take out a bank loan than to attempt a stock offering. The amount of capital that will be forthcoming is more predictable than in a stock offering, where you may not raise the amounts expected and where investment will only be forthcoming when the market is in good shape. This is especially relevant for major manufacturers trying to raise huge sums of capital relatively quickly. As long as business is going well, debt may be a preferable means of raising capital, but servicing that debt can become a crippling expense at a time of crisis. The 1978–80 financial restructuring at BSC was in essence a conversion of debt into equity. BL underwent a similar debt-equity conversion, although the firm's continued access to debt financing from private banks meant that the removal of debt from its balance sheet was not as complete as was the case at BSC. Both BL and PSA were anxious to reduce their debt burdens however and whenever they could in the 1980s, while one of the widely cited positive aspects of British Steel at the time of its privatization was that the firm did not carry an enormous debt burden, thanks to earlier write-offs by the government. For manufacturing concerns operating in a highly cyclical industry, debt can be a headache. At the same time, however, all of the firms studied here used enormous sums of debt as an additional source of financing for their operations—even PSA, which had better access to equity than the others in the mid-1980s.

The costs of equity financing were less direct but no less important in some of these cases. British Steel found the cost of maintaining its dividend in 1992 proved too high, as did PSA from 1980 to 1986. On the other hand, these firms had the option of waiving a dividend payment, where waiving loan payments would have been relatively much harder. PSA was able to forgo dividend payments over a long period of time, without suffering any unduly adverse reactions from its investors, and without jeopardizing its ability to raise additional funds when needed. However, British Steel's dividend reduction and subsequent waiver caused financial problems for the firm, in that its share price fell and its investors got skittish. Maintaining investor confidence is a cost of equity financing. In the case of the British auto industry, firms historically maintained high dividend payments even during severe market downturns, including BLMC, practically up to the eve of nationalization. The same was true for Jaguar in the mid-1980s and for British Aerospace more recently. The reason why the cost of equity financing in these British cases varied so markedly from the cost for Peugeot SA has to do with the attitudes of the investors involved and with the workings of the national system of finance and corporate governance.

The Attitudes of the Providers
The attitudes of the providers of financing toward the needs of a firm faced with a crisis of survival and adaptation proved to be the key issue for each of these firms, whether financed primarily by the state or by private capital.

The Peugeot SA case is one of a dominant stakeholder and a core of supportive investors. The dominant stakeholder is the Peugeot family, which holds a significant portion of the company's capital (and also has a long and high reputation in French financial and industrial circles). The family played an important role in managing the firm's expansion and restructuring from 1974 onward, bringing in outsiders at critical junctures and giving them the support necessary to carry out a clearly defined goal—expansion in the mid-1970s with Parayre; industrial and financial restructuring in the 1980s, including a standoff with labor, with Calvet. The family maintained its financial interest in the firm through a tumultuous and very expensive period of reorganization and investment. Equally crucial was the role of the so-called friendly investors. This core of investors supported the firm through its period of financial difficulties in the early 1980s, even when it paid no dividend for five successive years, and then went on to subscribe to new capital in the firm in 1985 and again in 1987.

In the case of the British Steel Corporation, the government basically acted as a dominant stakeholder by 1979, and even more so after the 1981 Iron and Steel Act. The state issued equity to the company in the form of New Capital, approved the board's actions, approved or denied further equity funding, and exercised overall control. The government had clear, if limited, goals for the company—survival, improved competitiveness and maintenance of market share, and financial independence from state aid by 1985, in line with ECSC requirements. It was able to dominate the agenda relevant to that goal, and was willing to cede control over other issues to the corporation's management. In addition, in a manner somewhat similar to the Peugeot family, the government brought in Ian MacGregor as an outspoken chairman in the early 1980s and supported him through standoffs with labor. Nevertheless, this was still a government and hence an inherently political animal, as seen by its decisions to keep the Ravenscraig complex operational through the 1980s, and by its intervention in the 1980 wage negotiations and subsequent strike.

The marked difference between these two cases and that of the French steel industry in the late 1970s is that there was no dominant stakeholder in the case of the French steel firms. At first sight, this seems paradoxical. Throughout the postwar period, the providers of finance to the French steel firms—the various state and para-public investment institutions, and ultimately the state itself—had been willing providers of funding, putting up capital for the long haul and seeing the firms through some rough times in the 1960s. Wasn't the state the ultimate guarantor of many of the firms' debts, even if via numerous other financial intermediaries? The crucial thing about the steel firms, though, was precisely that there were multiple interests involved in their financing. The GIS effectively acted as a screen between state and industry. The former seemed to assume that as long as they were pouring vast sums into the industry, all must be well; the latter did nothing to grapple with adjustment, as long as they could survive on government-guaranteed debt; and the banks didn't take a particularly active role in forcing the firms to get their act together because they were essentially only funneling state-subsidized credit into the industry, via the umbrella trade organization GIS.

The government, the apparent dominant stakeholder, could not play that role effectively with regard to the steel firms, even after nationalization. Between the complexity of the firms' debts and the number of institutions represented on their holding companies—not to mention the political and organizational problem of two firms with geographic and strategic rivalries— the government did not begin to act like a dominant stakeholder until the 1984 Steel Plan. Only then did the government begin to make long-term, strategic decisions for the industry, playing a more active role in overseeing the firms' restructuring strategies and then appointing Francis Mer and charging him with merging the two companies into a single, viable enterprise. However, there is also evidence that this situation already may be changing, with the development of new forms of financing since the mid-1980s, and with a significant percentage of Usinor's equity now held by an additional (albeit currently still state-owned) institution. The role of the state, and its ability to act as dominant stakeholder, may be being diluted again. On the other hand, we may also be seeing the development of a core of supportive investors in a way that is reminiscent of the corporate governance structure at PSA. This is certainly the situation favored by the new French government in the run-up to possible privatization.

British Leyland, or BL, never really had a dominant stakeholder. (Rover now does, in that the firm is 80 percent owned by BAe.) Although the government was BL's primary owner from 1975 to 1988, it never exercised that dominance to the extent that it did at BSC. Other interests also had a stake in the firm—namely private creditors—and the government was deeply ambivalent about the nationalized carmaker. In the case of BL, there is a sense of muddling through on the part of successive governments, and of the Thatcher governments in particular being very uneasy about the whole exercise. Maybe this was in part the result of the firm's being nationalized at a time of crisis, thus establishing the perception of a short-term government bailout during a state of emergency, rather than the perception of government involvement leading to long-term strategic improvement. The ambivalence was perhaps also due to the fact that BL was not the only, or even the biggest, carmaker in Britain. The government was also concerned about the fate of those other manufacturers, some of whom, although foreign-owned, had been established in the country for decades. In any event, the government never dominated the agenda at BL as clearly as it did at BSC in the 1980s. There were battles within the Cabinet over the best strategy for the firm, and between the government and BL over some of the early privatization proposals. Throughout the period of nationalization, the goals of both Labour and Conservative governments were never really any clearer than general desires not to be blamed for massive job losses if the firm folded altogether; to ensure the firm's short-term survival; and to be free of financial responsibility for the firm as soon as practicable by returning it to the private sector—the "proper" place for BL to deal with the issues of longer-term adaptation. Although the Labour government installed Michael Edwardes soon after nationalization and charged him with rescuing the firm, management and their assumptions about the firm were otherwise left in place. Management's focus on labor relations, and their misjudgment of the state of the market in 1975, were not challenged by the new owner. In this respect, the case of BL bears similarity to the nationalized steel firms in France, where the government also struggled to dominate the agenda.

Finally, the private British Steel has no dominant stakeholder. Investors on the London market took a very negative attitude toward the firm's unwillingness to make a full dividend, even though British Steel was caught in a recession and severe cyclical downturn. This attitude could pose a major obstacle to the firm's ability to raise additional investment funds from the market in the near term. Similarly, the volatile attitude of Jaguar's investors in 1984–88 had a very negative impact on the firm's ability to survive a market downturn, and made serious long-term industrial restructuring impossible until Jaguar was taken over by Ford. British Steel does not have a core of supportive or friendly institutional investors, as is likely to be the case for Usinor when it is privatized. Jaguar did not have this benefit either, nor that of PSA's dominant stakeholder.

With an analysis that starts from firm-level financial issues, we can see that when it came to the restructuring of the 1980s, the British Steel Corporation and Peugeot SA had more in common with one another than do the three nationalized cases, or than did PSA with the private French steel industry or the British auto industry. This is a conclusion that cuts across both national and sectoral lines.

In addition, the attitudes of the providers of financing do not break down along state-owned versus privately owned lines. Nationalization can mean that the government acts as a dominant stakeholder, but this depends on a number of issues, not least exactly how the firm is financed and how its ownership and corporate governance were structured both before and after nationalization. The French government has been less actively involved in the management of Usinor since the late 1980s, and the British government was not particularly active in the management of BL during the early years. On the other hand, privatization can include Special Shares, ensuring that the state retains the potential to play a vital role in the firm's affairs. Flotation on the private stock market—which is likely in the near future for both Usinor and Renault—can also vary enormously, from cases such as Jaguar to something like the case of Peugeot SA.

Long-term debt does not necessarily mean a long-term relationship between firm and creditor. The French banks were lending primarily government money, not their own funds. As part 2 describes, the long-term relationships between German banks and the firms they help to finance are based more on the fact that the banks own shares in the companies and have seats on their boards, than on their role as providers of debt financing. In addition, equity financing does not necessarily mean that exit is the only means of exercising influence over a firm. Peugeot's shareholders have a long-term relationship with the company, and the French government is planning to privatize firms with an established core of friendly institutional investors. How debt and equity financing really work, and how the kinds of relationships involved and the attitudes of investors affect firm survival and adaptation, depends on the national financial system and form of corporate governance. To put it another way, not all markets are created equal. A British pension fund is not the same kind of animal as a French institutional investor, when it comes to industrial financing.

From the four cases studied here, we can draw some conclusions about the preferred form of financing and governance for a major manufacturer undergoing restructuring upheavals and tremendous competitive pressures. Above all, the firm needs providers of capital that have one or more of the following characteristics:

(a) *patience*, and the willingness to support the firm over a long period of time with minimal short-term profit;

(b) the ability to play the role of *dominant stakeholder*;

(c) the willingness and ability to *support management's long-term strategies* for restructuring and adaptation; and

(d) the willingness and ability to *provide enormous sums of capital* at critical junctures.

This does not mean to say that a firm whose providers of capital meet one or more of these characteristics will always survive, adapt, and prosper. Given the competitive environment in which it was operating, BLMC might have ended up as a much smaller manufacturer looking for a larger partner by the end of the 1980s no matter who was the provider of its capital. For a major manufacturer's primary source of financing to lack any of these characteristics, however, does not augur well for its chances to survive and to adapt for the long term during a period of intense competitive pressures and rapid technological change.

The Role of the State

> [E]ven in the classical *laissez-faire* model, the ground rules for the market are set by the minimal state. The selection of one particular rule against another will create a different type of market. (Graham 1989, 210)

> He promised me that HMG would turn it all into a successful and profitable venture. . . . Whoever heard of the government being involved in a successful and profitable venture? Does he think I was born yesterday? (Lynn and Jay 1984, 158)

We have seen that each of the cases analyzed illustrates aspects of Graham's "com-penetration" of the public and the private sectors. As he points out, this is a notable feature of the modern state, a state that is thus always involved in industrial affairs. When it comes to industrial restructuring in particular, governments do not just have an impact on outcomes when there is some overt form of intervention such as nationalization, or the sponsoring of national champions and "*secteurs en mutation*" as seen in the first Socialist administration in France. For example, the state plays an obvious and overt role in maintaining protectionist trade policies and, in the case of steel, the EC's crisis regime (protectionism, subsidy, set prices and production quotas). Thus we could interpret BL as an example of a lack of a state role in managing the market, and PSA as an example of strong state intervention on behalf of a manufacturer. More fundamentally, however, as seen in the four cases, the individual firms' financial structure and form of corporate governance is derived from the national financial system as regulated and defined by the state.

Chapters 2 and 5 illustrated the dominance of the stock market in industrial financing in Britain, and the attitudes of the market's investors toward their investments. This market did give the newly privatized British Steel access to a potentially huge pool of capital in the booming days of 1988–90. The highly capitalized market is also highly liquid, however, and dominated by institutional investors who dumped the firm's shares when it announced a reduced dividend in 1991–92 and then no interim dividend in 1992–93. Womack (1982) aptly describes this kind of industrial financing as arm's-length, with investors making short-term assessments of business prospects and stock performance. The investors are rarely patient, there is not usually a dominant stakeholder in the sense defined here, and the providers of capital tend to have little in the way of detailed knowledge about management's long-term plans for the company. The system can provide enormous sums of capital, but not necessarily at the critical junctures when it is most needed. In addition, successive British governments have shied away from overt mixes of public and private capital, and have had only limited institutional resources for channeling investment funds to the private sector. Nor have governments developed mechanisms that would allow private capital to flow into otherwise state-owned companies, except in limited and one-off cases such as British Leyland and its relationship with a group of private banks.

Chapters 3 and 4 showed that the financial system in France is very different. Two particular aspects stand out. First, that governments have actively developed the institutional means both to channel public funding to the private sector and to allow state-owned firms access to private capital. Second, that a major manufacturer's corporate governance structure often includes a core group of supportive investors, whether in the form of a family and its "institutional friends" or in the form of a 20 percent stake held by a financial institution. Peugeot's investors were indeed patient during the tumultuous 1980s, and the firm has a dominant stakeholder and a core of supportive investors who are more likely to take an active role in tracking management's long-term strategies. These investors were also willing to provide considerable sums of capital during the critical period of the mid-1980s. Usinor appears to be moving toward a similar structure. Crédit Lyonnais already holds 20 percent of its equity, and the Balladur government has made it clear that state-owned firms now on the privatization list (which includes Usinor) will be provided with a core of supportive institutional investors—*noyaux durs*—in the same way as those firms transferred to the private sector in 1986–88. It should also be noted, however, that in the French cases analyzed here, much of the characteristics of patience, long-term support, and provision of enormous sums found in the financing of these firms was ultimately due to the government being overtly or covertly involved in industrial financing in ways not found in Britain.

It is also clear from these cases that national variations in industrial financing include more than just a tendency to, say, debt, retentions, or equity as the primary source of funding for most firms. The different forms of financing available across countries come with different costs, but the attitudes of the providers of that financing are the most important issue. In other words, the way in which ownership and control is organized—the form of corporate governance—is more important than how the balance sheet is structured on paper. Thus, it is not enough to define Britain as a "market-based system" and France as a "state-controlled system." In fact, to do so misses the real fundamental differences between the two countries. Although successive French governments have been more actively involved in industrial financing, this alone does not explain the differing outcomes between the French and British cases analyzed here. As we saw, the British governments got involved too, just in a more ad hoc manner and under a different set of labels. Not until we start the comparative analysis at the level of the firm does it become apparent that the providers of financing are the key in industrial survival and adaptation. It is not whether the state has an activist or hands-off stance toward industrial policy that counts, nor whether one state has more "structural capacity" to get involved in industrial affairs than another. Rather, the financial and governance structure of British Steel and Jaguar, of Peugeot and Usinor, are derived from a national system of governance and financing that is regulated and defined by the state. The state is thus always involved in the financing of industry; its role is crucial and unavoidable. More specifically, individual governments can change that system—the liberalization and development of the French financial markets during the 1980s are a very clear example of the role that government plays in regulating and defining markets and corporate-governance systems.

National financial markets differ, for example, in the extent to which banking and other financial services are kept separate, and in the nature of official supervision. In France, for example, a firm with a banking license may also provide a broad array of securities services and other financial activities. In the United States, on the other hand, the Bank Holding Company Act and the Glass-Steagall Act limit the in-house activities of banks and ownership linkages between banks and nonbank financial firms. There are also differences in the forms of finance available. Despite global, twenty-four-hour trading and investment, equities in particular still retain distinct national characteristics. This is due to national differences in accounting procedures, taxation requirements, disclosure laws, and legal or unofficial restraints on institutional investments in foreign shares. Even the legal definition of what constitutes corporate control varies across countries. The United States defines control of a company as owning 10 percent or more of that company. In Britain and France, 20 percent constitutes ownership. This also means different conceptions of what counts as direct investment from overseas.

Government has the power to alter the structure of the financial market, through legislation and regulatory moves. One of the first moves of the Thatcher government in 1979 was to abolish financial controls, triggering a massive and continuing outflow of British investment capital overseas, which some argue has had a marked effect on the sources of investment capital available within the country. As described in chapter 1, both the French and British governments legislated changes in the structure, operation, and supervision of their stock markets in the 1980s. The Socialist government in France has encouraged the major banks to become more involved in the affairs of industry, with potentially long-term consequences for the structure of French banking. It has also largely given up the state's historic ability to control the flow of funds through the credit markets.

The importance of national financial and corporate governance systems is especially relevant as we move into the 1990s, given not only the new crisis unfolding in the European steel and auto industries, and continuing intense competitive pressures, but also the extent to which state intervention is shifting away from the overt forms practiced in the 1970s and early 1980s. Furthermore, how major manufacturers are financed, and the forms of ownership and control that govern them, are issues of profound importance for the nations of Eastern Europe as they grope toward the creation of market-based economies. Before exploring these issues in part 3 of this chapter, the following pages turn to some examples from Germany, Japan, and the United States of financing a major industrial concern at a critical juncture for its survival and restructuring.

2. Other National Financial Systems

The premise of this comparative analysis of government-industry relations is that firm-level financial issues are both a direct result of the national financial system as defined and regulated by government and a powerful tool for explaining varying outcomes in cases of industrial crisis and adjustment. If this firm-level-financing perspective is to be of any use in comparative political economy, it must be applicable to other cases, and especially to other countries. This section begins that process with an overview of some examples drawn from Germany, Japan, and the United States, with the example of Fiat in Italy thrown in for good measure. The discussion is not intended to be exhaustive or very detailed, but merely a preliminary exploration of how the financing of major manufacturers, and particularly the varying attitudes of the providers of that financing, reveal fundamental differences in national financial systems and forms of corporate governance. It draws on historic examples from Womack (1982) and on current developments in these nations' steel and auto industries.

Germany

In analyses of industrial policy in Germany, the major banks are always at the heart of the story, usually in terms of their role in forging a consensus between the firm, workers, and financiers concerned. They are said to make "conspicuous use" of their privileged position as the primary source of capital by stepping in to enforce restructuring, even bringing in a new chairman of their choice and closely monitoring his performance, "frequently before the governments even take notice" (Abromeit 1990). However, as shown by the case of Volkswagen in 1974, the banks have played an equally—if not more— crucial role in providing firms with access to significant sums of financing at key junctures. In addition, the role of Federal and Länd governments also has been important in creating an atmosphere of long-term cooperation and in providing financial aid. The rescue of steel firms in the Saar in 1978 and the Ruhr in the early 1980s is illustrative. Today, however, the old ties between bank and firm are gradually loosening, and EC rules prevent the active subsidization of major manufacturers by national or local governments; yet firms such as VW still need access to enormous sums of capital.

Volkswagen was created by the Nazi state in 1937 to produce a small car for the masses. It survived the postwar period of deconstruction and denazification, and went into civilian production. In 1961, the firm was partially privatized: 60 percent of its shares were sold to the public, with the remaining 40 percent split between the Federal government and the Länd of Lower Saxony. The company was highly successful—and highly profitable—until 1971, when the end of the Bretton Woods system sent the deutsche mark soaring against the dollar, and turned Germany into a high-cost production site. Its new models performed badly, sales of the famous Beetle were in a slump, and the firm's troubles began to multiply. VW was facing the same critical juncture as Peugeot at this time: it could no longer survive as a one-model producer.

In September 1971 the new president of VW proposed boosting annual new capital spending almost fivefold, in order to press ahead with a host of new designs. Management had to convince the firm's banks and shareholders (including Federal and Länd authorities), as well as the trade union representatives on its supervisory board, that VW needed a new direction (Jones 1981). When it began to look as if the internal wrangling would lead to stalemate and no coherent strategy, Chancellor Helmut Schmidt (perhaps concerned that the economic consequences of failing to agree would be blamed on the government) stepped in to mediate. Consensus on the new strategy was eventually forthcoming. By mid-1972, the company's cash reserves were exhausted and "for the first time in its history VW embarked on a program of medium and long-term borrowing" (Womack 1982, 8). As the worldwide auto market slid into recession in 1974, VW posted a loss for the first time in its history, and its medium and long-term bank loans were increased to a total of $2.2 billion. In 1975, the firm's debt:equity ratio hit 2.2 (ibid.). However, the loans enabled the firm to launch new models—which proved highly successful—and by 1979 VW was making record profits, had built up a significant cash reserve, and had retired much of its debt.

A few years later, the unfolding international steel crisis hit first the old steel region of Saarland, then the industrial heartland of West Germany, the Ruhr. Again, we find the involvement of banks, "social partners," and, ultimately, the government, in reaching consensus on a solution to the crisis. The Federal government had not been actively involved in the postwar steel industry. It was the banks that encouraged industrial self-organization, with the formation of four steel-sales cartels in the 1960s that eventually became rationalization groups coordinating investment and production (Abromeit 1990). In 1978, the Saar steel companies faced imminent bankruptcy. After the major German steel firms in the Ruhr made it clear that they were neither willing nor able to come to the Saar firms' rescue, the Federal and Saar Länd governments negotiated a deal with the IG Metall union and the Luxembourg Arbed combine. The government gave Arbed financial aid to take over Saar iron and steel, in return for the combine implementing a restructuring program. Esser and Väth (1986) have dubbed this arrangement a "political regulation cartel for the organisation management of the crisis which trends, in terms of factual results, towards indirect nationalisation" (651).

The informal "cartel" of steel companies, union, and state authorities, centralized the formerly fragmented structure of ownership and decision making; restructured production; and used social provisions such as early-retirement programs to mitigate the impact on the work force. This was essentially the same outcome found over the next few years in France, except that in the latter case, financial intermediaries and local authorities did not become actively involved in initiating solutions to the crisis, and the central government took a much longer time to impose a solution on the French steel firms. When the steel crisis subsequently engulfed the Ruhr region, a similar solution was launched, strongly supported by Deutsche Bank and the federal government, whereby the two German companies Krupp-Stahl and Hoesch would form a new company and restructure the industry. The plan fell apart, however, because of negotiations between Krupp and a third firm, Thyssen, over a possible linkup in the special-steel sector. Meanwhile, Arbed Saarstahl received a sixth injection of aid from the Federal and Länd governments in 1983, to the tune of DM3 billion (DM3,000 million) (Wilks 1984b). Saarstahl was taken over by Usinor Sacilor in 1988, which took a 70 percent stake in a new holding company that owned all of Saarstahl, the Länd retaining the remaining 30 percent. In the spring of 1993, however, the venture folded. This time, there was no coordinated rescue.

Womack (1982) calls the German national financial system one of "banker coordination." The major banks perform both commercial- and investment-banking functions. They may own equity stakes of any size in German firms, have seats on the German stock exchanges, and can also act as proxy voters for individual shareholders. The banks can also exchange voting proxies without having to inform the shareholders, thus ensuring that a bank can control the largest block of shares of each enterprise to which it is lead lender. The banks use their proxies to vote on policy questions at annual meetings, and to elect the members of corporate supervisory boards. Comprised of outside directors, the supervisory board approves strategy, authorizes major investments, and in turn elects the operating board that manages the company day-to-day. The banks also trade each others' stock proxies "in order to preserve their own independence from bank stockholders" (Womack 1982, 3). All in all, the likes of Deutsche Bank can not only have considerable influence over a client firm's corporate strategy, but can also have a long-term view over investment and industrial adaptation, and the independence to ride out a downturn in the market.

Deutsche Bank has long been the dominant bank in the auto sector. In the early years of German auto production, the bank helped the specialist producers BMW and Daimler-Benz through the lean times, with Deutsche chairman Emil Georg Von Strauss supporting the firms because of what he saw as their potential as arms producers (Reich 1990). It was also the major banks, rather than the free-market-oriented Federal government, that took steps in the postwar period to resist foreign takeovers of major West German manufacturers. In the mid-1960s and again in the mid-1970s, the banks frustrated possible takeovers at Daimler-Benz. Large blocks of the shares of Daimler, and of BMW, are held by individual families, as well as by the banks (Jones 1981). In 1975, Federal legislation was passed explicitly protecting core German auto companies from foreign takeover, following an attempt by the Shah of Iran to take a significant stake in Germany's largest industrial company, Daimler-Benz.

Finally, the German financial system is also characterized by a large amount of intercorporate equity holding. According to research by Franks and Mayer (1992) on West Germany's 200 largest companies in 1990, 35 percent of the shareholdings in excess of 25 percent were held by other companies; 17 percent were held by families; and banks accounted for only 8 percent of the large stakes. Franks and Mayer dub this an "insider system" of corporate control. One outcome of such a system is a low level of hostile corporate takeovers—between the banks' wielding of proxy votes, large stakes already held by other corporations, frequent shareholder resolutions limiting the voting right of any one shareholder to a maximum of 5 percent of the total votes, and the difficulty of removing members of the supervisory board, German companies have long had "barriers to unfriendly takeovers that an Olympic hurdler would find difficult to overcome" (*New York Times*, November 5, 1989). However, such barriers are not insurmountable, if certain conditions hold. The recent case of the Italian firm Pirelli's bid for German tire manufacturer Continental was a case in point.

Continental was one of the few companies in the former West Germany that was both publicly quoted and widely held. When Pirelli launched its unwelcome bid in September 1990, there was a 5 percent limitation on voting rights. An extraordinary shareholder meeting resolved to remove the limitation, so allowing Pirelli to make a full bid for Continental. Pro-Pirelli forces reportedly were busy buying up shares from individual investors, as were promanagement forces, primarily BMW, Daimler-Benz, and Volkswagen.

The firm's management board was firmly opposed to the merger. The supervisory board was more willing to explore the possibility, however, and replaced the chairman of the management board with one more sympathetic to merger discussions in May 1991 (Franks and Mayer 1992). Meanwhile, the removal of voting restrictions was delayed (and never implemented) by a court action by some shareholders who said that the removal would violate minority interests. Pirelli agreed to compensate allies holding a third of Continental's shares, if no merger was agreed to by the end of November 1991. Finally, on December 1, Pirelli called off the attempt. Aware of Pirelli's pledge to its allies, Continental managers opposed to the scheme had only to stall negotiations for long enough to kill the bid. Although the case has been seen as proof of the insurmountable barriers to takeovers in Germany, part of the reason this one failed was that Pirelli's own senior managers were deeply divided over the venture. Most interesting, however, is the fact that Deutsche Bank, a big Continental shareholder, remained neutral throughout the affair (although this may have been because two members of the Deutsche board were themselves on opposite sides in the affair: see *Economist*, June 22, 1991). It was Continental's corporate shareholders, not its lead bank, that led the fight against the Italians. Nevertheless, it was the firm's system of corporate governance, in particular an ownership structure of corporate cross-shareholdings, that was instrumental in defeating the hostile bid.

Another recent takeover bid, this time in the steel sector, had a very different outcome. On October 15, 1991, with consolidation in the industry speeding up across Europe, German steelmaker Krupp revealed that it had acquired a 24.9 percent stake in its nearby rival, Hoesch. Krupp had decided to take the lead in consolidating the German steel industry, which at that point still had six major steel firms where most other European countries had only one. Not even Deutsche Bank, Hoesch's lead bank, had known what was in the offing. By the end of November, Krupp claimed to control, directly and indirectly, some 80 percent of Hoesch's shares. Although less than thrilled by the aggressive move of its rival, Hoesch agreed to the merger, which was to be finalized during 1993. Again, the lack of involvement by Deutsche Bank in the merger is striking. By the late 1980s, many analysts had been pointing out that consolidation in the western German steel industry (which accounts for a third of European steel output) was inevitable, but this time Krupp appears to have moved on its own, without the involvement of banks, governments, or unions. It also does not seem to have been put off by the presence of Deutsche Bank behind Hoesch. Could it be that the role of the banks—and of federal and local governments—is no longer what it was in Germany?

This brings us to the example of German carmaker Daimler-Benz AG, which plans to become the first German stock to be listed on the New York Stock Exchange later in 1993. Daimler will initially offer 2 to 3 percent of its existing shares through New York, and eventually wants to increase this to 10 percent. In order to do this, Daimler has had to agree to abide by American accounting requirements. This will undermine much of its comfortable support from the likes of Deutsche Bank, and will open up the firm to greater scrutiny by foreign investors who are likely to be less patient than their German counterparts. After four years of negotiations with the United States Securities and Exchange Commission, Daimler has agreed to a number of changes. It will abandon its main protection against unwelcome takeover, a special holding company, called Mercedes Holding, that was set up in 1975 at the initiative of Deutsche Bank to stop the Shah of Iran from buying a stake in the firm. Mercedes Holding owns 25.23 percent of Daimler's shares, which will be converted into Daimler shares later in 1993. Daimler also agreed to partial disclosure of its hidden reserves, which in 1992 added "extraordinary earnings" of DM4.49 billion to Daimler-Benz AG income (*Financial Times*, April 3, 1993). (At the time of writing, the full details of the deal between Daimler and the SEC have not been revealed.)

Daimler is putting itself through all of this because it badly needs investment financing. The firm wanted to hold a DM2 billion rights issue in 1992, but had to postpone due to poor conditions in the German equity market (*Financial Times*, April 3, 1993). With more German companies competing for investment funds to modernize the eastern part of the country and to expand into the markets of Eastern Europe, the banks can no longer always be counted upon to provide vast sums of capital. Daimler seems to feel that it has no choice but to turn to the biggest pools of equity capital—the pension funds of America and the insurance funds of Britain. With such a small percentage of its shares initially available in New York, Daimler is unlikely to find itself suddenly subject to the volatile reactions of Anglo-equity investors that so plagued Jaguar in the mid-1980s. Although there have been rumors of late that Deutsche Bank is interested in reducing the size of its stake, the bank still holds 28 percent of Daimler's shares: "We've had the Daimler stake for over 60 years and it's not our view to buy today and sell tomorrow. . . . That's why we can take such a hands-off approach. Daimler is like a fund managing assets for us, of which we own a certain part." (Deutsche Bank chief executive Hilmar Kopper, in *Financial Times*, March 19, 1993.) In addition, two holding companies, Stella Automobil and Stern Automobil, which are in turn owned by a number of banks and industrial companies (including Allianz, Dresdner Bank, Commerzbank, and components company Robert Bosch) hold half of Daimler's shares.

Finally, to return to the case that we started with, Volkswagen AG is reportedly struggling through "the worst group crisis and the most difficult market conditions since 1945" (*Financial Times*, April 1, 1993). In the fiercely competitive European market of the 1990s, Germany's Volkswagen

AG is aiming to become a pan-European company that offers a wide variety of cars and builds them in much-reduced cost structures. In 1991 Carl Hahn, then chairman of the board of management, estimated the price of expansion at $35 billion—on average, $7 billion a year, which was $3 billion more than the company's reported annual cash flow at that time (interview in *Harvard Business Review*, July–August 1991). The success of VW's plans is largely dependent on its ability to finance them. Hahn maintained that for VW "liquidity is not likely to be a problem. You simply cannot compare the profit and loss statement of a German company with that of a North American corporation. Different accounting laws and traditions play a significant role." (ibid., 109). He argued that VW, like many other German companies in the 1980s, was able to manage its depreciation allowances to build up its reserves. In the past decade, the company's capital increased from DM6 billion to DM16 billion, even though it raised only DM4 billion from the sale of capital.[1] In addition, said Hahn, its close relationship with a number of banks gives Volkswagen AG "deep pockets" (ibid.).

However, economic uncertainty and high interest rates have severely depressed the German car market (new car registrations in 1992 were down 5.5 percent on 1991), and with recession looming and consumer confidence at a ten-year low, things are not likely to improve before 1994. The German Automobile Industry Association predicts a 10 percent fall in production and sales in 1993. A new chairman, Ferdinand Piëch, took over at VW in January 1993, after the supervisory board changed its mind about pushing back Carl Hahn's retirement date (*Financial Times*, October 20, 1992).[2] Along with a team of outsiders brought into top management positions by the supervisory board in the past few months, Piëch is pushing a restructuring program to deal with what he calls "the emergency." Despite record-high sales of 3.5 million vehicles in 1992, the company's after-tax profits collapsed to just DM147 million, and the firm lost DM1.25 billion in the first three months of 1993. The company plans to cut some 36,000 jobs by 1997, 20,000 of them in 1993. Capital spending in 1993 will be cut from the previous year's DM9 billion to DM6 billion. The number of suppliers to the firm are to be drastically reduced. Piëch intends to introduce Japanese-style work and production practices into the firm over the next three years. All told, the scale and scope of this restructuring program are unprecedented in German industry. The Länd of Lower Saxony still owns 20 percent of the VW group's voting stock, and representatives of the workers and the Länd together can outvote private shareholders on the supervisory board (*Economist*, March 13, 1993). This means that management must continue to have the backing of labor and of the Länd in order to implement the plan. On the other hand, it also implies that as long as that backing is forthcoming, management stands a good chance of pulling it off.

In the midst of all of this upheaval, VW has embarked on a heavy investment program. In January 1993, the supervisory board approved a five-year plan to inject almost DM76 billion into the firm by the end of 1997. Although this year's spending will be less than in 1992, the company said that it plans to increase average annual outlays again once the market improves (*Financial Times*, January 14, 1993). Clearly, access to financing will continue to be a crucial issue for VW.

This quick survey of some selected cases from the German scene raises a number of issues. First, it seems that the banks are mostly deserving of their assigned place at the heart of the story of industrial policy in Germany. They played a dominant role in the postwar period in organizing restructuring programs such as those in the steel industry in the late 1970s and early 1980s. They were also instrumental in launching defenses of "key" industrial firms from foreign investors. However, they are not the only explanation for the availability of long-term investment capital in Germany. They rarely control the majority of seats on the supervisory boards of companies such as VW, and the various Länd governments have also been closely involved in the financial support of some major manufacturing concerns. Equally important, the role of the banks seems to be changing. Nevertheless, they have behaved in ways quite unlike those of their British or French counterparts. Deutsche Bank, in particular, has been the most influential of the banks in the industrial sphere. Aside from its holding in Daimler-Benz, Deutsche has a 30 percent stake in the Philip Holzmann construction company and owns 10 percent of Europe's largest insurance group, Allianz. Even if they are not in the majority, bank board members still hold more than 100 seats on various company supervisory boards (*Financial Times*, March 19, 1993). When Germany's fifth-largest steel company (and Western Europe's twelfth), Klöckner-Werke, filed for protection from creditors in December 1992, a complex rescue plan was drawn up by the leading creditor—Deutsche Bank.[3]

The second issue raised by these examples is that corporate cross-shareholdings seem to be an important part of the famed "patience" of long-term investment capital in Germany. A corporate shareholder may be less likely to bail out when a firm gets into trouble, especially if the shareholder is a supplier to, or customer of, the firm, or if the firm in turn has an ownership stake in the corporate shareholder. What emerges from these quick examples is, perhaps, less a system oriented around powerful banks or dominant supervisory boards, than one where the national financial system and form of corporate governance encourage a network of stakeholders that are more apt to take a long-term view of a firm's financial needs. It is also a network where there are likely to be one or more dominant stakeholders that can either force management into a restructuring plan at a time of crisis, or see to it that management receives the backing that it needs. It is this pattern of corporate governance that is the key to the attitudes of providers of finance to major manufacturers in Germany, and it is maintained in many and often subtle ways. For example, the German commercial paper (CP) market is still relatively new and underdeveloped, and Deutsche Bank has underwritten almost all of the CP issued. Most of this paper does not come with an independent credit rating, but the bank's name is sufficient to reassure investors, their trust based on the links that are known to exist between banks and their corporate clients ("A Survey of World Banking," *Economist*, May 2, 1992).

Finally, these examples raise some important questions. Can the system withstand the strains of unification with the former East Germany? The opposition Social Democratic Party (SPD) has proposed limiting the stakes that banks and insurers can take in industrial companies to no more than 5 percent, and limiting to five the number of board seats that could be held by officials from bank and insurance companies. The SPD argues that these moves would not only make companies' stock more appealing to individuals, but would also loosen the ties between financial institutions and industry, so making German managers more willing to take risks in an increasingly competitive environment. The demands on German investment capital are now considerable, and the Daimler example suggests that domestic sources will no longer be adequate (or, perhaps, even desirable) in a rapidly changing world.

If Daimler turns out to be only the first of many firms to turn to the American equity market, will this eventually alter its corporate governance and ownership structures into something decidedly non-German? On the other hand, might the kinds of changes sweeping the international auto industry, with all producers attempting to emulate what Womack et al. (1990) call the "lean production" techniques of the Japanese, eventually lead to the development in other countries of the kinds of corporate cross-shareholdings between major firms, or firms and their customers and suppliers, that we find in Germany? The EC's clamp-down on state aid to industry is widespread. In April 1993, the Commission rejected a proposed German government subsidy of nearly DM1 billion to the eastern company Eko Stahl, on the grounds that it would lead to increased capacity in warm flat steel. Might the elimination of state aid encourage major manufacturers across Europe to seek alternate sources of long-term financing—either from the markets in the United States, or from fellow manufacturers at home and abroad? What the impact of such changes might be on German-based manufacturers, and what their options are in terms of industrial adaptation in the 1990s, can best be answered by an analysis of German industrial financing and corporate governance that begins with developments at individual firms such as VW, Daimler, and Hoesch.

Japan

There is almost no direct state ownership of industrial companies in Japan. Where various European governments have tended over the years to build national champions with state equity, the Japanese government has instead restructured private markets, usually attempting to reproduce shifting market structures by fortifying the position of existing firms (see Samuels 1990). As markets are never totally stable, the state and firms are constantly working together to "order" markets. This leads to what Samuels characterizes as a system of reciprocal consent between market players and the state, with government-industry relations based around negotiation. "As in France, state bureaucrats or private firms have never held a priori that markets will adjust in the best interests of capital or citizens" (Samuels 1990, 53).

Discussion of industrial financing in postwar Japan centers around the industrial groupings known as *keiretsu*. These typically bring together a lead bank, one or more insurance companies, and a number of large industrial concerns from various sectors. The combination of interlocking stock ownership and boards of directors with expertise across industrial sectors, can make for a group that is both supportive and dynamic. It also gives troubled manufacturers access to some very deep financial pockets. A classic example of this is the rescue and restructuring of Toyo Kogyo (Mazda) in 1974, detailed by the MIT study on the future of the automobile (Altshuler et al. 1984). As in Germany, however, the fabled Japanese financial system is under some strain. The new pressures on the Japanese banks, along with the rapid internationalization and liberalization of financial markets, may mean some changes in the Japanese system of corporate governance down the road.

Toyo Kogyo was founded as a machine-tool company in 1920 and its first automobile entered the market in 1960. The firm decided the only way to challenge the likes of Toyota and Nissan was head-on, with a dramatic new technical innovation. It therefore launched full-scale development of a new type of engine, the Wankel rotary engine (Womack 1982). Mass production began in 1967. The Mazda cars were initially highly successful, and by 1973 Toyo Kogyo had secured the number-three spot among Japanese auto makers. Then came the 1973 energy crisis that sent fuel costs soaring and sales of the fuel-hungry Mazda plunging. Toyo Kogyo suddenly found itself needing to develop a whole new range of models with a newly designed engine, and to improve its far-from-lean production system. Sumitomo Bank—lead bank of the Sumitomo *keiretsu* of which Toyo Kogyo was a part—came to the rescue.

The Sumitomo group included another major bank, two large insurance companies, and an international trading company, all with considerable financial resources, as well as many suppliers to Toyo Kogyo who could advance trade credits (Womack 1982). The bank sent a team of executives to replace family management at the car firm. This team decided that Toyo needed to initiate a Toyota-style production system and that it should receive massive loans for new engines and a new model range in order to expand its market presence (Womack, Jones, and Roos 1990). Like VW and Peugeot, this was a one-model company that had to change drastically in order to survive. In

January 1975, the Sumitomo Bank and the Sumitomo trust loaned Toyo Kogyo sufficient operating cash to enable the firm to survive while the restructuring got under way. A number of Sumitomo senior executives were moved into senior management positions (i.e., outsiders were brought in to initiate the kinds of drastic changes that incumbent management were unwilling or unable to contemplate). To increase the firm's access to investment capital without overly draining the rest of the group, a 25 percent equity stake was sold to the Ford Motor Company in 1979. Although Ford made a $135 million investment in Toyo Kogyo (which improved the firm's debt:equity ratio), the American firm received "practically no dividends . . . and little control over T-K management or product policy" (Womack 1982, 7). The Sumitomo group had quickly bought up many of the shares held outside the group, so maintaining overall group control. By 1981, Toyo Kogyo "was securely back in third place among Japanese auto makers" (ibid.).

The contrast with BLMC in 1974–75 is instructive. When the British firm faced a similar financial crisis, its only options were a drastic retrenchment and a state financial bailout. Furthermore, to recall chapter 5, the British government accepted the incumbent management's analysis of the firm's problems, and their recommendations as to how to proceed. No doubt it would have been politically very difficult for the Labour government in power at the time to override the views of such "top capitalists." The important point, however, is that BLMC had little recourse other than to turn to state guarantees for its bank loans, followed by outright nationalization. Toyo Kogyo was rescued not only by its access to the financial resources of the group, but also by the attitudes of the providers of that capital, and by the expertise and industry-wide perspectives provided by managers brought in from other parts of the group.

According to the OECD (1992), a distinctive feature of the corporate financial system in Japan is the extent to which firms and financial institutions have mutual stockholdings. Just over two-thirds of all corporate-sector shares are held by "stable" share owners: banks and life-insurance companies hold 42 percent, enterprises a further 25 percent.

> Shareholdings are based on implicit self-enforcing agreements to hold shares as "friendly insiders." Inter-corporate relationships are strengthened by interlocking directorates among non-competing companies and deepened by exchanges of personnel at most levels. A corporation can thus establish multi-layered networks with its trading companies including sub-contractors, banks and trading houses. (ibid., 75–76)

As in France, such shareholdings by friendly investors inhibit hostile takeovers—doubly so in the case of Japan, in that the friendly investors tend to be members of the same group, making them in effect friendly insiders.

The group's main bank acts as ultimate overseer, directing negotiations in order to avoid any potential management-shareholder conflicts, and acting as a monitor, representing the concerns of all creditors. Finally, because these insider shareholders have access to a great deal of information about the financial health of the company, "profit and dividend fluctuations have been less important as indicators of Japanese corporate financial health . . . Japanese management has been allowed to choose a longer corporate-planning horizon, avoiding the emphasis on short-term profits and dividends for which the U.S. and U.K. systems are often criticised" (ibid., 76). There is also, therefore, less pressure to maintain a high and consistent dividend—one of the ways in which capital has been relatively less expensive in Japan in recent years than in, say, the United Kingdom, particularly for a firm in a highly competitive industry such as auto manufacturing, where developing new technologies and production processes is both risky and expensive.

Whether these *keiretsu* groupings are significant barriers to foreign entrants in Japanese markets, an efficient means of allocating risks and resources, or bloated groups propping up overmanned and inefficient firms, are questions that are the source of a great deal of debate in both the academic and the popular press. They are also beyond the scope of this study. For our purposes, however, the Mazda example shows that the system can make available to a manufacturer in crisis considerable financial resources, both for short-term survival and for long-term adaptability, and it can do so in ways that may be relatively inexpensive and come from providers with a supportive attitude toward restructuring. One study of the financial restructuring of the world auto industry in the late 1970s (Anderson 1982) found that the Japanese producers had garnered large financial reserves and achieved capital structures with little dependence on external capital, enabling them to change products rapidly, to improve production techniques, and, crucially, to make rapid gains when the auto market turned up and to cushion themselves during the inevitable downturns.

The 1990s will bring some severe tests of such laudatory analyses, and particularly for the Japanese auto makers. Domestic auto production fell for the second consecutive fiscal year in 1992–93, and by the sharpest drop (6.2 percent) since the crisis year of 1974. Although Japanese per capita car ownership is the lowest of the industrial nations at 286 cars per 1,000 people (1990 figures; in the U.K., the number was 400 cars per 1,000; in the United States, 667 per 1,000—*Financial Times*, October 20, 1992), the domestic market is close to saturation, thanks to an aging population and city streets that seem to be stuck in almost permanent traffic jams. The giant Japanese auto firms have no choice but to target other markets if they are to survive and prosper. Chapter 5 described how the Japanese producers are opening new facilities in Britain that target their output to the EC market. Nissan, Toyota,

however, Big Steel in Japan may have some financial options that could help to ease the pain of the process. Kobe Steel, Japan's fifth-largest producer, is planning to reduce steel sales from the current 50 percent of its total revenue to 25 percent by the year 2000 (*Wall Street Journal*, February 2, 1993). The firm needs to raise capital to invest in its new materials and semiconductor businesses, and to cover the costs of inventory adjustments. In March 1993, Kobe Steel announced that it would sell shareholdings in its subsidiaries to other members of its *keiretsu* over the next three years. The firm expects to post ¥6.9 billion in special profits from stock sales in the 1992–93 fiscal year, and plans to sell some ¥5 billion worth of shares over the next three years. Kobe reportedly said that, "by enhancing cross-shareholdings among affiliates, ties within the *keiretsu* would be strengthened, and would also contribute to growth of the whole group" (*Financial Times*, March 5, 1993).

The United States

Starting in the late 1980s, the steel firms of Europe began to enter into a series of joint ventures and cross-border alliances. The moves were part of the European industry's process of restructuring. About the same time, American steel firms also began forging international links and joint ventures—but for a rather different purpose. Where the Europeans' primary concern has been consolidation and rationalization, the Americans have been driven by the need for access to the latest productive technology, and for access to the kinds of capital resources necessary to fund the related research and development. Research-and-development expenditure as a percentage of sales was 1.5 percent in the Japanese steel industry in 1987, compared with just 0.5 percent in the United States (*Financial Times*, January 24, 1990). Antitrust regulations have also historically prevented American steelmakers from the kinds of European mergers that have resulted in one or two steel manufacturers dominating a domestic market. By 1990, all of the big United States integrated steelmakers except Bethlehem, as well as many of the smaller ones, had forged alliances with Japanese steel firms. The American firms have gained access to new technology, while the Japanese firms have gained access to the United States market by taking equity stakes in their American partners. Thus Nippon Steel took 13 percent of the voting stock of Inland Steel in December 1989. Nippon already had a 40 percent share of a cold-rolling complex built by Inland, and was involved in a joint venture with the American firm on a galvanizing line. Kobe Steel has purchased a USX steel and pipe works in Ohio, and has taken a 40 percent stake in Armco. Nisshin has begun a joint venture with Wheeling-Pittsburgh, in which it has a 10 percent stake. In January 1993 Sumitomo Metal announced a $200 million investment in LTV Corporation, giving it a potential stake of 10 percent in the nation's third-largest steelmaker. Sumitomo said that the investment will provide more support for the two joint ventures in Ohio set up by the firms in 1986 and 1991.

In recent years, the American steel industry has been undergoing the same kind of painful restructuring and retrenchment as its European counterpart, and behind a similar protective barrier in the form of voluntary restraint agreements put in place in the mid-1980s by the Reagan administration. (When these import quotas ran out in 1992, American steel firms filed dozens of unfair trade suits against foreign producers, resulting in January 1993 in the imposition of preliminary duties on imports from nineteen countries by the Commerce Department.) Over the course of the 1980s, the number of steel-mill employees in the United States plummeted from around 380,000 to some 170,000, while raw steel production capability dropped from a historic high of 160 million tons in 1977 to around 119 million by 1991. Meanwhile, the integrated steelmakers have invested in a mammoth modernization effort to provide continuous casting capacity. By the end of the decade, concasting accounted for around 67 percent of total United States steel output. The comparable figure for the Japanese firms by then was around 95 percent. Even as Big Steel has turned to Japanese partners for capital and know-how, it is increasingly being challenged in the domestic market by American mini-mills, which have already captured a significant percentage of the low value-added end of the market, and are now moving aggressively into higher-quality sectors. Most of these mini-mills make steel from scrap on a relatively small scale using an electric furnace, and tend to serve regional markets. Their capital costs tend to be lower than those of the integrated manufacturers, they can adapt to new technologies faster, their productivity levels tend to be higher, and, through the tumultuous years of the 1980s, they tended to be more profitable. The largest mini-mill is Nucor, which was profitable in every quarter from 1966 to 1990 (*Financial Times*, March 28, 1991).

The first American-Japanese joint venture of the 1980s involved National Steel and the NKK Corporation of Japan. National had been a public company from 1929 to 1983, then became a unit of a new holding company, National Intergroup. NKK bought 50 percent of National Steel in 1984. After a series of management shake-ups and unsuccessful diversifications at National Intergroup, NKK bought an additional 20 percent of National Steel in 1990. National Intergroup retained the remaining 30 percent. In the spring of 1993, National Steel Corporation (now the nation's fourth-largest steelmaker) announced that it was returning to public ownership, with an initial public offering valued at up to $178 million that will cut National Intergroup's holding to some 11 percent. National is anxious to raise capital, as some of its pensions are underfunded, and new accounting standards mean that the firm will face some $650 million in retiree health-care liabilities, which it will begin to recognize in the first quarter of 1993. With steel shares in general posting something of a rally in late 1992 and early 1993, the offering has been described as "trying to simply take advantage of the market being strong" (*Wall Street Journal*, February 8, 1993). As described in the previous section, Kobe Steel also announced in the spring of 1993 that it was trying to raise capital by issuing shares. Unlike National, however, Kobe can turn to other members of its *keiretsu* to take stakes in its subsidiaries over the next three years. National's only recourse, aside from its two current owners, is a public offering. At the time of the announced IPO (initial public offering), stock analysts in the United States were described as "lukewarm" about the company's long-term prospects (ibid.).

While National was planning its IPO, another steel firm was having an interesting experience with the American stock market. LTV Corporation, now the third-largest steelmaker, has been one of the nation's longest-running bankruptcies. It filed for Chapter 11 protection from its creditors in July 1986. Since then, creditors have allowed the firm to invest some $2 billion to modernize its plants, while at the same time shedding more than half of its capacity and employees. On January 20, 1993, the firm filed a complex reorganization plan that aimed to resolve the almost $6 billion worth of creditors' claims against five different entities in the company,[5] and a further $3 billion in pension-related claims. Part of the reason the bankruptcy has dragged on for so long is the dispute over funding the pension plans that has embroiled the company, the federal government, and other creditors. Two days after the story about the reorganization hit the newspapers, LTV "found itself in the odd position of having to calm raging stock-market enthusiasm for its shares" (*Wall Street Journal*, January 25, 1993). The company's common stock had jumped 50 percent to close at $1.25 on unusually heavy volume of 15 million shares. At one point, the price had peaked at $2, prompting LTV to issue a news release pointing out the actual worth of the common shares— under the reorganization plan, LTV common would be worth a mere 3.22 cents. Just what sparked this rally is a matter open to conjecture. Brokers may have seen the headlines that LTV was coming out of bankruptcy and started a buying wave, without reading the fine print about the details of the reorganization. One theory is that the stock may have been boosted by computerized stock-trading programs that are set up to issue buy orders for stocks that move up sharply.

The example of LTV is one of those bizarre cases that will no doubt be used in many business-studies courses to illustrate the dangers and vagaries of the modern stock market. It is, of course, an aberrant example that cannot in all fairness be used to judge an entire system of industrial financing, but it does perhaps illustrate the kinds of extreme results that can arise from "imperfect investor information" in a financial system notable for being very decentralized and extremely liquid. Womack (1982) characterizes the United States system as "arm's-length," with highly decentralized commercial banks barred from most forms of interstate banking and from equity participation in the industrial enterprises to which they lend. Much as in the United Kingdom, the equity market is dominated by large institutional investors—principally pension funds, insurance companies, and bank trust departments. By 1990, institutional investors had increased their share of total United States equity to 60 percent. The comparable figure in 1950 was 8 percent. Such investors tend to have legal restrictions placed on concentrated ownership, ensuring that they tend to have only small holdings in any one company. Thus Calpers, the huge California state-employee pension fund, in 1990 had stakes in over 2,000 firms, none of them bigger than 0.7 percent of a company's equity (*Economist*, June 27, 1992). Such investors also tend to be restricted from sitting on company boards and so do not have access to "inside information" about the company. Hence they make short-term analyses of their holdings based on assessments of business prospects and stock performance. Tough American financial reporting requirements (the kind that have caused headaches for Daimler) ensure that the investors have access to the kinds of data needed to make such judgments.

A recent ruling by the Securities and Exchange Commission (SEC) has made it easier for shareholders to communicate with each other and with management.[6] This could, for example, make it easier to find out which reforms at a company will get majority support from other shareholders, and make it cheaper to lobby them in advance of a proxy fight. Such possibilities have spawned numerous articles and analyses about the beginnings of a new shareholder activism in America. Calpers has released the names of twelve United States companies that it is targeting in 1993 in an effort to exact better financial performance from those in which it invests. The list includes Chrysler Corporation, where Calpers reportedly has had meetings with management to discuss the fund's concerns, and where it has filed a shareholder proposal seeking bylaw amendments requiring the chairperson to be an independent director. Although there is anecdotal evidence that institutional investors are communicating more with management and with each other, this is still a very long way from the kinds of long-term monitoring relationships found in Germany and Japan.

The implications of this kind of national financial system for a major manufacturer embroiled in a financial crisis are illustrated by the case of the Chrysler Corporation in 1979. The firm was founded in 1924, and by 1946 "had sales second only to GM, healthy profits, and no debt" (Womack 1982, 9). From 1953, however, the firm started to slip, its emphasis on a practical, well-engineered car no longer so profitable, as customers began to demand fancier styling and more variety. Over the next two decades, the corporation tried a number of different strategies and a number of changes in management, none of which were pursued for long enough or consistently enough really to reorganize the firm's "ramshackle system" (ibid.). Every division reported directly to the president, there was no coordinating committee structure, and instead of sophisticated financial controls the company retained a simple bookkeeping system. As the firm slipped further behind Ford and GM, its bankers and stockholders frequently criticized management's performance, or produced analyses of the firm's financial problems, but there was no organized critique of a strategic nature, and no mobilization of the firm's shareholders in favor of a long-term reorganization plan. By the mid-1970s, Chrysler was drawing not only on domestic lenders but also on foreign creditors for its financing needs, while slashing product-planning outlays and firing large numbers of engineers in order to try and cut costs. Meanwhile, its shares were so widely held that no individual or corporation held more than 1 percent (Altshuler et al. 1984). By 1979, after struggling unsuccessfully to respond to the auto recession and crisis of 1974 with more cutbacks and more borrowing, the number of lenders had reached 400 and the firm was facing bankruptcy.

Chrysler Corporation's investment-banking advisor at this time was Lazard Frères. According to Womack (1982), Lazard proposed bringing together the firm's suppliers, commercial bankers, major union (the United Auto Workers), and management, to work out a plan of mutual concessions to save the company. As there was no German or Japanese-style lead bank to organize this process (and no dominant family shareholder as at Peugeot), "Lazard Frères offered to take on the task but Chrysler's management and board immediately balked. In their view, a party with no equity interest in Chrysler and no loans to the company was essentially proposing to take it over!" (ibid., 11) Without a coordinated behind-the-scenes rescue by its creditors, Chrysler's only other option was the government. In the American political context, a BLMC-style nationalization was out of the question. Instead, Chrysler applied to the state for a bailout in the form of federally guaranteed loans. The administration and its key congressional allies decided that the firm should be given "the absolute minimum" to ensure its day-to-day survival, while it scaled back operations, cleaned up its balance sheet, then looked for some form of partner, perhaps from overseas. "The amount of the guarantees was such that Chrysler was eventually forced to sell just about every property not connected with day-to-day automotive operations, including the highly profitable defense subsidiary" (ibid.).

Chrysler was not alone among the American automakers in facing financial problems after the crisis triggered by the first and second oil shocks. According to Anderson (1982), the market downturn at the end of the 1970s almost totally consumed the short-term liquid reserves of the United States auto companies. GM and Ford were also laden with record debt levels at this time, increasing their costs, and limiting their ability to modernize their plants and to bring new models to market. In the event, all three firms did survive. With the benefit of the minimal funding it managed to raise via the federal government, Chrysler was able to scale back its operations drastically, focusing on a few core models to return to profit. By 1984, the firm had repaid the government loans and raised an additional $5 billion in equity and debt financing from the private market. The firm went on to restructure how it did business, studying Honda in order to learn how to forge close links with its suppliers and create production systems based on platform teams. Nevertheless, it took another financial near-crisis in 1990 for Chrysler to slash its operating costs and introduce the new production techniques.

After some rough years in the mid- to late 1980s, the American Big Three have begun to reclaim some of their domestic market share from their Japanese competitors. The Japanese share of the market seems to have peaked at 30 percent in 1992, sliding to 27 percent in the early months of 1993, compared with 68 percent for GM, Ford, and Chrysler together. The Big Three have even begun to cooperate on research and development projects in nine key areas (with the blessing of the government in the form of the 1984 National Cooperative Research Act allowing that some R&D in "precompetitive" fields does not violate antitrust laws). Still, the pressures continue to be relentless, as is the need to access huge sums of capital. GM has said that it expects capital spending to top $7 billion in 1993, compared with $6.4 billion in 1992 and $7.1 billion in 1991—a level of spending that the firm anticipates will continue for the next few years. In March 1993, GM announced that seventeen banks are expected to commit $1 billion each to the firm's new credit lines, as GM works its way toward assembling some $20.75 billion in syndicated bank credit and an additional $4 billion in lines with individual banks, in what may end up being the largest-ever bank-credit package (see *Wall Street Journal*, March 11, 1993, A8). GM will reportedly use the new lines to refinance maturing bank lines and other debt coming due. Press reports cite banks involved in the deal as saying that it is unusual even for GM to seek such large commitments from so many banks at once, and that the big banks involved are expected to resell most of their loan commitments to smaller institutions. This comes hard on the heels of 1992, when GM again posted massive losses; announced a major restructuring of its North American operations that included the closure of twenty-one plants and the loss of 74,000 jobs over the next two-to-three years; and saw an overthrow of senior management by a disgruntled board of directors. The company also made five large stock offerings over the course of the year, including the biggest conventional common-stock offering ever done for an American company—a $2.167 billion global offering of 55 million shares distributed around the world by four syndicates. By the end of 1992, however, the firm's shares had fallen from the June price of $39 to around $31, and GM had announced that its dividend would be halved to 81 cents a share. Institutional investors owned some 40 percent of GM's common stock at the end of June; by December, the proportion reportedly had fallen to some 32 percent (*Economist*, December 12, 1992).

Chrysler continues to be the weakest of the three United States auto giants. In its 1992 annual report on the auto industry, Moody's singled out Chrysler as the most vulnerable American manufacturer. The report noted that, with the large sums of investment necessary for companies to produce new models and improve production efficiency, unless Chrysler's latest range of models achieves strong market acceptance, the firm may have no choice but to forge some form of strategic alliance with another producer in order to survive. This prognosis at first seemed overly pessimistic. Chrysler's share price quadrupled over the course of 1992 and into the first two months of 1993, even after the company raised $1.78 billion gross in an international share offering of 46 million new common shares. However, almost half of these funds will be used to reduce the underfunding of Chrysler's pension obligations. With the pension shortfall running at some $4 billion, Chrysler has left open the possibility that all of the cash raised could go straight to the pension fund. Meanwhile, of course, the American market isn't getting any less competitive and the firm must still raise enormous sums to finance the incorporation of the latest technologies into its production processes.

In April 1993, Chrysler posted a first-quarter loss of $4.2 billion, or $12.81 a share (dragged down by a big one-time charge for retiree medical benefits), and its shares promptly tumbled on fears that its recent surge in operating profit was now a thing of the past. An analyst summed up the attitude of Chrysler's investors succinctly: "More people will question whether Chrysler will be able to produce the kind of earnings in the next two quarters that we thought they could a quarter ago" (*Wall Street Journal*, April 20, 1993). The emphasis on earnings above all other indicators of the firm's financial health, and the incredibly short time frame—measured in months, not years—stand in strong contrast to the attitude and perspective of Deutsche Bank cited earlier, or those of Kobe Steel's *keiretsu* affiliates.

The Unfolding Case of Fiat

The Italian carmaker Fiat is now facing the same kind of challenge as BLMC, Chrysler, Peugeot, and Volkswagen did in the mid-1970s. Group earnings have fallen steadily since their peak in the late 1980s, mostly due to problems at Fiat Cars. In 1988 the automotive wing (which includes Lancia, Alfa Romeo, Ferrari, and Innocenti) was challenging VW for leadership of the new-car market in Western Europe. By 1992, it had fallen to fourth place behind VW, GM, and Peugeot, by far the sharpest slide among the major European car producers. The Fiat model range is aging and out-of-date and the few new models introduced in 1991 didn't do nearly as well as expected. Fiat's share of its home market—Europe's second-largest after Germany, where for years Fiat reigned supreme behind import restrictions—shrank rapidly from a peak of 60 percent in 1988 to 44.3 percent in 1992, as foreign competition suddenly undermined its position. As the Japanese plants in Britain begin to export to the continent, the competitive pressure on Fiat will increase markedly. Fiat has earmarked some 40 trillion lira in spending between 1992 and 1999, to renew its models and build new factories. It has announced plans to unveil eighteen new models between 1992 and 1998. Meanwhile, it has slashed its profit margins with generous customer incentives in an effort to retain market share. These deals, and the need for huge new investment levels, have reportedly bitten deep into the firm's cash reserves, and forced it to raise its borrowing, while also turning increasingly to asset sales to generate one-off profits to tide the firm over (*Financial Times*, January 1, 1993). Fiat's net financial position worsened to a L3.8 trillion deficit at the end of 1992, compared with L270 billion a year earlier. The devaluation of the lira since September 1992 should help to buy Fiat some breathing space, in much the same way that the fall of sterling has helped the Rover Group in recent months—the firm's exports to other European markets have suddenly become more competitively priced, while importers will have to raise their prices. Overall, however, the picture for the next few years looks bleak.

The case of Fiat is a particularly interesting one for two reasons—its dominant position in the Italian financial market, and its ownership structure. Fiat and its subsidiaries account for some 11.4 percent of the capitalization of the Milan stock exchange, while its work force of 300,000 makes the group one of the biggest employers in Italy. Some 40 percent of the company is still owned by the Agnelli family, who founded the firm at the turn of the century. Giovanni Agnelli is chairman of the company, and his younger brother, Umberto, has been tapped to succeed him in the position in 1994. Meanwhile, the Italian financial system is now beginning the kind of extensive liberalization and development of new products and markets that swept through France in the 1980s. Although the pace of liberalization has slowed down significantly in recent months, as charges of widespread corruption have led to political convulsions and constitutional upheaval (the charges now extending to top management at Fiat itself), the firm is likely to face quite a different national financial system five years from now. How such a dominant private-sector company adapts to these myriad new challenges, and whether it even manages to survive the upheavals, will make for a fascinating study in the saga of industrial restructuring and the financing of major manufacturers in Europe.

These examples, drawn from the steel and auto industries in Germany, Japan, and the United States in the late 1970s and the early 1990s, illustrate the kinds of differences that are found from one national financial system to the next. Drawn with a large brush, these pictures are oversimplified and, as such, fall somewhat into the trap of overreliance on a "national characteristics" approach that cannot account adequately for the great variety of outcomes that occurred, both within and across nations. These examples serve, rather, to illustrate some of the great national variations in the forms of financing available to major manufacturers, particularly at times of crisis, and in corporate governance practices and the attitudes of the providers of financing. A more detailed study that begins with an analysis of firm-level financial issues would reveal a more subtle and more complete picture.

Nevertheless, this quick survey of other cases has served to underline some important points. For example, debt and equity do not necessarily carry the same costs and implications in every country. An American bank does not get involved in industrial financing in the same way as might its German or French counterpart. When a Japanese firm lists "debts" in its financial statements, they don't necessarily carry the same implications for the firm's long-term financial health as would a similar item for a British firm. Although national differences are breaking down as capital becomes ever more internationalized, it is still the case that the German credit markets work very differently from their British or American counterparts—and differently again from the debt markets of France and Japan. Stock markets are by no means always the same kinds of institutions as we are used to seeing in London and New York. Institutional agents hold by far the largest percentage of equity in the United States, at some 60 percent, with individual investors the next-largest percentage (around 25 percent), and institutional owners and corporations at a scant 5 percent or so between them. In contrast, the share of equity held by institutional agents in Japan or Germany is between 5 and 10 percent, while institutional owners and corporations between them account for roughly 70 percent of each market (institutions being the larger group in Japan, and corporations somewhat more dominant in Germany). Individuals hold just under 20 percent of Japanese equity, and less than 5 percent of Germany's (*Economist*, Business Brief, June 27, 1992).

These examples, like those in the case-study chapters, have focused on capital-intensive manufacturers during a period of crisis and profound upheaval. They suggest that the decentralized—in Womack's phrase "arm's-length"—financial systems in Britain and the United States fail in comparison with their German or Japanese counterparts, and perhaps their French counterparts also, when it comes to dealing with manufacturers going through intense change. On the other hand, it is also possible that the more fluid American financial system (and, by implication, its British cousin) may be more flexible and more responsive when it comes to channeling investment capital to industry. Does the focus on earnings and short-term profitability lead to more rapid reallocation of capital from unprofitable to profitable industries? Would the German or Japanese financial system be more likely to keep financing the modern-day equivalent of a buggy-whip maker, the quintessentially doomed industry once the automobile had been invented, in the hopes of keeping the firm going until its market picked up, instead of reallocating capital toward, say, tire manufacturers instead? There is also the question of which national financial system is better at financing new industries, especially ones that are not so capital intensive. To date, the new steel mini-mills have been extremely successful in establishing themselves in the United States market. Is part of the reason for this the fact that financial resources in this market are quick to flow to a new and profitable venture? Similarly, as noted in chapter 5, the fledgling U.K. auto firms in the early years of the twentieth century apparently had no trouble getting access to financing.

3. The Challenges of the 1990s

From the previous section, and from the four case-study chapters, two things are obvious. First, that access to enormous sums of financing will be just as crucial for such firms' survival and adaptation in the 1990s as it was in the decade-and-a-half after the first oil crisis. Second, that the world has changed. This final section looks at the politics of financial change and the globalization of financial markets. The financial options open to the likes of British Steel, Peugeot, Usinor, and the Rover Group in the 1990s are in many ways quite different from their options in 1978. Major manufacturers everywhere are facing increasingly globalized financial markets, which means opportunities as well as challenges—Daimler is looking to tap into the United States equity market, while Peugeot is both helping to create and benefiting from the creation of new financial instruments and markets in France and across Europe. The importance of national financial and corporate governance systems is especially relevant for European firms as we move into the 1990s, given not only the new crisis unfolding in the European steel and auto industries, and continuing intense competitive pressures, but also the extent to which state intervention is shifting away from the overt forms practiced in the 1970s and early 1980s. Of particular relevance are the provisions of the European single market (especially concerning services and capital), governments' removal of capital controls, and the attempt to make national markets more compatible. How far will national differences break down, and in what ways will they linger the longest? Will there eventually be a single EC-wide financial system, and what will it look like? Finally, how major manufacturers are financed, and the forms of ownership and control that govern them, are issues of profound importance for the nations of Eastern Europe as they grope toward the creation of market-based economies.

EC 1992, National Financial Markets, and State Aid to Industry

> . . . a level playing field where individual talent, effort and comparative advantage lead to victory, rather than an inclined pitch with moving goalposts, a biased referee and an opposing team full of steroids. (Former EC Competition Commissioner Peter Sutherland on EC 1992. Quoted in Giles 1991)

> Humphrey chuckled . . . at the idea that the Community was united . . . "The game is played for national interests, and always was . . . We went in [to the EC] to screw the French by splitting them off from the Germans. The French went in to protect their inefficient farmers from commercial competition. The Germans went in to cleanse themselves of genocide and apply for readmission to the human race." (Lynn and Jay 1984, 273)

The impact of the single-market program known as EC '92 on financial markets and structures goes beyond making the Bank of England as independent as the Bundesbank, and allowing the proverbial Belgian dentist a wider range of investment options. It also goes beyond the obvious constraints on governments' macroeconomic maneuverability with the loss of control over exchange and interest rates. The attempt to create a single market is having a big impact on government-industry relations, as governments lose their ability to support financially major manufacturers. Nevertheless economic nationalism, on the part of both firms and governments, is proving slow to die, and governments are still just as concerned with protecting "their" industries. The German steel industry survived to 1980 with relatively little government aid and was reluctant to accept EC crisis measures restricting output in subsequent years. In November 1989, Italy refused to close a steel plant near Bagnoli, on the grounds that the market had now picked up; at the insistence of Britain and Germany the case went to the European Court.

The EC's single market was formally launched by a June 1985 EC White

Paper, "Completing the Internal Market." The aim was to bounce the EC twelve toward the original goal of the six founding members—a common market in which goods, people, services, and capital could move without obstacles. The plan therefore has many dimensions, from general immigration policy to regulations stipulating the acceptable dimensions of the proverbial widget. The basic theory behind the single-market idea is that it will overcome the limits to economic growth posed by national markets and by international competition. In this sense, EC '92 is trying to overcome the very limits that government financing of troubled industries was itself trying to correct or compensate for during the 1970s and 1980s.

"Completing the Internal Market" lists three aims of the capital liberalization part of the program: to increase the effectiveness of financial intermediaries and markets; to maintain monetary stability; and to promote the optimum allocation of savings by "decompartmentalizing" financial markets. In theory, this means freedom of capital movement, the right to sell financial services across borders, and the right of financial firms to become established in other EC countries. First came a 1986 directive requiring liberalization of capital movements in connection with long-term commercial transactions, bond issues, and unquoted securities. An ambitious package of measures was subsequently announced in 1987 that aimed to remove the last barriers to the free movement of capital, including short-term monetary instruments and personal bank accounts. (Greece and Portugal have until 1995 to implement these measures fully.) The move toward closer financial and monetary integration led France to scrap its last remaining exchange controls. It also provided much of the impetus for liberalization of French capital markets and for clearer regulatory structures in the British markets. It is proving much harder to liberalize and regulate exchanges across Europe as a whole. For example, France, Italy, Spain, and Belgium want to protect domestic exchanges by banning off-market trading. Members have also found it hard to agree on common capital-adequacy standards for securities firms.

The program covering financial services as a whole has, to date, had mixed success. Financial-service companies are supposed to have the right to operate throughout the EC on the basis of a single "passport" issued by the supervisory authority in their home country. Out of banking, investment, and insurance, only the banking directive was close to operational by the end of 1992. The freedom of financial firms to sell and establish across borders will remain hazily defined in the immediate future. It remains to be seen, for example, whether a British clearing bank will really be able to offer floating-rate mortgage loans to German home buyers. Creating a European regime that covers brokers, dealers, and investment managers will be even harder than creating universal standards of banking practice. Nevertheless, it is certainly true that major corporate customers increasingly expect their banks to understand the legal and regulatory details involved in doing business in other EC countries.

The program is having a clear impact, however, on the major European banks, who increasingly have sought mergers as a means of creating stronger national institutions.[7] Reforms are also developing at Deutsche Bank. There has been anecdotal evidence that members of the bank's executive board are gradually giving up the seats that they hold on German companies' supervisory boards, on the grounds that clashes of interest can arise that hurt Deutsche Bank, and that supervisory board chairmen should be professionals with direct experience of the industry concerned. Meanwhile, as discussed in chapter 1, the French banks are changing their relationships with French industries in quite a different direction. Thus for many reasons, and across countries, the European banking industry is gradually changing the shape and scope of its involvement in industry.

The move to create a single market has also led to a welter of regulations and directives concerning acceptable standards for specific products. In most cases, the principle of mutual recognition applies, with members recognizing one anothers' standards as acceptable. This means that a great deal of the minutiae of product standards and regulation will continue to be dealt with at the national level. The clearest standardization impact is on those sectors that traditionally depend on public procurement—telecommunications, electrical equipment, energy and railway equipment, and pharmaceuticals (*European Community News*, April 6, 1990). Public procurement is a prime example of the ways in which national patterns can continue to dominate in an ostensibly common market. The public sectors of the EC members have been obliged to put their larger contracts out for Europe-wide tender since 1971. The procurement part of EC '92 seeks to broaden the scope of EC-wide tender requirements, and to extend open procurement to sectors that have until now been exempt, namely energy, transport, water, and telecommunications. In reality, however, government procurement is most likely to remain within national boundaries:

> How can any rulebook cope with the blend of patriotism, government pressure, tactical sacrifice and straight cheapness that moves, say, Lord King, when he orders Rolls-Royce engines for British Airways? (*Economist*, July 9, 1988)

The Commission is facing its toughest political challenge in trying to harmonize fiscal regimes across the member states. There are as many national fiscal regimes as there are EC members, with variations in the proportions of tax revenues raised from social security contributions, taxes on income, and excise taxes; and with different Value-Added Tax (VAT) rates. In theory, if the EC does manage to more-or-less unify its various tax codes, particularly those relating to company taxes, one result would be that the financing practices of firms would harmonize, at least in terms of how they viewed the value of debt versus equity on their balance sheets.[8] This is the kind of assumption about the benefits of harmonization that lies behind the creation of a single market. The reality is that tax structures are one of the hardest of all national differences to harmonize.

The sum total of all of these EC proposals, directives, and rulings is immense. In many respects, EC '92 and the move toward economic and monetary union has already had a profound impact on government-industry relations in Europe. The industrial cases analyzed here demonstrate some of that impact. Nevertheless, national governments in the Community still intervene in the financial affairs of restructuring manufacturers, as they did in the 1980s. The way they do so, however, is changing, thanks to moves by the EC's Competition Commission preventing governments from overt financial intervention in firms' affairs. History suggests that European governments will certainly get involved in financial aid to major manufacturers in trouble in the 1990s, but with many of the options described in these cases now off-limits, how will they do so?

The Treaty of Rome prohibits the European Commission from favoring or discriminating against state-owned companies. But Article 92 of the treaty also outlaws state aid that distorts competition. The vast discretionary powers awarded the Commission allowed it to ignore this contradiction for decades. The EC's competition requirements once affected private firms more than governments or state enterprises. In the early 1980s, the growing number of exemptions threatened to make the EC's policies redundant (Butt Philip 1983). The preparations for a single market led to a tightening up of such contradictions that quickly developed its own independent dynamic, dedicated to "leveling the playing field." The whole issue periodically becomes a veritable battleground between the still formally more *dirigiste* governments such as France and Italy, and officially antiaid governments such as Britain.

The rules governing state aid to industry now define subsidies to include almost any action where the state, as owner, behaves differently from a private investor. This includes not only grants but also government accepting a below-market rate of return on its investment in a state-owned company, implicitly guaranteeing the company's borrowings from private lenders, injecting additional equity capital when private investors clearly would not buy shares in the company, or forgoing dividends. This would preclude many of the forms of aid used by the French and British governments to assist the steel and auto firms in the late 1970s and early 1980s. For example, since 1989 all government investments in the auto industry worth over Ecu12 million, and which include any element of subsidy, must be cleared by Brussels. In the summer of 1989 alone, the EC told the West German and Spanish governments to scrap or alter forty-seven state-aid packages to their auto industries, each worth more than $13 million (*Economist*, August 5, 1989).

The impact of these moves on national government-industry relations was illustrated in chapter 4 by the French firms Peugeot and Renault. Chapter 5 described how the Commission ordered British Aerospace to repay £44 million in secret subsidies that it had received from the British government as part of the Rover Group purchase. In the first six months of 1991, the Competition Commission launched more than fifteen aid investigations across a variety of industries. One of the biggest involved France's decision to give FFr4 billion in aid to the state-owned computer maker Groupe Bull, which lost FFr7 billion in 1990 (Giles 1991). Another involved Belgium's $1 billion plan to recapitalize the state-owned airline, Sabena (ibid.). In clamping down on state aid, the Commission has had to deal with some enormous variations in national attitudes and practice. In Italy, the nationalized industries are an important source of patronage for politicians. In France, they have formal, constitutional justification. In Germany, some are co-run by the Länder, giving a source of local economic power (Vickers and Wright 1988).

During the crisis period of the 1980s, the French and British governments used a variety of financial measures to influence and support the firms' restructuring plans. How each of these measures worked has been discussed in detail in the case-study chapters. If similar crises were to arise in the 1990s, many of these measures could not easily be used again—specifically, debt write-offs, aid masquerading as equity investments, loans or grants for survival only, and loans at a below-market rate or guaranteed by the government.

Given the size of the debts accumulated by the nationalized industries, it is not surprising that each government, at one time or another, wrote down the debt carried by the firms, or wrote it off altogether, and restructured the firms' finances away from interest-bearing loans. Without the earlier debt write-offs, neither BSC, the Rover Group, nor Usinor would have looked like viable commercial companies by the end of the 1980s.

The prohibitions against governments accepting a below-market rate of return on their investments, injecting additional equity capital when private investors clearly would not, or forgoing dividends, would also have had a big impact in three of these four cases. Both states provided massive injections of capital to their nationalized firms in this form. The precise mix of equity and debt in the financing of the firms varied, as did the way in which each state issued the equity. At no time, however, did any of the governments involved expect any return on the capital so invested. In each case there was either an overt or covert understanding that dividends were being waived until some vague future date when the firm would again turn a profit. Calling the funds equity preserved the appearance that the state was "investing" in a firm with a future, rather than simply bailing out one that was otherwise bankrupt.

The restrictions on grants and lending would have had a clear impact in the case of Usinor and Sacilor in 1981. In most instances when loans and grants were given by the governments, it was said to be for some greater end than simply shoring up a company's finances—for industrial reorganization through mergers; for investment in underdeveloped regions; to create independent, private producers, and increase competition in the industry; to facilitate modernization and the acquisition of the latest computer-based technologies. In the case of Usinor and Sacilor in 1981, the grant was made purely for survival purposes, to keep the companies solvent until after the presidential and National Assembly elections.

The prohibition against loans at below-market rates, and against loans from private lenders implicitly guaranteed by the state, would also have affected much of government-industry relations in the two industries in the 1980s. Each government made a number of direct state loans to each of the companies analyzed here. Some were directly subsidized, as in the loans to the French steel industry. In other cases, the methods used by the government would probably pass the more stringent tests of today—for example, the public-private Phoenix schemes in the British steel industry, where the government used BSC as the vehicle to make loans to establish the new companies. There are other methods a government can use that, while less direct, ultimately have the same results. In the case of Allied Steel and Wire (ASW) or Phoenix One, the government advanced large sums of cash, via BSC. Ostensibly a form of special aid to help the new company to become independent of the state, it also effectively provided backing for additional bank borrowing by ASW. Although the government was not officially guaranteeing their loans, similar arrangements in other Phoenix schemes no doubt encouraged private capital to invest in the new companies at a time when their markets were anything but stable.

If today's EC rules had existed in 1977–87, these case studies could have told some very different tales. Even the borrowing limits set by each government on the funds made available to their nationalized industries—rigid External Financing Limits in Britain, negotiated contracts in France—would no longer be applicable. The combination of EC regulations and national budget constraints amount to severe limits on the ability of nationalized firms to borrow from the state. The impact on private firms such as Peugeot is less obvious, but no less great. Although Peugeot itself remained aloof from direct government subsidy in the 1980s, it received significant aid for its takeovers of Citroën and Chrysler-Europe in the 1970s. The new limits on a government's ability to "assist" a private manufacturer's purchases are well illustrated by the case of British Aerospace and Rover.

Despite the new restrictions, as the earlier examples have shown governments are still giving financial aid to their state- and privately owned firms, even though they now risk a conflict with the Commission. However, they are also using new methods to get financing to firms that need it, or to prevent them from falling victim to hostile takeovers. In the late 1980s, a number of the nationalized manufacturers and financial institutions in France began to swap each others' shares, while Usinor-Sacilor began issuing convertible bonds in 1985, with subscription reserved for the state and other public-sector companies. This allowed the firm to raise capital without violating the EC regulations on state aid to the steel industry. The British government, on the other hand, came up with state-held Special Shares in newly privatized companies as a means of maintaining British ownership of strategic companies. The French government's *noyaux durs* may have the same effect.

The changes promised by EC '92 also have broad implications for wholly privately owned firms. The case of Peugeot SA is a prime example. M. Calvet, Peugeot's PDG, is no fan of the single market. Although his public statements focus on the single market's implications for increased competition from Japanese carmakers, from the case study presented in chapter 4 we can surmise that his fears go deeper. First, the source of major trade and competition-policy decisions affecting the industry is shifting from Paris to Brussels. As the largest privately owned firm in France PSA could have considerable influence in decisions affecting the auto manufacturers, and could manipulate government regional aid schemes to its own advantage. As just one of six major carmakers in Europe, Calvet's voice is far less influential in Brussels. In fact, in November 1990 his fellow European carmakers formed a new industry lobby without him, in order to isolate his extreme demand that the EC block Japanese imports altogether (Giles 1991).

Second, PSA may witness the demise of those national financial regulations and structures that have served the firm so well until now. If harmonization stretches to the kinds of products offered and traded on Europe's exchanges, will Anglo-American ownership patterns become dominant? Will the French still be willing, or able, to set up complex holding companies with closely held shares and cross-holdings in shares, to protect the financial flows of firms such as Peugeot? A "successful" capitalist firm is based on more than just smart management and lucky breaks in the market. The wider network of relationships in which it is involved also plays a role.[9] It is here, in terms of its impact on wider financial relationships, that the effects of EC '92 may, eventually, have both profound and unforeseen impacts on government-industry relations.

However, these impacts will be slow to arrive, as twelve member governments go through the tortuous process of passing into national law the 282 measures needed to remove internal barriers. Meanwhile, there have been some moves to try to create an EC-wide industrial policy that uses a combination of subsidized financing and trade-protection measures to promote "Euro-champions" in "strategic sectors." In June 1991 it was reported that Renault's chairman Levy claimed Europe's big auto manufacturers were going to ask the EC for massive subsidies to finance layoffs and restructuring (*Economist*, June 17, 1991). Many European electronics companies in particular are argu-

ing that a more *dirigiste* Euro-policy is essential "to prevent Europe's indigenous capacity in the industry from being eliminated by Japanese competition"
(ibid.).

Changes in the Community's competition and trade rules have gone too
far for there to be much risk of a sudden swing to a Europe-wide industrial
policy that is interventionist and protectionist. As one Competition Commission official stated, however, "you have to be realistic. In a very bad recession, politics come into play. We won't change our policy, but we may tailor
it a little" (*Financial Times*, June 17, 1991). More to the point, it doesn't take
a particularly severe recession to persuade governments that intervening in the
financial health of a major manufacturer is "in the national interest." The EC
as a whole may not end up with a strictly *dirigiste* industrial policy, but the
role of national governments in structuring financial markets and aiding firms
is not about to disappear overnight.

Conclusions and Conjectures

The international economic system has altered a great deal over the past two
decades. Many of the changes are ongoing, and arise from the actions and
decisions of national governments. More countries are industrializing and
competing with the manufacturers of Europe and the United States. Technological development is ever more rapid, revolutionizing products and production
processes across national boundaries. The auto industry alone saw three major
developments in one decade—the incorporation of robots and computer-aided
design and manufacturing, Just-In-Time delivery systems, and now modular
production. The international capital markets are increasingly integrated, yet
international trade seems to be polarizing into separate regions such as Europe,
Asia, and the American continents.

All of which suggest that states will increasingly be involved in mitigat-
ing the effects of rapid international economic change on their domestic
economies. As Zukin points out (1985), the role of government in advanced
industrial states is shifting from mediating among domestic interests, to acting
as intermediary between national industries and their foreign rivals. A crucial
aspect of that mediation will be ensuring that firms have access to sufficient
capital for their research and investment needs. The problems of firms such as
Usinor and Rover were not just ones of overcapacity in the 1980s. They were
also struggling to keep up with the latest technological developments and new
overseas competitors. These struggles are likely to continue for many years to
come. As this research has shown, however, capital is not neutral. Aside from
issues of availability and cost, the attitudes of the providers of the vast sums
of capital that these firms need have a profound impact on their ability to
survive a crisis of competition and restructuring, and to adapt over the longer
term. The study of contemporary government-industry relations must incor-

porate the role of government in defining and regulating national financial systems, and must analyze firm-level financial issues, in order to discern the fundamental differences between national systems of industrial finance and corporate governance.

This research has focused on two industries that are characterized by high capital intensity, high labor intensity, and long-lived fixed assets. Financial structures at the national and firm level may not be of such critical importance in other sectors. Nevertheless, it is only at the level of particular industries and firms that the subtlety and complexity of government-industry relations emerges. The study of those relations must, therefore, analyze specific industries and specific policy areas, in a comparative context, as suggested by Wilks and Wright (1987). This will enable us to advance explanations for the differences and variations that are found, and to deepen our understanding of industrial politics and policies.

These questions about national financial systems and forms of corporate governance are vital issues for European manufacturers and, ultimately, for the competitiveness of the EC economy. Major manufacturers are, in a sense, the financial system, and changes in national financial systems—driven by globalization of markets and by the regulatory actions of governments—are played out at the firm level. The French government is likely to create a corporate pension-fund system in the coming years. This will have a profound impact on the French equity market, which may become more Anglo-American in style. Or perhaps French pension funds will operate differently from their American counterparts when it comes to investment decisions, maybe themselves evolving into *noyaux durs*. The answer is crucial to a firm such as Peugeot, and to the likelihood of friendly investors continuing in the 1990s to be the patient and supportive providers of capital that they were in the 1980s. And for Usinor, how will its network of debt and equity holders function if the state no longer plays the role of dominant stakeholder? One tantalizing suggestion that emerges from the previous pages is that the French financial system and form of corporate governance may be moving toward a German or Japanese-style system—although the history of French government-industry relations suggests that a Gallic version may include more active state involvement in building or maintaining networks of corporate cross-shareholdings.

Across the Channel, who will be the provider of the long-term funds needed to keep British Steel and Rover/BAe viable through the next restructuring crisis, if not the state? U.K. managers tend to complain that "life would be better if we had Deutsche Bank behind us." Yet Deutsche Bank may be losing some of its famed proclivity to retain large shareholdings in industrial clients through thick and thin. On the other hand, the gradual creation of a single EC market for goods, services, and capital may give British manufacturers access to sources of finance whose providers have attitudes quite different from those of the investors in the London International Stock Exchange. Ultimately, how rapidly such changes in national financial systems occur, and the directions in which forms of corporate governance evolve, will depend on the actions of the national governments, and the reactions of major manufacturers.

This brings us to the developing capitalist economies of Eastern Europe, where industrial contraction and restructuring is proportionately far greater now than anything experienced in the West in the 1980s. In the steel industry alone, output in the Eastern European region has virtually halved, and employment has fallen by a third, over the last three years (*Financial Times*, February 19, 1993). Both the United States and the European Community have slammed antidumping measures on sales of steel from the region, even as demand from the former Soviet Union has all but disappeared. In addition, the costs of modernization and catching up with the West in terms of technological processes will be astronomical. The bulk of Poland's steel, for example, comes from open-cast equipment, with only 7 percent produced by continuous casting. A plan to replace the old plants with electric arc furnaces and mini-mills comes with an initial $4.5 billion price tag (ibid.).

Privatization of formerly state-owned firms in Eastern Europe is not the end of the issue. Nations such as Poland, Hungary, and the Czech Republic must also create an entire market economy. In Latin America, privatizing companies and markets has included privatizing pension systems. Chile, in particular, has earned much praise for the successful creation of a private pension system that generates funds for investment from the nation's own savings. Similar developments will be needed in Eastern Europe. As the case studies from Britain and France have shown, the state will always be involved in assisting major manufacturers, but the form of that involvement can vary a great deal, depending on the very national financial system that the state helps to create, regulate, and maintain. The national financial system created will be of fundamental importance for firms' adaptation and survival prospects. The kinds of overt public-private capital mixes found in France and being actively developed there may give large manufacturers greater flexibility and more financing options than found in Britain. The French (and also German and Japanese) system of building networks of core private investors may be equally important. Although a network of providers is potentially highly problematic due to the lack of a dominant stakeholder, it does also give a firm more options than the stock market versus state bailout that seems to be the choice in Britain and the United States.

Not all markets are created equal. Some may be much better at supporting and nurturing capital-intensive and globally competitive industries than others.

Appendixes

The Steel and Auto Industries

In order to make the context of the four case studies clearer, this appendix outlines the manufacturing processes for European steel and auto production in the 1970s and 1980s.

The Steel Industry

Steel is a very international industry in terms of its products, raw materials, and markets. Its market environment is somewhat determined by leaders such as US Steel and Nippon Steel, and is also very sensitive to business cycles. In all industrialized nations, governments have become closely involved in the industry's affairs in one way or another. As in the auto industry, technological changes have transformed steel production in the past two decades, with more producers moving toward adding value to basic products.

Steel is essentially an alloy of iron and carbon. The chief technical innovation of the postwar period was the basic oxygen furnace using a chemical reaction, rather than heat, to reduce the carbon and other impurities in the iron. The oxygen furnace is a much faster operation and the process now dominates bulk-steel production in OECD countries. Modern integrated plants can produce up to 500 tonnes of steel an hour with large oxygen converters. The various stages of production can now be combined into integrated units from coke manufacture to finished steel products. This was a major reason for increased concentration of production in the industry in the 1960s and 1970s (Messerlin and Saunders 1983).

Liquid steel requires an additional finishing process. The cast steel is rolled and shaped to produce flat products such as sheet and coil, long products such as rods and bars, and tubular products. Plain carbon steel can be modified by adding alloying elements to produce alloy and stainless steels. Hot-rolling mills manipulate the cast steel at extremely high temperatures to achieve major shape changes. In the conventional technology, molten steel is cast into ingots that are then reheated into more finished forms. The newer process of continuous casting (concast) creates semifinished forms directly from molten steel, skipping the ingot stage and using less energy. Finally, the semifinished forms pass through cold-rolling mills at lower temperatures, to produce the final shape and surface quality.

By the end of the 1980s electric arc furnaces, or mini-mills, accounted for a larger percentage of steel production. Mini-mills use scrap in electric arc furnaces, and at first mostly produced specialty steels. Some of the mills now produce thin slabs for the flat-products market. In addition, direct one-step smelting can produce thin strips of hot material that can be tailored to a customer's specific needs with little further processing. Thin-slab casting lowers the cost of entry into a once highly capital-intensive industry. The trend in the 1990s will likely be toward "super-mini" direct-smelting mills, implying still more changes for the industry.

The Auto Industry

Auto manufacturing has a different set of technological and international market dynamics than steel. Automobile manufacturing began on a small scale in the 1880s in Europe and North America. The introduction of the assembly line in the United States around 1910 led to a mass-volume industry dominated by the North Americans. After the Second World War diversification of the industry spread rapidly. European producers began seriously to challenge American-based production as the auto markets of the various producing countries began to differ in terms of consumer preferences. Then, in the late 1960s, Japanese producers combined the latest technologies with new forms of production organization and quickly developed low-cost, high-quality models.

In the mid 1970s the industry's growth rates slowed as markets approached maturity, the Japanese emerged as strong competitors, and recession and the oil shocks hit demand. The sudden shifts in energy prices drastically cut sales at the same time that producers had to reinvest in more fuel-efficient models. As auto production is a highly capital-intensive industry, manufacturers were anxious to maintain large production runs to achieve economies of scale, while simultaneously trying to introduce new technologies.

There are three distinct categories of auto manufacturer. The smaller, specialist producers such as Jaguar produce a few select models for a narrow range of the market. The mid-size producers such as Rover and Peugeot produce almost a full range of models, but tend to focus on their own domestic or regional market. The multinational mass producers, such as Ford, GM, and Toyota, produce a full range of models for worldwide sale. Car production and assembly is organizationally highly complex, involving hundreds of components. Major investment decisions have a long gestation period—a model can last up to eight years, an engine even longer. The sheer scale of financial risk involved in auto manufacturing means that the largest producers have become the dominant force in the industry.

Yet this picture is changing as auto firms of every kind link together to ensure economies of scale and to spread the otherwise prohibitive costs of research and development. Common arrangements include equity exchanges or the creation of jointly held corporations, and joint production agreements, such as the Honda-Rover and GM-Toyota agreements. Firms increasingly buy in components from other manufacturers, particularly those with whom they have equity ties. These agreements not only help to share the risks of failure, they also benefit importers. (The Acclaim was counted as of British origin, allowing Honda to skirt the British import quota on Japanese cars.)

Technical change in the industry has progressed rapidly in recent years. In the early 1980s, the microelectronics revolution offered new opportunities for process automation, and industrial robots are now found in auto plants along with computer-aided design, engineering, and manufacturing. Advances in manufacturing systems have developed rapidly, from the introduction of Just-In-Time supply techniques, to the latest in flexible manufacturing systems. By the end of the 1980s modular production was the new watchword. Modular manufacturing gives firms the ability to rapidly change the product/model mix, without needing extremely expensive and time-consuming retooling. Parts are made that can fit into a greater variety of cars, and more of the design and engineering work is delegated to the outside suppliers of those parts. In the long run, the entire car can be designed and assembled as a series of subassemblies or modules, many supplied by component suppliers. These developments are reducing interim financing needs and are lowering the economies of scale sought by mass producers.

The manufacturers themselves increasingly concentrate on styling, overall packaging, marketing, and distribution to differentiate their products. Peugeot and Citroën cars, built by the PSA group, look and drive differently, and appeal to different market segments, yet use many common components. The industry is no longer characterized by massive scale economies, a mature product and mature production process. As Lee Iacocca succinctly put it: "We gotta do cars differently. We gotta do modular stuff" (*Economist*, July 29, 1989).

Corporate survival in the car industry thus depends on the ability to keep pace with technological and marketing changes, and on the ability to make the right long-term investment and planning decisions. Generating sufficient funds to finance these long-term, costly activities is crucial to an individual producer's ability to survive with a competitive edge—"mistakes may only become evident after a long time and take years and large sums of money to correct" (Jones 1983, 118).

Abbreviations Used in Text

ASW	Allied Steel and Wire
AUEW	Amalgamated Union of Engineering Workers
BAe	British Aerospace
BISPA	British Independent Steel Producers Association
BL	British Leyland
BLMC	British Leyland Motor Corporation
BMC	British Motor Corporation
BNP	Banque Nationale de Paris
BS	British Steel
BSC	British Steel Corporation
BT	British Telecom
CAPA	Caisse d'Amortissement pour l'Aciér
CDC	Caisse des Dépôts et Consignations
CFDT	Confédération Française Démocratique du Travail
CGP	Commissariat Générale du Plan
CGPS	Conventions Générale de Protection Sociale de la Sidérurgie
CGT	Confédération Générale du Travail
CIASI	Interministerial Committee for Management of the Industrial Structure
CODEVI	Compte de Développement Industriel
CP	commercial paper
CSSF	Chambre Syndicale de la Sidérurgie Française
DATAR	Délégation à l'aménagement du territoire et à l'action régionale
DoI	Department of Industry (U.K.)
DTI	Department of Trade and Industry (U.K.)
EC	European Community
ECSC	European Coal and Steel Community
EFL	External Financing Limit
ENA	École Nationale d'Administration
FDES	Fonds de Développement Economique et Social
FIM	Fonds Industriel de Modernisation
FIS	Fonds d'Intervention Sidérurgique

FSAI	Fonds Spécial d'Adaptation Industrielle
G&MWU	General and Municipal Workers' Union
GIS	Groupement de l'Industrie Sidérurgique
GM	General Motors
IPO	initial public offering
IRC	Industrial Reorganisation Corporation
ISC	International Steel Cartel
ISTC	Iron and Steel Trades Confederation
JFB	Johnson and Firth Brown
LIFFE	London International Financial Futures Exchange
LTOM	London Traded Options Market
MATIF	marché à termes des instruments financiers
MOFF	multiple-option financing facility
MONEP	marché des options négociables de Paris
NEB	National Enterprise Board (U.K.)
NEDC	National Economic Development Council (U.K.)
NLF	National Loans Fund
OECD	Organisation for Economic Cooperation and Development
PCF	Parti Communiste Française
PDC	Public Dividend Capital
PDG	Président-Directeur Général
plc	public limited company
PM	Prime Minister
PS	Parti Socialiste
PSA	Peugeot Société Anonyme
PSBR	Public Sector Borrowing Requirement
ROSW	Round Oak Steel Works Ltd.
RPR	Rassemblement pour la République
SEC	Securities and Exchange Commission
SFFP	Société Foncière, Financière et de Participation
SMMT	Society of Motor Manufacturers and Traders
SPD	Social Democratic Party (Germany)
TGWU	Transport and General Workers Union
TI	Tube Investments Limited
TUC	Trades Union Congress
UDF	Union pour la Démocratie Française
UES	United Engineering Steels
VAT	Value-Added Tax
VER	Voluntary Export Restraint
VW	Volkswagen

Notes

Chapter 1

1. Much of this approach is taken up with explaining how some states have capacities for intervention that others lack, and with discussing the relative "strength" of a particular state institution compared with others (Skocpol and Finegold 1983) or compared with organizations within the society (Weir and Skocpol 1985). Ikenberry (1988) wonders what capacities the modern American state possesses to cope with rapid international political and economic change.

2. Cox (1986) counters that France may have such a financial system because it chose to have a state-led economy rather than the other way around, and that Britain may have a capital-market financial system because it chose not to have a state-led economy.

3. Similarly, the severity of the steel crisis in Britain in the late 1970s is often attributed to the fact that Britain industrialized earlier than its competitors, and without active state involvement. Yet France led Western Europe in the development of car manufacturing earlier in this century (Laux 1976), successive French governments did not get involved in the industry's development, and the French auto industry was not in a severe crisis by 1979.

4. Especially since the work of Modigliani and Miller after 1958 showed that lower-risk debt is not necessarily cheaper than higher-risk equity, and that all things being equal and tax distortions apart, the debt-equity ratio has no effect on a firm's value. The original paper from Modigliani and Miller was "The Cost of Capital, Corporation Finance and the Theory of Investment," in *American Economic Review*, June 1958.

5. In general, the French law, introduced in 1985, pays little heed to the interests of creditors, whereas Britain's 1986 Insolvency Act may be biased to put creditors' interests first.

6. I am indebted to Fred Block for his insight on this point. Grant (1989) makes a similar argument about "the blurring of the public and the private."

7. Young (1986b) has identified seven distinct forms of privatization in Britain, only one of which involves the sale of state-owned assets or industrial privatization: selling off public sector assets; relaxing state monopolies; contracting services out; changing to private provision of services; attempting to bring investment into deprived areas; extending private sector organizational practices into the public sector; and reducing subsidies and increasing charges for some services provided by the public sector.

8. The one location where M.P.s can be more active is in the select committees that shadow the work of government departments. These were introduced by the Conservatives in 1979, to create a review system modeled on the U.S. Congress. The committees request evidence from civil servants and ministers, question outside experts and interested parties, and issue reports. Their power lies in their ability to attract public attention. They cannot force the government to pay attention to their reports, and their findings usually come too late to influence the policy-making process. However, by the mid-1980s the committees had established the power to subpoena witnesses and evidence. This became especially relevant in 1988–89, over the sale of the Rover car group to British Aerospace. See chapter 5.

9. "Five 'types' of governmental involvement . . . applied to the shipbuilding industry: 'pure' private enterprise (pre-1959); assisted private enterprise (e.g., Swan Hunter prior to 1977); hybrid enterprise (e.g., Upper Clyde Shipbuilders, 1967–71); state-owned enterprise (e.g., Govan Shipbuilders, 1974–77); statutory nationalized industry (post-1977)" (Steel 1982).

10. The most significant are the stakes in National Power, PowerGen, and British Petroleum.

11. The *projet de loi* on nationalization, covering all but the steel groups, was finally passed in February 1982. The five big industrial groups were Compagnie Générale d'Electricité, Saint-Gobain-Pont-à-Mousson, Pechiney-Ugine-Kuhlman, Thomson-Brandt, and Rhône-Poulenc. These were totally nationalized by legislative expropriation. Other industrial groups included two big manufacturers tied to arms making, Dassault and Matra (government took majority control), and three enterprises with strong foreign shares, CII-HB (Honeywell Bull, government increased its majority holding), Roussel-Uclaf (government moved toward an equal public-private control), and Compagnie Générale Communication Téléphonique (government took majority control). See Delion and Durupty 1982.

12. The major sales were: Saint-Gobain, Matra, Banque IndoSuez, Paribas, Sogénal (a small bank), and Crédit Commercial de France, all nationalized in 1982; and long-time public companies Crédit Agricole, Société Générale, and the TV station TF1.

13. For the sake of consistency, the American definition of *billion* is used throughout (i.e., 1,000 million), rather than the British or French definition of a million million.

14. According to Veljanovski, the British government's initial plans for British Telecom (BT) had not included privatization, but rather focused on devising some scheme whereby the corporation could borrow on the capital market. Patrick Jenkin tried to create special bonds for BT but couldn't overcome the protests that these amounted to borrowing on privileged terms. Frustration over the bonds caused him to hit on the idea of privatization of BT as a way of overcoming the problem of financing capital expenditure programs by creating a viable borrowing vehicle (Veljanovski 1987).

15. Economic weight measured based on employee numbers, value added, and investments.

16. Many theorists have pinpointed a lack of access to investment capital as a major "blockage" to the rapid development of French industry in general in the late nine-

teenth and early twentieth centuries. Laux (1976) debunks that myth, at least with respect to the nation's fledgling auto industry, arguing that the firms were not starved of capital. Rather, it was a lack of bolder marketing strategies that held the firms back from more rapid development after 1909.

17. That is, obligations that require cash payment within one year, such as accounts payable, accrued wages, taxes and other expenses payable, and notes payable.

18. Measuring the cost of equity capital is a contentious issue, particularly when it comes to making international comparisons. Accounting practices alter price-earnings ratios; differing relationships between companies and shareholders can have an impact on the flow of information and the uncertainties and risks of investment; and firms in a particular sector may be operating in a higher-risk environment in one country than in another. In general, a less risky firm is likely to enjoy a lower cost of capital—but measuring relative levels of risk internationally is far from straightforward.

19. A large number of other departments such as the Planning Commission and DATAR (Délégation à l'aménagement du territoire et à l'action régionale—Delegation for Space Planning and Regional Action) are involved in industrial policy. It was DATAR rather than the Ministry of Industry that worked on attracting Peugeot to specific regions (chap. 4).

20. Report of the Commissariat Général du Plan: *Aides a l'Industrie* (Documentation Français 1982). On the other hand, a complex system of credit restrictions tended to encourage conservative lending patterns by the banks while creating very profitable situations for only a few firms. See Préparation du IXeme Plan, vol. 4: *Le Financement des Entreprises et l'Allocation des Resources Financières*, "Allocation," Pierre Gourdin, Banque de France (Documentation Français: janvier, 1983).

21. The FDES is divided into subcommittees for sectors of the economy, dispensing funds in the form of capital and soft loans directly from the state budget to public and privately owned industries. Set up in 1974, the CIASI promises state funds, on a case-by-case basis, to encourage small business owners and their bankers to develop rescue or merger plans.

22. Commission de reforme de la Planification: *Rapport au ministre d'Etat, ministre du Plan et de l'Aménagement du Territoire* (Documentation Française, 8 juin, 1982), (Christian Goux, président de la commission).

23. Préparation du IXeme Plan, vol. 3: Rapport, 31 janvier, 1983: *L'industrie au futur* (Jean-Claude Pelissolo, Ingénieur). "Un secteur bancaire encore trop peu orienté vers le développement industriel" (my translation).

24. Since the early 1970s, state-controlled corporations and financial institutions could borrow on favorable terms on the international markets, due to the state's solid credit rating. From the late 1980s, the government gradually withheld its signature from new bond issues by state-owned borrowers. The outstanding volume of guaranteed loans fell from FFr412 billion at the end of 1984 to FFr280 billion at the end of 1990 (*Wall Street Journal*, January 23, 1991).

25. The following statement, from a work of fiction, is a delightful summary of how the British policy process supposedly works:

I mean that [the Department] will give it the most serious and urgent consideration, but will insist on a thorough and rigorous examination of all the proposals, allied to a detailed feasibility study and budget analysis before producing a consultative document for consideration by all interested bodies and seeking comments and recommendations to be incorporated in a brief for a series of working parties who will produce individual studies that will form the background for a more wide-ranging document considering whether or not the proposal should be taken forward to the next stage. (Lynn and Jay 1987, 231)

Similarly, Sir Michael Edwardes, one-time chairman of the nationalized British Leyland, concluded that: "If the Government is to involve itself . . . in industrial matters . . . then it needs the degree of interchange between civil service and industry which makes the French civil service so much more effective in this area" (Edwardes 1983, 218).

26. There have been exceptions. The Industrial Reorganisation Corporation (IRC) operated under the Labour government from 1966 to 1971, promoting mergers. IRC loans assisted in mergers in the auto industry (chap. 5). It had a £150 million financial limit and potentially wide powers, but lacked clear operating criteria (Hague and Wilkinson 1983). The National Enterprise Board (NEB) took over the IRC's functions but operated as a holding company, with union and private sector members, and £1 billion in funding (Zysman 1983). The NEB was supposed to extend state ownership and investment into profitable sectors, but ended up involved mostly in troubled firms such as Leyland. It was wound up in 1981. The National Economic Development Council (NEDC) was a tripartite forum established in 1962 to discuss economic issues, but it was only a consultative body. After 1979 even this limited status was much reduced and it was finally abolished in June 1992.

27. However, the Bank's relationship with the City was more clearly defined in the Banking Acts of 1979 and 1987, and the Bank increasingly intervenes between the City, the Department of Trade and Industry (DTI), and the Treasury, to apply these regulations. The Financial Services Act (1987) set up a new system for regulating investment businesses in Britain, stating who is allowed to sell and trade investment products, and how much information they must disclose to customers. There are now self-regulatory organizations covering securities dealing, investment and management, futures and options. These report to the new Securities and Investments Board which in turn reports to the DTI, but is paid for by its subjects. The financial markets look increasingly to the Bank, rather than the Treasury, as regulator (*Economist*, April 30, 1988). The securities industry was not widely consulted about the act.

28. In late 1989 it was revealed that the chancellor had a plan to establish the independence of the Bank of England. The Bank was apparently very interested in switching its accountability from the Treasury to Parliament. Its status and role continue to be matters for discussion in the context of European Monetary Union. The plan, revealed by newly resigned Chancellor Nigel Lawson, was apparently rejected by Thatcher as implying that she had failed to control inflation. It was drawn up in secrecy within the Treasury and discussed only with the P.M. Lawson's plan would have made the Bank subject to the authority of Parliament rather than the chancellor, and given it authority analogous to that of the U.S. Federal Reserve. Sir George Blunden, deputy governor of the Bank, said: "most of us would admit that we envy the authority and power of the Bundesbank and the Federal Reserve System, and believe

that countries with independent central banks have an advantage over the rest" (*Financial Times*, November 9, 1989). Increasing the Bank's independence "would be very strongly welcomed in the City" (*City Programme*, Thames TV, January 4, 1990). It is apparent that given the will, governments can and do try to change the institutional structures with which they are faced. It is also clear that without the backing of the City, changes in the status of the Bank of England would not have been discussed this far.

29. The issuer insures against the risk that its shares will not be fully taken up by paying underwriters, including pension funds, insurance companies, and mutual funds, a fee for their promise to buy at the issue price any shares that are left; and it prices the new shares at a discount to its old ones.

30. Personal communication, 1991.

31. In 1981 the state gave some FFr100 billion (3.5 percent of GDP) to industry as a whole in the form of direct grants or loans, aid to R&D, export aids, compensation for employment cuts, and tax incentives (Wright 1984).

32. A further clear difference between Britain and France is the latter's use of national planning, with the Commissariat Général du Plan generating and coordinating strategies for industrial development through the preparation of five-year national plans. The Seventh Plan (1975–81) was concerned with adjusting to the recession and reducing French dependence on energy imports. The Eighth (1981–85) focused on industrial competitiveness, but was abandoned in 1981 after the Socialist election victories. The replacement Ninth Plan (1983–88) had the same industrial priority but rejected a sectoral strategy. By 1980 the plans had become an adjunct to the government's industrial policy rather than the work of objective technocrats (Hall 1986). The 1980s further eroded the policy impact of the plans, in part due to the unpredictable effects of reflation and recession.

33. The 1982 Auroux laws contractualized the labor-management relationship, obliging firms to negotiate each year on wages and working conditions, and guaranteeing basic workers' rights (Hall 1985).

34. The controls were actually a system of authorization procedures. Industrial price restraint agreements were either hammered out centrally between industry-sector representatives and the Ministry of Economics, or were direct controls on a firm-by-firm basis, administered by the ministry's Direction des Prix (Adams 1989).

35. A succession of Employment Acts limited union rights to picket, compelled majority approval of industrial action by secret ballot, and made the unions liable for monetary damages if the laws were violated.

36. Until the 1980s the Department of Trade and Industry (DTI) had a wide range of responsibilities, including trade, assistance to industries, regional policy, inward investment, and the nationalized industries. The Departments of Trade and Industry were reunited in 1983. However, the DTI is the industry ministry for England only. The departments for Scotland, Wales, and Northern Ireland are responsible for industrial policy in their areas, with separate budgets controlled by the Treasury. The existence of regional departments "accentuate[s] the fragmentation of the decision-making process" (Grant 1989, 90). It has also accentuated the role of regional considerations in industrial policy. See chapter 2, on Ravenscraig.

37. The reforms also ended the old system whereby large proportions of investment,

including investment financed by borrowing, could be written off over extended periods of time. In 1982, Ford UK's annual report showed it had written off over £260 million in either depreciation, amortization, or accelerated capital allowances, whereas it had received just £21 million that year in regional aid. Cited in Quinn 1988.

38. Unlike the carefully specified R&D write-off schemes in France, the British tax credit is allowed for "expenditures for the purposes of scientific research," the secretary of state having sole discretion over whether an activity counts as "scientific research," and to what extent (Inland Revenue and H.M. Treasury 1987).

39. In the early 1980s in particular, many reform proposals for British government-industry relations stressed the need for an industrial strategy, and a positive commitment to industrial concerns by the government. Wilks (1986a, 495) gives an example of this attitude, quoting Trevor Holdsworth of industrial firm GKN: "There is no better evidence of this lack of commitment [to positive policy] than by the promotion in 1986 of 'Industry Year.' What other developed economy could conceive of the necessity for such an event in 1986?"

40. Calls for more active cooperation between government and industry in order to plan industry's economic performance were particularly prevalent in Britain in the 1980s. In the 1970s, under the more concerted Labour governments of Wilson and Callaghan, the prescription was usually for less government involvement in the affairs of industry and less consultation with economic actors.

41. The classic example, repeated by Zysman (1983) is of the buggy whip industry, which was indeed doomed when the automobile was invented.

42. Despite the changes in the industry, however, charges of cartelization are still leveled at the big heavy-steel makers in some markets. In May 1992, for example, the European Commission started an investigation into an alleged cartel in steel beams produced by Usinor, British Steel, Luxembourg's Arbed, and Germany's Saarstahl and Peine Salzgitter. In January 1991, the Commission had also launched a major inquiry into alleged illegal price fixing and market sharing in other sectors of the EC steel industry.

43. On the earlier period of EC industrial policies see, for example, El-Agraa 1983; Jacquemin 1984; Joliet 1981; Swann 1983.

44. The Rome Treaties of March 1957 created the European Economic Community, which began operation in 1958. The EEC and ECSC were merged in 1967 to create the European Community, or EC. France was a founding member of the Community; the United Kingdom joined in 1976. At time of writing, there are twelve EC member-states, with negotiations under way to admit Austria, Finland, Norway, and Sweden.

45. "The worst thing that ever happened to the steel industry was the invention of the Mini because that used one-third less of anything that was used before." Executive Director of the National Association of Steel Stockholders (Britain), to the Trade and Industry Committee 1983–84, HC 344.

46. Proportion of imports from non-EC members to total apparent consumption in the EC, in tonnage. The largest imports came from Eastern Europe, Austria, Sweden, and Spain. Exports from the EC rose from 20 percent of output in 1961 to 27 percent in 1980 (Messerlin and Saunders 1983).

47. In 1992, Belgium had some of the lowest car prices, and Britain some of the highest. In the late 1980s, taxation levels on car sales ranged from 12 percent in

Luxembourg to over 200 percent in Denmark and Greece (Commission of the European Communities 1988). Policies on VAT refunding of company purchases of vehicles also vary enormously between countries.

48. These are located in the United Kingdom, with Nissan established since 1987. The Toyota and Honda plants began producing in October 1992.

Chapter 2

1. Between 1967 and 1975 BSC estimated it lost £783 million in revenue due to state price controls (Trade and Industry Committee, 1980–81, HC 336-I).

2. Note on steel statistics: output and capacity are usually measured in either money or volume; a very different picture may result, depending on the method used. Small finishing plants usually produce little in terms of volume, but a great deal of value-added. This makes it difficult to make accurate interplant and international comparisons. Employment figures can also be deceptive when compared internationally, due to great variation in the category of workers included. For example, in the early 1980s BSC usually counted research staff; trainees; cleaning and catering staff; nursing, health, and safety staff; coke production staff; stock holding staff; and even maintenance staff in their manpower figures. The French producers often included employees in their mining subsidiaries under steel employment.

3. "The steel industry is particularly vulnerable to the capital goods cycle [and] we have special problems in the United Kingdom because of the decline in the production of consumer goods made from steel, especially those that use steel heavily like motor cars, appliances . . ." Chairman MacGregor (Trade and Industry Committee 1982–83: HC 212, 1).

4. There were eight other craft unions and the two mass unions, the Transport and General Workers Union (TGWU) and the General and Municipal Workers' Union (G&MWU).

5. The campaign was orchestrated by the Strathclyde Regional Council, and included Motherwell District Council, the Scottish Development Agency, the Scottish TUC and, ultimately, the Scottish Office. The sense of a Scottish regional-national identity helped to include a broad array of interests in an effective publicity campaign. The primary argument was the impact of closure on the region's economy, with estimates that unemployment in the region would quickly rise to over 30 percent.

6. Billion = 1,000 million.

7. The government may also have used the financing limits to affect the outcome of the 1980 strike. Papers leaked to Granada TV showed that BSC management was originally prepared to offer the unions a pay increase of 10.5 percent to 14 percent, with no strings attached. The government, having received BSC's plan to meet the government's cash limits, apparently vetoed this. The DTI instructed MacGregor to make a lower offer and so tighten the cash limits still further ("World In Action," Granada TV, 1980). These allegations led to legal battles between the government and Granada TV, complete with impounded evidence and an injunction against the station.

8. British Petroleum, in October 1987, raised £7 billion; British Gas, in December 1986, £5.4 billion; and British Telecom, in November 1984, £3.9 billion.

9. There had been a number of previous management and employee buyouts, among them National Freight in February 1982 (net Treasury gain of £5 million); a number of the operating companies being created at that time out of the National Bus Corporation; the Unipart spare parts business hived off from BL and bought out by employees and financial institutions in January 1987 (Treasury received a net £52 million); and Leyland Bus, another BL hive-off, sold to a management consortium with a 16 percent employee stake in January 1987 (Treasury net receipt £4 million).

10. Some firms, such as Lees of Sheffield, founded in 1885, had a long history of steel manufacturing. Others were significant employers, such as Sheerness Steel in Kent, the major U.K. mini-mill, which employed some 700 by the mid-1980s (British Independent Steel Producers Association 1986). There was also an oft-forgotten fourth strip mill in Britain in the 1980s, at Alpha Steel in South Wales. See Trade and Industry Committee 1983–84, HC 344.

11. Assistance was available for redundancy payments that were part of rationalization; for other costs of closure or restructuring; and for industry-organized schemes of financing closures by means of a levy on those remaining in business (Industrial Development Act 1982: Annual Report, 1986). Still, BISPA continued to object to what it called "the payment of State subsidies to steel producers by Governments anxious to avoid the social or political consequences of change" (BISPA 1988, 7).

12. Under the initial proposal, 67 percent of the new company's trading assets were to be provided by GKN, and 33 percent by BSC. BSC would provide for the company's present and future cash requirements and would also supply it with low-priced steel billets for its first three years. But the DTI felt that transferring assets on the basis of net book values favored GKN, and asked the two sides to reconsider in line with the government's own requirements. The revised proposal was approved. GKN contributed 71 percent of fixed assets, and BSC had to increase the amount of cash it contributed to ASW (Committee of Public Accounts 1984–85, HC 307).

Chapter 3

1. Ascométal was actually a holding company, merging the two enterprises' interests in engineering steels. Unimétal was a more straightforward merger of plants, directly held by the two enterprises (*Financial Times*, April 18, 1984).

2. When the steel industry increased its prices in the early 1960s against government wishes, the government raised the cost of transportation and coal for the steel companies by price increases in the relevant nationalized industries. In contrast, in the 1966 steel agreement the government agreed to reduce the cost of domestic coking coal and coke, with subsidies to the nationalized Charbonnages de France (Adams 1989).

3. Following the 1983 law on democratization in the public sector, one-third of the boards of Usinor and Sacilor were trade-union representatives, the remainder appointed by the government. The actual leverage of the unions over government industrial policies was limited. In statements reminiscent of the TUC Steel Committee in Britain, the representatives complained that they were asked "to approve the conclusions of reports we have never discussed and of which we have no knowledge" (Smith 1989, 12).

4. Since the early 1970s, steel employers had signed regular agreements with the unions, called *conventions générale de protection sociale de la sidérurgie*. These were negotiated collective agreements that were applicable to the entire industry, setting general conditions of employment that were then implemented in the various enterprises. As the crisis accelerated, the conventions increasingly involved state provision of financial benefits to workers and became a regular part of the industry's affairs. The 1979 convention granted assistance and retraining for redundant steelworkers. The 1982 and 1984 agreements were signed by all of the big steel unions except the CGT. They added a 35-hour week for those still employed and extended the unemployment-relief measures until December 1987. In July 1987, the agreements were extended once again, to December 1990 (Chambre Syndicale de la Sidérurgie Française 1987).

5. Groupement d'équipement pour le traitement des minerais de fer; Groupement pour le financement des économies d'énergie; Groupement interprofessionnel financière antipollution; Groupement des industries de matériaux de construction.

6. Thus la Société financière Usinor held 52.84 percent of Usinor's capital directly, and 51 percent of the holding company Valmétal's capital, which itself held 11.83 percent of Usinor's capital. La Société financière Sacilor held 23.2 percent of Sacilor's capital directly, and 67 percent of the capital of the holding company Société financière sidérurgique, which itself held 53.7 percent of Sacilor's capital (Gendarme 1985).

7. "Il revient, de ce fait, aux Pouvoirs Public, d'organiser un soutien diversifié aux efforts d'adaptation de notre industrie. Le développement de notre economie, de l'emploi et finalement du bien-être des citoyens en est l'enjeu" (Ministère de l'Industrie 1979, 35).

8. The installments were as follows: March, FFr 1.2 billion; May, FFr 0.8 billion; July, FFr 0.4 billion; September, FFr 2.4 billion (Gendarme 1985).

9. Proposal No. 2220, registered December 18, 1980, by Jean Laurain, deputé of Moselle.

10. "Le Gouvernement tient à donner à ces enterprises une réelle autonomie de gestion qui s'exercera dans le cadre des contrats passés avec le Gouvernement pour la durée de chaque Plan." *Projet de loi de nationalisation*, presented to the Assemblée Nationale on September 23, 1981.

11. Sacilor's major agreements were to modernize its steel plants, with a FFr3.5 billion investment program over the next four years; to increase its downstream operations by reorganizing its raw materials plants with a FFr 200 million investment; and to increase its research budget by 7 percent per annum. Usinor's contract was more detailed, specifying seven objectives, but some of these were very vague. The most important was a massive investment program of FFr9 billion to modernize production facilities and return to profitability by 1986. Usinor also agreed to double its research spending within five years; to diversify its downstream operations and strengthen its steel subsidiaries; to initiate an energy conservation program; and to reinforce its position in various steel markets in order to alleviate the country's balance-of-payments problems.

12. " . . . it would be disastrous for France to let the big nationalized enterprises, which carry a large part of French industrial hope, become marginal for want of capital" (my translation).

13. The buyers must provide new capital for the state partner, and they must form an industrial, commercial, or financial cooperation accord.

Chapter 4

1. Known from 1896 to 1966 as Société Anonyme des Automobiles Peugeot, the firm became Peugeot SA in 1966; became PSA Peugeot-Citroën in 1976; went back to Peugeot SA again in 1979; and now, once again, is called PSA Peugeot Citroën.

2. French data treat each legally distinct company as a separate statistical and decision-making entity. Thus Peugeot, Citroën, and Talbot are considered three distinct auto sellers, although Peugeot controls the other two. SA = *Société Anonyme*, a firm that has at least seven shareholders, and either a board of directors headed by a *Président-Directeur Général* (such as Peugeot), or a supervisory board with an executive committee underneath. Unless otherwise noted, "Peugeot" refers to the PSA group as a whole.

3. These paragraphs on the early history of Peugeot are drawn extensively from Laux 1976, a detailed and fascinating study of the beginnings of the auto industry in France, the families and men associated with the early firms, and the impact of the industry on French industrialization.

4. The firm concentrated nationalities in particular factories and made membership in the company's own "union" compulsory. Linhart's 1978 *L'établi* was the most famous exposé of conditions among the immigrant workers at Citroën's factory at Choisy (translated, 1981, as *The Assembly Line*. University of Massachusetts Press). The percentage of immigrant workers at Citroën has declined, however, from a high of over 20 percent at the start of the decade to barely 13 at the end (*Financial Times*, March 1, 1988).

5. The public statement was that the French government couldn't approve the measure since it could not guarantee a common approach by the EC member states (*Financial Times*, July 22, 1988).

6. In an interview with *Le Monde*, June 6, 1989, Fauroux stated that he and Finance Minister Bérégovoy welcomed foreign investment: "Il faut faire venir des investisseurs étrangers, car ils nous apporteront des capitaux, des emplois et surtout une culture nouvelle qui nous stimulera. Un Japonais en France doit travailler avec des cadres et des ouvriers français, des syndicats français, des banquiers français, des soustraitants français, une administration française." But imports, that's another problem: "Je distingue bien, d'une part, les investissements qu'il faut accueillir . . . et, d'autre part, les importations." In the latter case, Europe must negotiate restraints, but with time limits, "pour favoriser la transition." One mustn't believe that French industry can develop with eternal protection.

7. Renault has entered into more joint ventures over the years than Peugeot. Until 1987, it had a 46 percent share in AMC in the United States. It had a 15 percent stake in Volvo Car in the early 1980s and in late 1989 it entered a major commercial vehicle linkup with DAF.

8. Previously, Renault had published its capital figures gross of past losses, giving it

published capital of FFr16.5 billion at the start of 1989. By writing off FFr32.8 billion of accumulated losses against FFr16.5 billion of shareholders' funds, the company now publishes its capital net of accumulated losses. This is purely an accounting maneuver, having no impact on Renault's borrowings or profits (*Financial Times*, November 25, 1989).

9. Renault also gained a 10 percent share in AB Volvo, the parent company, and a 45 percent share in the truck-making subsidiary, Volvo Truck. Aside from its 20 percent share in Renault, AB Volvo also received a 45 percent share in the truck-making subsidiary, Renault V.I.

10. Laux (1976) finds that at least some of these bonds were placed by Banque Renauld of Nancy, a successful provincial investment bank.

11. The $200 million eight-year loan had a 0.75 percent spread throughout its term and a five-year grace period for repayment.

12. Caisse des Dépôts et Consignations—Deposits and Consignments Bank—is a major financial institution; even more so in the controlled credit markets of the late 1970s. It pooled the cash from a number of public savings networks, and the nation's long-term lending institutions in turn drew funds from the Caisse. It also made its own investments in loans and securities, and financed public infrastructure investment and the work of local authorities. See Zysman 1983.

13. Peugeot and Citroën each have 25 percent of Sevel, Fiat has 50 percent. Some of the joint ventures with Renault are in research and development, some are joint ownership of overseas subsidiaries or components manufacturers.

14. Family Ownership of the French Top 500

	As percentage of net worth of first 500	Number of Sociétés
1975	30.4	212
1981	17.2	158
1984	18.6	151

"Propriété et Pouvoir dans L'Industrie," Laboratoire d'études et de Recherches sur l'économie de la Production. Université des Sciences Sociales de Toulouse, 1987.

15. A warrant gives the holder the right to buy common stock for cash. Warrants are usually combined with either privately placed bonds or new issues of stock. In the Peugeot case, the warrant holder would have been given the right to buy shares of common stock directly from the company at a fixed price, for a given period of time. The holder is not obliged to buy. The warrant specifies the number of shares the holder is entitled to, the exercise price, and the expiration date. In some cases, a warrant may be perpetual, with unlimited maturity periods. If a holder exercises a warrant, the firm must issue new shares of stock, thus spreading the firm's net income over a larger number of shares and decreasing the earnings per share. The percentage ownership of existing shareholders also declines (Ross and Westerfield 1988). As of December 31, 1987, warrants were outstanding for subscription of 2,029,668 unissued new PSA shares (*Moody's International*).

16. The plant was established as a subsidiary, Société de Mécanique Automobile du

Nord, owned 75 percent by Peugeot, 20 percent by Talbot, and 5 percent by Citroën, in order to maximize the financial benefits that could be received. See Hayward 1986.

17. In 1982, the Socialists replaced the FSAI and five smaller regional aid schemes with the Regional Development Grant, and the Regional Employment Grant, dispersed in the first instance by the new regional councils established under the 1983 Defferre decentralization laws. The state now makes block grants to the regional councils for employment generation and industrial development, but control over the various incentive schemes remains highly centralized (Morvan 1985).

Chapter 5

1. In May 1989, DAF floated 63.6 percent of itself on the market, and Rover agreed to sell a 24 percent stake in the firm as part of the deal. In the spring of 1993 the firm collapsed and sought court protection from creditors. At the time of writing, its future remains uncertain.

2. The currency shift had specific effects on BL models sold mostly in the United States, such as the TR7 and MG sports cars. MG lost £26 million in its last year of production. In 1982, sterling weakened against both the yen and the dollar, making some of BL's exports more profitable (Trade and Industry Committee 1981–82, HC 194). Vauxhall suffered from the deutsche mark/sterling exchange rate, claiming that it would otherwise have been in profit in 1986–87 (ibid.). The industry's long lead times make it hard to predict when currency-rate changes will have an effect.

3. Analysts such as Wilks blame this multinational presence for helping to preserve an industry structure of "too many manufacturers with too many models, too many plants and too much capacity" (Wilks 1984a). Adeney finds that the story of the British motor industry in the 1980s "is not so much about the continuing difficulties and disappointments of . . . BL . . . but of a major switch of car and component making and design out of Britain into other parts of the world" (Adeney 1988, 308).

4. The government has, however, required 80 percent local European Community content.

5. The Westland affair was a furious row over whether American or European companies should take rescuing shares in Westland, an ailing helicopter firm. The Cabinet had decided in favor of the American company, Sikorski.

6. Reportedly, larger applicants for shares in Jaguar plc were squeezed out in favor of small, individual bids. Of the initial 125,000 holders on the register, however, only 49,000 remained by May 1985, according to R. Buckland (1987).

7. Ford had tried to take over Alfa-Romeo in late 1986, but was outmaneuvered by the Italian state and Fiat. In 1987 Ford took a 75 percent stake in the British Aston Martin Lagonda, for an unrevealed price. AML's Chief Executive Gauntlett holds the remaining 25 percent, the condition for his staying on (*Financial Times*, December 15, 1989). GM purchased Lotus in 1986 for £22 million (*Financial Times*, December 15, 1989). By 1989 Chrysler had taken over Lamborghini, Saab of Sweden was ailing, Daimler-Benz was protected by Deutsche Bank, and BMW by the Quandt family, while Porsche was protected by the Porsche and Piech families.

8. Britain's top 100 exporters, for fiscal 1988–89 (*Financial Times*, September 27, 1989):

Ranking	Company	Exports, £ million
1	British Aerospace	4,389.0
6	Ford U.K.	1,471.0
8	British Steel	1,341.0
12	Jaguar Cars	704.0
44	United Engineering Steels	201.2
72	Peugeot Talbot	134.4

The British Aerospace figure includes Rover's exports, but even without them, BAe would still have been in first place. BAe was responsible for about 6 percent of Britain's manufactured exports in 1988.

9. BAe had paid £190 million for Royal Ordnance, and had closed a number of production facilities and redeveloped the sites, which were on prime areas of land. The House of Commons Public Accounts Committee was drafting a report on Royal Ordnance criticizing the sale as hasty and undervalued when the Rover purchase went through (Trade and Industry Committee, 1987–88, HC 487).

10. DAF floated 63.6 percent of itself on the market. Rover had a 40 percent stake in DAF at this point, and agreed to sell a 24 percent holding as part of the deal (*Financial Times*, December 7, 1989).

11. The Hawker Siddeley Group (formed in 1935) and the British Aircraft Corporation (formed in 1960), were merged by the Labour government in 1977 to form British Aerospace.

12. Between 1985 and 1989, some 25 percent of foreign investment in manufacturing in Britain was attracted to the region. Toyota picked nearby Derbyshire for its greenfield site partly because there are so many auto-components producers in the region (*Financial Times*, October 18, 1989).

13. For example, the Support for Innovation Scheme; the Microelectronics Applications Project; and a scheme for using computer aided design and manufacturing systems (CADCAM). There have also been complaints about the arbitrary and unhelpful nature of DTI assistance from some components manufacturers: see Trade and Industry Committee, 1986–87, HC 407, qu.734.

14. The government holds ten other Special Shares in companies that say the Shares make little difference to their business and are effective in limiting foreign control (*Financial Times*, December 14, 1989).

Chapter 6

1. "Normally, a German business may depreciate an investment 10 percent over ten years. But the German government has supported an accelerated pace of investments near the old East Germany—an advantage we were able to exploit because Wolfsburg is less than ten kilometers from the old border. So we were usually able to depreciate 50 percent of our investments here during the first year" (Interview in *Harvard Business Review*, July–August 1991, 109).

2. Formerly chairman of Audi, the VW division that makes the group's top-of-the-line models, Ferdinand is also the grandson of Ferdinand Porsche, who designed the legendary VW Beetle.

3. At the time of writing, the plan envisages creditors forgiving some DM1.4 billion of the DM2.7 billion in debts, in an out-of-court settlement.

4. Japan was formerly the second-largest producer of crude steel, after the USSR.

5. The parent company, and four operating divisions—steel, aerospace, energy, and AM General.

6. Previously, a shareholder would have to contact all shareholders if it lobbied more than ten—a potentially phenomenally expensive and complex exercise. Now, a shareholder can contact, say, the company's 1,000 largest shareholders who between them hold 70 percent of the votes, for far less money. This is what the United Shareholders Association, a group of small shareholders, did in the spring of 1993, when trying to separate the jobs of chief executive and chairman at Sears, Roebuck.

7. Three Danish banks merged into Unibank in 1990, four Dutch banks have merged into two separate institutions, and similar moves have occurred elsewhere. This pressure to consolidate is also being felt outside the EC itself. Two Austrian banks announced merger plans in May 1991 that will create that country's largest bank. The two said the move was to meet the "challenges created by the prospects of a unified, single European market" (*American Banker*, May 17, 1991).

8. For example, in the United States, corporate income is effectively taxed twice— once as corporation tax, and a second time as personal income tax on dividends. Interest payments on debt, however, are deductible from profits before tax, as a cost of doing business. Thus, the value of a firm in theory rises as it takes on more debt, because it is paying out less of its earning in taxes. See discussion of Modigliani and Miller in Emmott 1991, pages 13/14.

9. I am indebted to Fred Block for drawing my attention to this point.

Bibliography

Abromeit, H. 1986. *British Steel*. New York: St. Martin's Press.

————. 1990. "Government-Industry Relations in West Germany." In M. Chick, ed., *Governments, Industries and Markets*. Aldershot: Edward Elgar.

Adams, W. 1989. *Restructuring the French Economy*. Washington, D.C.: Brookings Institute.

Adeney, M. 1988. *The Motor Makers: The Turbulent History of Britain's Car Industry*. London: Collins.

Altshuler, A., M. Anderson, D. Jones, D. Roos, and J. Womack. 1984. *The Future of the Automobile*. Cambridge, Mass.: MIT Press.

American Banker. Various issues, weekly.

Anderson, M. 1982. "Financial Restructuring of the World Auto Industry." Paper presented at MIT Auto Program, International Policy Forum, Japan, May 1982.

Balassa, B. 1985. "French Industrial Policy under the Socialist Government." *American Economic Review*, May.

Barsoux, J. L., and P. Lawrence. 1991. "The Making of a French Manager." *Harvard Business Review* July–August.

Bayliss, B. T., and A. A. S. Butt Philip. 1980. *Capital Markets and Industrial Investment in Germany and France*. England: Saxon House.

Bellon, B. 1985. "Strengths and Weaknesses of French Industry." In S. Zukin, ed., *Industrial Policy: Business and Politics in the U.S. and France*. New York: Praeger.

Benoit, F. 1982. *Citroën: le printemps de la dignité*. Paris: Editions Sociales.

British Aerospace Business Review. London. Various issues, monthly.

British Independent Steel Producers Association (BISPA). 1986. *Industry Report*.

————. 1988. *Annual Report*.

Buckland, R. 1987. "The Costs and Returns of the Privatization of Nationalized Industries." *Public Administration* Autumn.

Business International Money Report. 1987. "How Centralization and Deregulation Helped Peugeot Restructure its Debt." June 29.

Butt Philip, A. 1983. "Industrial and Competition Policies." In A. M. El-Agraa, ed., *Britain within the EEC*. London: MacMillan.

Capie, F. 1990. "The Evolving Regulatory Framework in British Banking." In M. Chick, ed., *Governments, Industries and Markets*. Aldershot: Edward Elgar.

Central Statistical Office. 1988. *Annual Abstract of Statistics*. London: HMSO.

Chambre Syndicale de la Sidérurgie Française. *La Sidérurgie Française*. Various issues, annual.

Cheval, J. 1987. "France." In C. Saunders, ed., *Industrial Policies and Structural Change*. New York: St. Martin's Press.

Chick, M., ed. 1990. *Governments, Industries and Markets*. Aldershot: Edward Elgar.

Commission de Reforme de la Planification. 1982. *Rapport au ministre d'Etat, Ministre du Plan et de l'Aménagement du Territoire*. N. P.: Documentation Française.

Commission of the European Communities. 1988. *Research on the "Cost of Non-Europe."* Vol. 2, *The EC 92 Automobile Sector*. Luxembourg: Commission of the EC.

Committee of Public Accounts, session 1983–84. *Third Report: Department of Industry Supervision and Monitoring of BL*. House of Commons Paper 103.

———, session 1984–85. *Thirty-Fourth Report: Control and Monitoring of Investment by BSC in Private Sector Companies—the Phoenix Operations*. House of Commons Paper 307.

Comptroller and Auditor General. 1983. *Memorandum to Committee of Public Accounts*. House of Commons Paper 103, 1983–84.

———. 1985. "Memorandum." Reprinted in Committee of Public Accounts, session 1984–85, HC 307.

Cowling, K., P. Stoneman, J. Cubbin, J. Cable, G. Hall, S. Domberger, and P. Dutton. 1980. *Mergers and Economic Performance*. Cambridge: Cambridge University Press.

Cox, A. 1986. "State, Finance and Industry in Comparative Perspective." In A. Cox, ed., *State, Finance and Industry*. New York: St. Martin's Press.

Delion, A., and M. Durupty. 1982. *Les Nationalisations 1982*. Paris: Economica.

Department of Trade and Industry (DTI). 1984. "Memorandum." Reprinted in Trade and Industry Committee, session 1983–84, HC 540.

———. 1988a. *DTI: The Department for Enterprise*. London: HMSO, cmnd 278.

———. 1988b. *Mergers Policy*. London: HMSO.

Documentation Française. 1980. *Notes et Etudes Documentaires, No. 4583—L'Industrie Automobile en France*. Documentation Française.

———. 1981. *Profil Economique de la France, au Seuil des Années 80*. Documentation Française.

———. 1982. *Aides à l'Industrie, Commissariat Général du Plan*. Documentation Française.

———. 1985. *Notes et Etudes Documentaires, No. 4798—Le Commerce Extérieur de la France*. Documentation Française.

———. 1987. *Notes et Etudes Documentaires, No. 4831—L'Avenir de L'Industrie Automobile Mondiale*. Documentation Française.

Downing, L. 1981. "A Consideration of the 1980 Strike Within the British Steel Corporation With Particular Regard to the Government's Role." Sheffield City Polytechnic.

Dudley, G. 1984. "The British Steel Corporation and Problems of Political Management." *Political Quarterly* 55(4).

Durand, C. 1981. *Chômage et Violence: Longwy en Lutte*. Paris: Editions Galilée.

Dyson, K., and S. Wilks, eds. 1983. *Industrial Crises: A Comparative Study of the State and Industry*. Oxford: Martin Robertson.

Economist. London. Various issues, weekly.

Economist. 1988. *France on Business.* London: Economist Business Publications Ltd.

Edwardes, M. 1983. *Back From the Brink: An Apocalyptic Experience.* London: Collins.

Eisenhammer, J. 1986. "Longwy and Bagnoli: A Comparative Study of Trade Union Response to the Steel Crisis in France and Italy." In Y. Mény and V. Wright, eds., *The Politics of Steel.* Berlin: Walter de Gruyter.

El-Agraa, A. M., ed. 1983. *Britain Within the EEC.* London: MacMillan.

Elbaum, B., and W. Lazonick, eds. 1986. *The Decline of the British Economy.* Oxford: Clarendon Press.

Emmott, B. 1991. "The Ebb Tide: A Survey of International Finance." *Economist,* April 27.

Esser, J., and W. Väth. 1986. "Overcoming the Steel Crisis in the Federal Republic of Germany 1975–1983." In Y. Mény and V. Wright, eds., *The Politics of Steel.* Berlin: Walter de Gruyter.

European Community News. New York. Various issues, weekly.

Federal Reserve Bank of New York. 1987. *Quarterly Review.* Winter 1987–88.

Financial Times. London. Various issues, daily.

Financial World (FW). London. Various issues, weekly.

Franks, J., and C. Mayer. 1992. "Corporate Control: A Synthesis of the International Evidence." Paper presented at UC Davis Conference on Corporate Control, San Francisco, May 15–17.

Fridenson, P. 1981. "French Automobile Marketing, 1890–1979." In A. Okochi and K. Shimokawa, eds., *Development of Mass Marketing.* University of Tokyo Press.

Fridenson, P., and A. Straus, eds. 1987. *Le Capitalisme Français XIX–XXe: Blocages et Dynamismes d'une Croissance.* Paris: Fayard.

Genay, H. 1991. "Japan's Corporate Groups." *Federal Reserve Bank of Chicago: Economic Perspectives.*

Gendarme, G. 1985. *Sidérurgie Lorraine: Les Coulées de Futur.* Nancy: Presses Universitaires de Nancy.

Gerschenkron, A. 1962. *Economic Backwardness in Historical Perspective.* Cambridge, Mass.: Harvard University Press.

Giles, M. 1991. "Second Thoughts: A Survey of Business in Europe." *Economist,* June 8.

Graham, C. 1989. "Regulating the Company." In L. Hancher and M. Moran, eds., *Capitalism, Culture, and Economic Regulation.* Oxford: Clarendon Press.

Graham, C., and T. Prosser. 1987. "Privatising Nationalised Industries: Constitutional Issues and New Legal Techniques." *Modern Law Review,* January.

Granada Television. 1980. *World In Action.* February 4.

Grant, W. 1984. "The Business Lobby: Political Attitudes and Strategies." In H. Berrington, ed., *Change in British Politics.* London: Frank Cass.

————. 1989. *Government and Industry: A Comparative Analysis of the US, Canada and the UK.* Aldershot: Edward Elgar.

Green, D. 1981. *Managing Industrial Change: French Policies to Promote Industrial Adjustment.* London: HMSO.

————. 1983. "Strategic Management and the State: France." In K. Dyson and

S. Wilks, eds., *Industrial Crises: A Comparative Study of the State and Industry*. Oxford: Martin Robertson.

————. 1986. "The State, Finance and Industry in France." In A. Cox, ed., *State, Finance and Industry*. New York: St. Martin's Press.

Hague, D., and G. Wilkinson. 1983. *The IRC: An Experiment in Industrial Intervention*. London: George Allen and Unwin.

Hahn, C. 1991. "A European Platform for Global Competition." *Harvard Business Review*, July–August.

Hall, P. 1985. "The Struggle to Define a New Economic Policy." In P. Cerny and M. Schain, eds., *Socialism, the State and Public Policy in France*. New York: Methuen.

————. 1986. *Governing the Economy*. New York: Oxford University Press.

Hancher, L., and M. Moran, eds. 1989. *Capitalism, Culture, and Economic Regulation*. Oxford: Clarendon Press.

Harris, J. 1988. *The British Iron Industry 1700–1850*. London: MacMillan Education.

Hayward, J. 1986a. "The Nemesis of Industrial Patriotism: The French Response to the Steel Crisis." In Y. Mény and V. Wright, eds., *The Politics of Steel*. Berlin: Walter de Gruyter.

————. 1986b. *The State and the Market Economy*. New York: New York University Press.

Heal, D. 1974. *The Steel Industry in Post War Britain*. London: David and Charles.

Her Majesty's Stationary Office (HMSO). 1978. "British Steel Corporation: The Road to Viability." Cmnd. 7149. London: HMSO.

————. 1983–84. "Public Expenditure White Paper, 1984–85 to 1986–87." Cmnd. 9143-II. London: HMSO.

————. *Industrial Development Act 1982: Annual Report*. Reports for years ending 3/85; 3/86; 3/88. London: HMSO.

Hoffmann-Martinot, V., and P. Sadran. 1986. "The Local Implementation of France's National Strategy." In Y. Mény and V. Wright, eds., *The Politics of Steel*. Berlin: Walter de Gruyter.

Howell, T. 1988. *Steel And the State: Government Intervention and Steel's Structural Crisis*. Boulder, Colo.: Westview Press.

Hudson, G. 1986. "Capital, Labour and the State in North-East England." In R. Martin and B. Rowthorn, eds., *The Geography of De-Industrialisation*. London: MacMillan.

Ikenberry, G. J. 1988. *Reasons of State: Oil Politics and the Capacities of American Government*. Ithaca, N.Y.: Cornell University Press.

Inland Revenue and H.M. Treasury. 1987. *Fiscal Incentives for R & D Spending—An International Survey*. HMSO. March.

Institute of Manpower Studies. 1989. *Economic Significance of the UK Motor Vehicle Manufacturing Industry*. London: Society of Motor Manufacturers and Traders.

International Labour Organisation (ILO), Iron and Steel Committee. 1986. *Conference Report II*. Geneva: International Labour Organisation.

Jacquemin, A. 1984. *European Industry: Public Policy and Corporate Strategy*. Oxford: Clarendon Press.

Jacquillat, B. 1987. "Nationalization and Privatization in Contemporary France." *Government Union Review*, Fall.

Jaguar Annual Report, various issues.

Jensen, M. 1989. "Eclipse of the Public Corporation." *Harvard Business Review*, September–October.

Joliet, R. 1981. "Cartelisation, Dirigism and Crisis in the European Community." *World Economy* 3(no. 4).

Jones, D. 1981. "The Auto Industry and Government: Analysing National Industrial Policies." Paper presented at MIT Auto Program, International Policy Forum, London, June.

————. 1983: "Motor Cars: A Maturing Industry?" In G. Shepherd et al., eds., *Europe's Industries: Public and Private Strategies for Change*. Ithaca, N.Y.: Cornell University Press.

Jones, K. 1986. *Politics versus Economics in World Steel Trade*. London: George Allen and Unwin.

Katzenstein, P. 1985. *Small States in World Markets*. Ithaca, N.Y.: Cornell University Press.

Kay, J. A., and M. A. King. 1986. *The British Tax System*. 4th ed. Oxford: Oxford University Press.

Keohane, R. O. 1984. "The World Political Economy and the Crisis of Embedded Liberalism." In J. Goldthorpe, ed., *Order and Conflict in Contemporary Capitalism*. Cambridge: Cambridge University Press.

Keyder, C. 1985. "State and Industry in France, 1750–1914." *American Economic Review*, May.

Laboratoire d'études et de recherches sur l'économie de la production (LEREP). 1987. *Propriété et Pouvoir dans L'Industrie*. Toulouse: Université des Sciences Sociales de Toulouse, LEREP.

Laux, J. 1976. *In First Gear: The French Automobile Industry to 1914*. Liverpool: Liverpool University Press.

Lévy, R. 1986. "Industrial Policy and the Steel Industry." In W. Adams and C. Stoffaës, eds., *French Industrial Policy*. Washington, D.C.: Brookings Institution.

Lewchuk, W. 1986. "The Motor Vehicle Industry." In B. Elbaum and W. Lazonick, eds., *The Decline of the British Economy*. Oxford: Clarendon Press.

Linhart, R. 1978. *L'établi*. Trans 1981. *The Assembly Line*. Amherst, Mass.: University of Massachussets Press.

Love, J., and J. Stevens. 1986. "Scottish Steel at the Crossroads." *Quarterly Economic Commentary*.

Lynn, J., and A. Jay. 1984. *The Complete Yes Minister*. London: BBC Books.

————. 1987. *Yes Prime Minister*. Vol. 2. London: BBC Books.

McArthur, J., and B. Scott. 1969. *Industrial Planning in France*. Boston, Mass.: Harvard Business School.

Marklew, V. 1989. "Privatisation in Britain: Government-Industry Relations and the Role of Management." Paper presented at the American Political Science Association annual meeting, Atlanta, September.

Masson, J-L. 1986. *Demain: L'Acier Français*. Paris: Editions Cujas.

Melitz, J. 1990. "Financial Deregulation in France." *European Economic Review* 34.

Mény, Y., and V. Wright, eds. 1986. *The Politics of Steel: Western Europe and the Steel Industry in the Crisis Years.* Berlin: Walter de Gruyter.

Messerlin, P., and C. Saunders. 1983. "Steel." In G. Shepherd et al., eds., *Europe's Industries: Public and Private Strategies for Change.* Ithaca, N.Y.: Cornell University Press.

Milner, H. 1988. *Resisting Protectionism.* Princeton, N.J.: Princeton University Press.

Ministère de l'Industrie. 1979. *Une Politique pour l'industrie Française.* N. P.: Documentation Française.

Ministère de L'Industrie et de la Recherche. 1983. *Débat de Stratégie Industrielle.* Documentation Française.

Ministère du Travail. 1981. *Le Processus de Restructuration Industrielle du Groupe Sacilor-Sollac Depuis 1948.* N. P.: Documentation Française.

Modigliani, F., and M. Miller. 1958. "The Cost of Capital, Corporation Finance and the Theory of Investment." *American Economic Review,* June.

Monde, Le. Paris. Various issues, daily.

Moody's International. Various issues, annual.

Moore, B. 1966. *Social Origins of Dictatorship and Democracy.* Harmondsworth: Penguin Books Ltd.

Moore, B., J. Rhodes, and P. Tyler. 1986. *The Effects of the Government's Regional Economic Policy.* London: HMSO, Department of Trade and Industry.

Morgan, K. 1983. "Restructuring Steel: The Crises of Labour and Locality in Britain." *International Journal of Urban and Regional Research,* June.

Morse, T. 1985. *BL: A Case Study in Frustration.* London: Policy-Search Ltd.

Morvan, Y. 1985. "Industrial Policy." In H. Machin and V. Wright, eds., *Economic Policy and Policy-Making under the Mitterrand Presidency 1981–1984.* New York: St. Martin's Press.

National Economic Development Council (NEDC). 1981. *TUC Memorandum: Financing the Nationalised Industries.* NEDC (81) 28.

———. 1986. *Committee on Finance for Industry: Financial Aspects of Industrial Restructuring.* NEDC.

National Economic Development Office (NEDO). 1987. EI(88)10. *Government IT Policies in Competing Countries.* London: NEDO. November.

Nikkei Weekly. Tokyo. Various issues, weekly.

Norton, P. 1989. "The Lady's Not for Turning: But What about the Rest of the Party?" Paper presented at the American Political Science Association Annual Meeting, Atlanta, September.

Organisation for Economic Cooperation and Development (OECD). 1987. *Economic Survey: UK.* Paris: OECD.

———. 1992. *Economic Survey: Japan.* Paris: OECD.

Pauly, L. 1988. *Opening Financial Markets: Banking Politics on the Pacific Rim.* Ithaca, N.Y.: Cornell University Press.

Perrin-Pelletier, F. 1986. "Industrial Policy and the Automobile Industry." In W. Adams and C. Stoffaës, eds., *French Industrial Policy.* Washington, D.C.: Brookings Institute.

Peugeot Annual Report, various issues.

Phoenix: Journal of the Iron and Steel Trades Confederation. Various issues, 1986–1989.

Price Waterhouse. 1989. *Doing Business in France*. Price Waterhouse.

Prosser, T. 1986. *Nationalised Industries and Public Control*. Britain: Blackwell.

Quinn, D. 1988. *Restructuring the Automobile Industry*. New York: Columbia University Press.

Reich, S. 1990. *The Fruits of Fascism: Postwar Prosperity in Historical Perspective*. Ithaca, N.Y.: Cornell University Press.

Richardson, J., and G. Dudley. 1986. "Steel Policy in the U.K." In Y. Mény and V. Wright, eds., *The Politics of Steel*. Berlin: Walter de Gruyter.

Riddell, P. 1989. *The Thatcher Decade*. Oxford: Basil Blackwell.

Ross, G. 1982. "The Perils of Politics: French Unions and the Crisis of the 1970s." In P. Lange, G. Ross, and M. Vannicelli, eds., *Unions, Change and Crisis*. London: George Allen and Unwin.

Ross, S., and R. Westerfield. 1988. *Corporate Finance*. St. Louis: Times Mirror.

Roume, J. 1986. "Sidérurgie: Vers la Rentabilité." *L'Usine Nouvelle* 49.

Samuels, R. 1990. "The Business of the Japanese State." In M. Chick, ed., *Governments, Industries and Markets*. Aldershot: Edward Elgar.

Scottish Affairs Committee, session 1982–83. *Second Report: The Steel Industry in Scotland*. House of Commons Paper 22.

———, session 1985–86. *First Report: The Proposed Closure of BSC Gartcosh*. House of Commons Paper 154(i).

Shonfield, A. 1969. *Modern Capitalism*. Oxford: Oxford University Press.

Signora, A. 1980. "La Restructuration de la Sidérurgie Française." *Revue d'Economie Politique* 90e année, no. 6.

Skocpol, T., and K. Finegold. 1983. "State Capacity and Economic Intervention in the Early New Deal." *Political Science Quarterly* 97.

Smith, W. 1989. "The Politics of Industrial Adjustment in France: Mitterrand, the Left, and the Steel Crisis, 1981–86." Paper presented at the American Political Science Association Annual Meeting, Atlanta, September.

Society of Motor Manufacturers and Traders (SMMT). 1988. *Statistical Review*. London: SMMT.

Steel, D. 1982. "Review Article: Government and Industry in Britain." *British Journal of Political Science*, October.

Stevens, A. 1985. "'L'Alternance' and the Higher Civil Service." In P. Cerny and M. Schain, eds., *Socialism, the State and Public Policy in France*. New York: Methuen.

Swann, D. 1983. *Competition and Industrial Policy in the European Community*. New York: Methuen.

Tolliday, S. 1987. *Business, Banking and Politics: The British Steel Industry Between the Wars*. Cambridge, Mass.: Harvard University Press.

Trade and Industry Committee, session 1980–81. *Third Report: Finance for BL*. HC 294.

———, session 1980–81. *Fourth Report: Effects of BSC's Corporate Plan*. HC 336-I; 336-II.

——, session 1981–82. *Third Report: BL Limited*. HC 194.

——, session 1981–82. *Fourth Report: British Steel Corporation*. HC 308.

——, session 1982–83. *Second Report: The British Steel Corporation's Prospects*. HC 212.

——, session 1982–83. *BL plc: Minutes of Evidence*. HC 353.

——, session 1983–84. *First Special Report: Observations by Government*. HC 181.

——, session 1983–84. *First Report: The British Steel Corporation's Prospects*. HC 344.

——, session 1983–84. *Third Report: BL plc*. HC 490.

——, session 1983–84. *Third Report: Observations by Government*. HC 540.

——, session 1984–85. *Second Report: The British Steel Corporation*. HC 474.

——, session 1984–85. *BL plc: Minutes of Evidence*. HC 569.

——, session 1985–86. *BL: Minutes of Evidence (Land Rover-Leyland)*. HC 291.

——, session 1985–86. *BL plc: Minutes of Evidence*. HC 423.

——, session 1985–86. *British Steel: Minutes of Evidence*. HC 539.

——, session 1986–87. *Third Report: The UK Motor Components Industry*. HC 407.

——, session 1987–88. *First Report: The UK Motor Components Industry: Supplementary Report*. HC 316.

——, session 1987–88. *First Special Report: Monitoring the Department of Trade and Industry*. HC 343.

——, session 1987–88. *British Aerospace/Rover: Minutes of Evidence*. HC 487.

——, session 1987–88. *British Steel: Minutes of Evidence*. HC 631.

Trades Union Congress (TUC). 1984. *TUC Motor Industry Study*. London: TUC.

Transport and General Workers Union (TGWU). 1980. *British Leyland: The Next Decade*. TGWU, AUEW, TASS.

U.K. Iron and Steel Statistics Bureau. *Annual Statistics*. Various issues, 1981–87.

L'Usine Nouvelle. Paris. Various issues, weekly.

Utton, M. 1986. "Developments in British Industrial and Competition Policies." In G. Hall, ed., *European Industrial Policy*. New York: St. Martin's Press.

Veljanovski, C. 1987. *Selling the State: Privatisation in Britain*. London: Weidenfeld and Nicolson.

Vickers, J., and V. Wright. 1988. "The Politics of Industrial Privatisation in Western Europe: An Overview." *West European Politics* 11(4).

Vickers, J., and G. Yarrow. 1988. *Privatization: An Economic Analysis*. Cambridge, Mass.: MIT Press.

Walker, B. 1987. *Changes in the UK Motor Industry: An Analysis of Some Local Economic Impacts*. Birmingham: Motor Industry Local Authority Network, University of Birmingham.

Wall Street Journal. New York. Various issues, daily.

Ward's Auto World. Various issues.

Weir, M., and T. Skocpol. 1985. "State Structure and the Possibilities for Keynesian response to the Great Depression in Sweden, Britain, and the United States." In P. Evans, C. Rueschmeyer, and T. Skocpol, eds., *Bringing the State Back In*. Cambridge: Cambridge University Press.

Wilks, S. 1984a. *Industrial Policy and the Motor Industry*. Manchester: Manchester University Press.

————. 1984b. "The Practice of the Theory of Industrial Adaptation in Britain and West Germany." *Government and Opposition* 19 (Autumn).

————. 1986a. "Government-Industry Relations: A Review Article." *Policy and Politics* 14(4).

————. 1986b. "Has the State Abandoned British Industry?" *Parliamentary Affairs*, January.

————. 1987. "From Industrial Policy to Enterprise Policy in Britain." *Journal of General Management*, Summer.

Wilks, S., and M. Wright, eds., 1987. *Comparative Government-Industry Relations*. Oxford: Oxford University Press.

Williams, K., J. Williams, and C. Haslam. 1987. *The Breakdown of Austin Rover*. Leamington Spa: Berg Publishers Ltd.

Womack, J. 1982. "The Corporate Significance of National Financial Systems in the Auto Sector." Paper presented at MIT Future of the Auto Program, International Policy Forum, Japan, May.

Womack, J., D. Jones, and D. Roos. 1990. *The Machine That Changed the World*. New York: Rawson Associates.

World in Action. 1989. *Jaguar: The Race for Survival*. Program Transcript, June 5.

Wright, V. 1984. "Socialism and the Interdependent Economy: Industrial Policy-Making under the Mitterrand Presidency." *Government and Opposition* 19.

Young, H. 1989. *One of Us: A Biography of Margaret Thatcher*. London: Macmillan.

Young, S. 1986a. "The Implementation of Britain's National Steel Strategy at the Local Level." In Y. Mény and V. Wright, eds., *The Politics of Steel*. Berlin: Walter de Gruyter.

————. 1986b. "The Nature of Privatisation in Britain, 1979–85." *West European Politics*, April.

Zukin, S., ed. 1985. *Industrial Policy: Business and Politics in the US and France*. New York: Praeger.

Zysman, J. 1977. *Political Strategies for Industrial Order*. Berkeley and Los Angeles: University of California Press.

————. 1983. *Governments, Markets and Growth*. Ithaca, N.Y.: Cornell University Press.

Index

Allied Steel and Wire (ASW), UK, 74–75, 78–79, 220, 231
Auto Industry, 42–45, 228–29; and role of EC, 45–49, 58–59, 104, 106. *See also* British Leyland (BL); and Peugeot SA (PSA)
Avesta, 71

Balladur, Edouard, 19, 25, 30, 122, 123, 189
Bank of England, 32, 33, 215
Banque de France, 25
Banque Nationale de Paris, 107
Banque Nationale de Paris (BNP), 26, 28, 116, 137
Barre, Raymond, 38, 91, 97, 131, 135
Bérégovoy, Pierre, 29, 120, 133
BMW, 3, 144, 150, 194
Britain: National Financial System, 31–35, 188–90; privatization in, 15–17
British Aerospace (BAe), 17, 25, 70, 141, 142, 146, 163–67, 169, 173, 174, 180, 183, 185, 219, 220, 223
British Independent Steel Producers Association (BISPA), 72, 75, 108
British Leyland (BL), 2, 5, 11, 13, 14, 16, 22, 41, 52, 53, 56, 65, 66, 83, 111, 119, 124, 134, 138, 140, 141–74, 176, 178–79, 188, 189; financing of, 153–58, 170–74, 180–87; government policy and, 147–51; labor relations, 148; privatization, 145–47, 155–61; restructuring and nationalization, 142–45, 152–53
British Leyland Motor Corporation (BLMC), 142, 143, 151, 152, 168, 170, 172, 173, 181, 183, 187, 201, 209, 211
British Steel (BS), 6, 9, 16, 17, 35, 36, 49, 93, 94, 125, 136, 139, 166, 169, 170, 188, 190, 214, 223; financing of, 70–71, 180–87; Special Share, 79–80
British Steel Corporation (BSC), 2, 5, 11, 12, 13, 14, 38, 41, 52, 53, 55–83, 85, 89, 95, 100, 103, 108, 110, 111, 124, 138, 139, 141, 145, 147, 151, 155, 158, 167, 172, 173, 174, 175, 176, 178, 219; financing of, 63–68, 81–83, 180–87; labor relations, 59–60; privatization, 62, 68–70; Phoenix schemes, 72–79; restructuring, 57–59

Caisse des Dépôts et Consignations (CDC), 25
Calpers, 208
Calvet, Jacques, 25, 53, 116–20, 128–31, 133, 134, 137, 184, 221
Certificats d'investissement, 18
Chambre Syndicale de la Sidérurgie Française (CSSF), 86, 91, 95, 96, 111, 182
Chirac, Jacques, 17, 39, 90, 104, 115, 121, 137
Chrysler Corporation, 20, 115, 126, 129, 131, 135, 136, 149, 157, 172, 179, 208–11, 220; Chrysler UK, government aid to, 168–69
Citroën, 113, 115, 116, 117, 125, 126, 129, 130, 131, 134, 135, 139, 172, 220, 229

City, The (UK), 32, 33, 68, 146, 158,
    159, 160, 162, 166, 170
Compte de Développement Industriel
    (CODEVI), 26, 131
Confédération Français Démocratique
    du Travail (CFDT), 92, 118
Confédération Générale du Travail
    (CGT), 89, 92, 118, 119, 131
Conservative Party, 38, 41, 60, 176
Continental (Germany), 194
Contrats de plan, 103
Crédit Lyonnais, 19, 28, 105, 107,
    109, 189
Crédit National, 28, 95, 98, 131, 136,
    138
Creusôt Loire, 25, 87, 95, 102, 106–8

Daimler-Benz, 144, 166, 194, 195–96,
    198, 199, 208, 214
Davignon Plan, 46
Department of Trade and Industry
    (DTI), UK, 38, 39, 60, 62, 65–67,
    73–78, 145, 147, 150, 151, 155,
    164
Deutsche Bank, 29, 70, 71, 193, 194–
    96, 198, 199, 211, 217, 223

Edwardes, Michael, 143, 144, 147,
    148, 153–57, 159, 168, 186
European Coal and Steel Community
    (ECSC), 45, 46, 49, 72, 80, 184
European Community (EC): and auto in-
    dustry, 49–51, 163–65, 218; and sin-
    gle market program, 215–18; and state
    aid to industry, 218–22; and steel in-
    dustry, 45–49, 58–59, 104, 106
External Financing Limits (EFLs), 52,
    66–69, 80, 103, 110, 176, 220

Fabius, Laurent, 103, 122
Fiat, 49, 127, 191, 211–12
Fils de Peugeot Frères (LFPF), 114,
    127
Fonds de Développement Economique
    et Social (FDES), 26, 28, 95, 97–
    101, 131

Fonds d'Intervention Sidérurgique
    (FIS), 104
Fonds Industriel de Modernisation
    (FIM), 26, 130–32
Fonds Spécial d'Adaptation Industrielle
    (FSAI), 108, 131, 135, 136, 179
Ford, 49, 114, 135, 142, 143, 146,
    149–52, 160–62, 169, 173, 174,
    186, 201, 209, 210, 228
Français de Participations Financières,
    127
France: National Financial System, 25–
    31, 189–90; nationalization in,
    17–20
French Bourse, 21, 28, 30, 35, 123,
    126, 137
French steel industry, 2, 5, 8, 12, 21,
    22, 25, 28, 52, 56, 65, 66, 81, 82,
    83, 85–112, 117, 124, 137–39, 143,
    145, 153, 172, 178, 193, 220; con-
    centration and restructuring, 86–90,
    93–94; financing of, 95–96, 102–6,
    110–12, 180–87; Giraud Plan, 20,
    25, 96–100, 109, 110; government
    planning and, 90–91; labor relations,
    92–93; nationalization, 101–3

Gandois Report, 90
Gandrange, 86, 89, 92
General Motors (GM), 49, 142, 146,
    149, 150–51, 161, 208, 209, 210,
    212, 228, 229
Giraud Plan, 20, 25, 96–100, 109, 110
Groupement de l'Industrie Sidérurgique
    (GIS), 26, 91, 95, 96, 98, 109, 111,
    182, 185

Hoesch, 193, 195, 199
Honda, 51, 127, 142, 145, 146, 149,
    150, 165, 167, 203, 210, 229

Industrial Reorganisation Corporation
    (IRC), 143, 152, 167, 179
Industry, financing of, 22–24, 179–91;
    financing of, in Germany, 191–99; fi-
    nancing of, in Italy, 211–12; financ-

ing of, in Japan, 199–205; financing of, in United States, 205–11; politics of adaptation, 175–77; similarities in national policies, 177–79
Inland Steel (U.S.), 205
International Steel Cartel (ISC), 45
Iron and Steel Act, 1949 (UK), 56
Iron and Steel Act, 1967 (UK), 57
Iron and Steel Act, 1981 (UK), 59, 61, 64, 65, 82, 175, 184
Iron and Steel Trades Confederation (ISTC), UK, 59, 73

Jaguar, 2, 5, 17, 21, 22, 43, 71, 80, 139–44, 146, 150, 151, 156, 158–63, 166, 167, 169–70, 172–74, 180–87, 190, 196, 228
Joseph, Keith, 67, 157, 176
Judet Report, 88

Kobe Steel, 204, 205, 207, 211
Krupp, 193, 195

Labour Party, 16, 143, 164
Land Rover, 144, 151, 155, 156
Lévy, Raymond, 87, 88, 96, 102, 120, 121, 122, 133
London International Stock Exchange, 34, 35, 55, 69, 70, 126, 170, 174, 224
LTV Corporation (U.S.), 205, 207

MacGregor, Ian, 57, 58, 60, 61, 64, 67, 72, 139, 184
Mazda, 200, 201, 202, 203
Mer, Francis, 90, 101, 105, 185
Michelin, 115, 126, 129
Ministry for Industry (France), 18, 26, 90, 100, 109, 132
Ministry of Finance (France), 10, 25, 91, 96
Mitterrand Governments, policies of, 37–42

National Enterprise Board (NEB), 153, 154, 155, 156

National Loans Fund (NLF), UK, 63, 64
National Steel Corporation (U.S.), 206
New Capital (BSC), 64, 65, 67, 82, 110, 184
Nippon Steel, 62, 85, 90, 204, 205, 227
Nissan, 51, 119, 120, 142, 149, 150, 168, 169, 200, 202, 203
NKK Corporation (Japan), 204, 206
Noyaux durs, 19, 189, 221, 223

Parayre, Jean-Paul, 115, 130, 135, 137, 184
Paribas, 17, 26, 28
Parti Socialiste, 17, 28, 38, 41, 85, 90, 101, 102, 121, 130
Peugeot SA (PSA), 2, 5, 6, 9, 10, 13, 14, 18, 20, 21, 22, 25, 26, 27, 31, 36, 39, 49, 51, 52, 53, 81, 108, 112, 113–40, 142, 146, 147, 148, 149, 158, 160, 168, 170, 172, 173, 174, 176, 177, 179, 188, 189, 190, 192, 209, 211, 214, 219, 220, 221, 223, 228, 229; expansion and restructuring, 114–17; financing of, 123–34, 136–39, 180–87; labor relations, 117–19; regional policy and, 135–36; relations with government, 119–20, 130–34
Peugeot, Armand, 114, 124, 127
Phoenix Schemes, 72–79
Pirelli, 194
Planning Commission (France), 25
Public Dividend Capital (PDC), UK, 63–64

Ravenscraig, 56–61, 63, 67, 71, 82, 175, 184
Renault, 19, 49, 51, 52, 108, 113–15, 118–23, 127, 131, 132, 133, 135–39, 146, 148, 172, 178, 187, 219, 221
Ridley, Nicholas, 80, 161, 164, 169
Rover Group, 2, 3, 25, 51, 53, 62, 70, 140–46, 148–51, 155, 156, 158,

Rover Group (*continued*)
169, 172, 173, 174, 178, 180,
181, 185, 212, 214, 219, 220, 222,
223, 228, 229; privatization of,
162–67
RPR-UDF, 19, 39, 90, 105
Ryder Report, 152–53

Saarstahl, 93, 94, 193
Scholey, Robert, 58, 68, 69, 70, 71
Schweitzer, Louis, 122
Sheffield Forgemasters, 76, 79
Simonet Plan, 46
Société Foncière, Financière, et de Par-
ticipation (SFFP), 127, 129
Société Générale, 19, 28, 107, 124,
126
Special Shares, 14, 17, 41, 69, 72, 79,
80, 160, 161, 166, 169, 170, 178,
221
Steel industry, 42–45, 227–28; and
Mini-Mills, 42, 43, 48–49, 206,
214, 224, 228; and role of EC, 45–
49, 58–59, 104, 106. *See also* Brit-
ish Steel Corporation (BSC), and
French steel industry
Steel Plan, 1984 (France), 111, 185
Sumitomo, 200, 203–5

Talbot, 57, 59, 67, 113, 115, 117,
131, 139, 149, 168
Thatcher Governments, Policies of, 37–
42
Thyssen, 193
Titres participatifs, 18
Toyota, 51, 120, 142, 149, 150, 200,
202, 203, 228, 229
Trades Union Congress (TUC), UK,
59, 80, 145
Trésor (France), 25, 33, 95, 110

United Engineering Steels (UES), UK,
75, 181
Usinor, 13, 17, 19, 27, 38, 48, 53, 62,
71, 121, 136, 189, 190, 214, 219,
221, 222, 223. *See also* French steel
industry

Volkswagen (VW), 49, 160, 191–92,
196–99, 211
Voluntary Export Restraint Agreements
(VER), 50, 147
Volvo, 122, 160, 172

Young, Lord, 158, 164

Zysman, John, 10–11, 14, 21, 41, 179